Learning Theory and Online Technologies

Learning Theory and Online Technologies offers a powerful overview of the current state of elearning, a foundation of its historical roots and growth, and a framework for distinguishing among the major approaches to elearning. It addresses pedagogy (how to design an effective online environment for learning), evaluation (how to know that students are learning), and history (how past research can guide successful online teaching and learning outcomes).

An ideal textbook for undergraduate Education and Communication programs, and Educational Technology Masters, Ph.D., and Certificate programs, readers will find *Learning Theory and Online Technologies* provides a synthesis of the key advances in elearning theory, and the key frameworks of research, and clearly links theory and research to successful learning practice.

Linda Harasim is a Professor in the School of Communication, Simon Fraser University, Vancouver, Canada.

Learning Theory and Online Technologies

Linda Harasim, Ph.D.

Routledge
Taylor & Francis Group

NEW YORK AND LONDON

First published 2012
by Routledge
711 Third Avenue, New York, NY 10017

Simultaneously published in the UK
by Routledge
2 Park Square, Milton Park, Abingdon, Oxon OX14 4RN

Routledge is an imprint of the Taylor & Francis Group, an informa business

Library of Congress Cataloging-in-Publication Data
Harasim, Linda M. (Linda Marie), 1949–
  Learning theory and online technology / Linda Harasim.
  p. cm.
  Includes bibliographical references and index.
  1. Internet in education. 2. Computer-assisted instruction. 3. Educational technology. 4. Learning.
  I. Title.
  LB1044.87.H365 2011
  371.33'4–dc22

2011008278

ISBN: 978-0-415-99975-5 (hbk)
ISBN: 978-0-415-99976-2 (pbk)
ISBN: 978-0-203-84693-3 (ebk)

Typeset in Minion by Wearset Ltd, Boldon, Tyne and Wear

Dedication

To educators and learners everywhere!

Contents

Illustrations

Tables

1

Introduction to Learning Theory and Technology

It is the theory that decides what we can observe.

—Albert Einstein

20th century theories 21st century knowledge age advancing knowledge appropriate knowledge community bad guy theory behavioral learning theory behaviorist learning theory civic knowledge cognitive theory cognitivism cognitivist learning theory constructivist epistemology constructivist learning theory constructivist theory discipline education educational practice educational psychology first major theory first theories good guy theory imparting knowledge knowledge building discourse knowledge building processes knowledge communities learning theories learning theory major learning theories major theories metaphysics new knowledge new learning theories new theories ocl theory online collaborative learning theory online learning environments own knowledge particular knowledge communities particular knowledge community particular knowledge problems particular theory pedagogies positivism rival behavior theory scientific learning theories scientific method scientific theories scientific theory soft social science theories theory building

Chapter 1 covers the following topics:

- Introduction to learning theory in the Knowledge Age
- What is learning theory?

  - Theory and epistemology: the nature of knowledge
  - Theory and scientific method
  - Knowledge communities

- Learning theories in the 20th century

  - Behaviorist learning theory
  - Cognitivist learning theory
  - Constructivist learning theory

- Learning theory for the 21st century

  - Online collaborative learning theory.

Introduction to Learning Theory in the Knowledge Age

Our personal, professional, social and cultural lives have been affected and transformed by the computer networking revolution: email, cellphones, text messaging, Twitter, participating in social networks, blogging and accessing powerful search engines using computers and/or mobile devices are common aspects of everyday life. Moreover, as aspiring or current members of the education profession (teachers, instructors, professors, trainers), the world in which we work and teach has been particularly impacted by networking technologies. The 21st century is referred to as the Knowledge Age, a time in which knowledge has key social and economic value. And today's youth are described as the Net Generation, raised in the culture of the Internet and viewing the Web as integral to socializing and work. Yet educational practice does not significantly reflect or address this new reality.

In such a technology-driven world, it is critical and timely to study the intersection of learning theory and technology. Opportunities for educators to reflect on the implications of how we might shape and apply new communication technologies within our practice have been limited. The field is characterized by training teachers in the use of specific online tools, but a theory-informed approach to transforming our educational practice remains elusive.

In our personal lives, we have embraced new technologies for social communication. New technologies are reshaping the way we function within our communities and how we form them. We use email, Twitter, texting; participate in online forums and social networks (such as Facebook, MySpace); search massive databases; access wikis, blogs and user-generated content sites (YouTube, Flickr); or shop online with Amazon. But in our professional lives, despite our interest or need, there has been little opportunity to consider and explore new learning paradigms.

Rather than transform pedagogy by using opportunities afforded by new technologies and the changing socio-economic context of the 21st century, a common tendency of educators has been to merely integrate technology into traditional ways of teaching. Examples of traditional didactic approaches to the Web are common and include the use of email, wikis and web portals for:

- transmission of course information and content to students;
- communication between student and teacher/tutor;
- transmission of lectures (PowerPoint slides, videoconferences, podcasts);
- administering quizzes, assessing quizzes and posting grades.

Such use of the Web for traditional teaching methods represents the most common educational applications of the Web, and for many educators, the only way of using the Web. Adopting the new technologies to serve traditional practices may not be bad in itself, but educators who restrict their use of the Internet and the Web to making traditional didactic teaching easier or more efficient are missing opportunities to introduce better, different or more advanced ways of learning.

While the Internet, Web and mobile communication technologies reshape the potential of both our professional and personal modes of communication, the challenge of how to transform how we think about learning and how we practice our profession confronts us. The transformative potential of the Internet for learning has thus far been largely limited to quantitative change; for example, improvement in educational efficiency. But qualitative change in how we perceive and practice teaching and learning remains in the early stages of development largely because it is not yet well understood by educators and researchers and the field lacks a theoretical framework to guide educational design, pedagogies and use of online technologies. There are few theory-based or research-based guidelines to assist educators to develop more effective pedagogies for online learning environments. Hence educators have adopted new technologies largely through trial-and-error methods and by adapting traditional didactic practices to online environments, both within formal (primary, secondary or tertiary) and nonformal (training, certification, professional development) educational settings.

Educators are challenged to respond to the Internet and the Web. There is a need to reflect on our theory of learning (even if it is implicit), and to rethink and reassess our teaching practices and pedagogical approaches in relation to the opportunities afforded by online technologies. Most professions are faced with this challenge; new technologies are transforming the world of work and the nature of the organizations in which we work. Educators are not alone in confronting the paradigmatic shift. But perhaps as educators we have the greatest responsibility and most powerful opportunity because this shift is, above all, one of learning: learning to function, survive and thrive in new contexts. For educators, learning new ways and new ways of learning are the nature of our profession.

Learning Theory and Online Technologies addresses the need for a theory of learning for 21st-century realities and presents educators with new ways of thinking about teaching and learning using online technologies. This book offers insight into and illuminates the type of learning and communication essential for educational practitioners and researchers today; it is both a guide to and an explanation for new educational practice that considers the ubiquity of online technology in society today.

The book is organized into four main components:

1. Introduction to learning theory and technology (Chapters 1 and 2)
2. Three major theories of learning and technology in the 20th century: behaviorism, cognitivism and constructivism (Chapters 3, 4 and 5)
3. Online collaborative learning: a theory of learning for the 21st century (Chapter 6), illustrated by exemplars and cases drawn from formal, nonformal and informal educational settings (Chapters 7, 8 and 9)
4. Conclusion (Chapter 10).

Learning Theory and Online Technologies begins with an overview of learning and technology from a theoretical perspective, exploring the role of learning theory in advancing knowledge. Learning has also historically been linked to technology in human development. Understanding the historical shifts in learning and technology as well as the advances in learning theory during the 20th century provides a valuable framework and context for identifying new theories of learning related to online technologies and social communication.

The second section of the book examines three major theories of learning in the 20th century—behaviorism, cognitivism and constructivism. Each theory introduces a new perspective on what learning is and how it can be facilitated through pedagogies and technologies. Learning theories and technologies reflect the changing view of education in the context of the rapid technological advances of the 20th and 21st centuries. The historical context helps us to understand how education was perceived, shaped and practiced at different stages of human development. We can see how education was perceived and to some degree how it was shaped and practiced. We can also see 20th-century learning theories as part of a continuum and as a context for learning theory and practice for the 21st century.

The third section of the book introduces a new theoretical perspective, online collaborative learning (OCL), to frame learning and teaching in the 21st century. To illuminate the OCL theory, this section provides real examples of contemporary educational practice based in both blended and fully online environments with learners of all ages, in all settings.

The final chapter concludes the book with a brief review of the trajectory the book has covered and preview of future opportunities.

What Is Learning Theory?

A theory is an explanation for why something occurs or how it occurs. Typically theory is generated by a question or by our curiosity, and offers a response to that question. A theory is an explanation that has been scientifically developed by scientists and scholars using state-of-the-art research methods and information of the day. A theory of learning aims to help us to understand how people learn. Many theories of learning were generated in the 20th century, and in this book we will examine the major theories and how each provides an overview and guide, or a lens, whereby education professionals (and others) gained a perspective on their field of work. As Albert Einstein stated, "theory provides the framework or lens for our observations." The theory that we employ (consciously or not) determines what we see, what we consider to be important and thus how we will design and implement our practice. By understanding learning theory, educators can reflect on their practice, improve upon, reshape and refine their work and contribute to advancing the discipline.

Theory should not be viewed as something divorced from how we work as educators or how we understand our professional activities. Theory is integral to practice and vice versa, although not all theoreticians, or practitioners for that matter, have respected and addressed that relationship. Understanding the major theories of learning that emerged in the 20th and 21st centuries and how they were shaped by (and shaped) contemporary technologies and educational practice can help us understand how the field of education has developed and changed. As we will see, theories of learning reflect the times in which they emerged and gained precedence.

A theory is a historical construct and reflects what was possible and deemed necessary and valuable at that time. It is essential that educators understand the context of a learning theory, to understand it as a product of the discourse of that time.

Moreover, theory not only provides ways to see and understand what already has happened or is happening, but is also a means to "envision" new worlds and new ways to work. Theories establish a language and discourse whereby we can discuss, agree, disagree and build new perspectives and ways to become knowledgeable, in this case, in the use of online technologies for learning. In his article "Thoughts on Theory in Educational Technology," Brent Wilson writes,

> Theory helps us formulate ideas; it informs the creative process. When we see the world differently, we act to make things different via the relationship between theory and design or between science and technology. Such relationships allow for new technology or conversely, "…a new technology spawns new theory." (1997a, p. 23)

TABLE 1.1 What Is a Theory?

The Role of Theory			
Explains:	Provides:	Shapes:	The theory we employ
Why?	A framework or lens	Understanding	(even unknowingly)
How?	A guide for practice	Discourse	shapes how we design
Where?	A means to envision	Ideas	and implement our
When?	change	Technology	practice
What?		Methodology	
		Actions	

Theory is also a kind of modus operandi; it influences, shapes and determines our actions, even unknowingly. Whether or not we consciously intend to "operationalize" a particular theory of learning, we are nonetheless operating according to some perspective on how to teach (and concomitantly, even if unconsciously, a perspective on how people learn). As Wilson noted, "Theories shape our world just as surely as physical forces do, albeit in a different way" (1997a, p. 23). Theories shape how we make sense of ideas and information and how we then act.

Approaches to scientific theory are also competitive. By the 20th century, theoretical approaches became compartmentalized into what can be viewed as two polar opposites: the battle between what is called "scientific" (hypothesis-driven or experimental) theory and "social" or critical theory. Other related theoretical terms include "hard" science versus "soft" social science theories, pure science versus applied science, quantitative versus qualitative scientific research.

This polarization continues to exist but there are increasing attempts to diminish the divide. The growing use of interdisciplinary collaborations in research is reducing some of the separations. Researchers are increasingly employing both quantitative and qualitative methods, especially within online applications. Moreover, while there are differences in what constitutes scientific theory, there are also important commonalities. Theories intend to explain how or why phenomena are understood in a certain way. Moreover, theories are usually linked to observations and are governed by what can be deemed as constituting evidence and reasonable explanation. Theories can also be viewed as a historical snapshot of ongoing discussions and conversations among those committed to the discipline, its study and advancement.

The history of theory development is relatively recent, the product of the scientific revolution that gained precedence in the 19th century. Understanding learning theories as part of this scientific ethos is critical and will form a key undercurrent of this book.

At the same time, theories of learning have an important philosophical component. Thoughts on learning are not new and did not emerge a mere 100 years ago. Reflection on human experience and behavior, its causation and implications, is part of human consciousness. Thousands of years of philosophical, social and religious perspectives on learning preceded the development of learning theories.

The ancient philosophers developed many important and illuminating insights into learning, and contributed to how we view "epistemology" and "knowledge." The term "epistemology" comes from the Greek word *episteme*, meaning knowledge. In simple terms, epistemology is the philosophy of knowledge or of how we come to know.

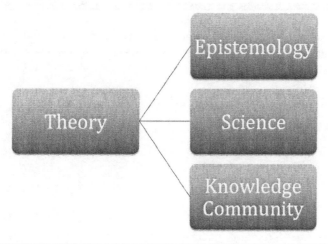

Figure 1.1 Three Aspects of Theory.

The discussion of learning theories in this book has an epistemological and a scientific component, and emphasizes as well the role of knowledge communities. Knowledge communities are the forums or processes of discourse and debate, whereby scholars advance the state of the art in that discipline. These three terms are discussed below as providing the cornerstones of theory. Deciding what to study when we seek to explain how people learn or deciding how to teach depends upon our disciplinary beliefs and perspectives: theories of learning are based on epistemologies, scientific methods and the views of knowledge communities of the time.

Theory and Epistemology

The term "epistemology," when we first encounter it, may seem complex and daunting. Not user-friendly. But it is worth befriending this term since it illuminates important concepts we educators need to understand. Epistemology asks: what is knowledge? How do we know? These questions are important because 20th- and 21st-century learning theories are based on epistemologies that began to nudge the concept of knowledge beyond the view of knowledge as divine that was dominant up until the 19th century. The two major epistemologies of the 20th and 21st centuries are objectivist epistemology (reflected in behaviorist and cognitivist theories of learning) and constructivist epistemology (reflected in constructivist and the online collaborative learning theories).

Until recently, epistemology in the Western world had a relatively simple foundation: we know because God told us. Kenneth Bruffee, in his book *Collaborative Learning: Higher Education, Interdependence, and the Authority of Knowledge* (1999), writes that up until the time of Descartes (what is called the pre-Cartesian world),

> people tended to believe that the authority of knowledge lodged in one place, the mind of God. Most teachers were priests—or priestly. They derived their authority from what they and their students regarded as their godliness, their nearness to the mind of God. (p. 151)

Formal education was "authorized" by the church, the temple, the synagogue or the mosque. The teachers in ancient civilizations such as Persia and Athenian Greece were to some degree exceptions given their focus on civic laws and virtues. But even civic knowledge was viewed as having a divine origin.

"Post-Cartesian assumptions emerge in roughly the seventeenth century. They remain potent and unquestioned today in the 'cognitive sciences' and implicitly in the persuasion of most members of every other disciplinary community, professional and academic" (Bruffee, 1999, p. 151). These assumptions posit knowledge as existing objectively beyond our own minds, as a kind of finite truth. The implication for education and learning is the search for knowledge and truth, and imparting it to others.

> One kind of knowledge that traditional college and university education especially values because it is long-lasting is knowledge of the conventions of traditional education themselves. Professors are responsible not only for imparting knowledge that was imparted to them, but also imparting knowledge *as* it was imparted to them. (1999, pp. 152–153)

Eric Mazur, well-known professor of physics, illustrates this view as part of his own teaching experiences:

> Discussions of education are generally predicted on the assumption that we know what education is … When I started teaching introductory physics to undergraduates at Harvard

University, I never asked myself how I would educate my students. I did what my teachers had done—I lectured. I thought that was how one learns. Look around anywhere in the world and you'll find lecture halls filled with students and, at the front, an instructor. This approach to education has not changed since before the Renaissance and the birth of scientific inquiry. Early in my career I received the first hints that something was wrong with teaching in this manner, but I had ignored it. Sometimes it is hard to face reality. (2009, p. 50)

Didactic methods of teaching are the accepted and traditional way of imparting knowledge. Didactic teaching involves transmitting knowledge from the teacher to the student, just as it was earlier transmitted to the teacher when she or he was a student. This is imperative if the view of knowledge is *objectivist*, *foundational* and *absolute* according to Bruffee, who writes that the objectivist view holds that

> knowledge is a kind of substance contained in and given form by the vessel we call the mind. Professors' mental vessels are full, or almost full. Students' mental vessels are less full. The purpose of teaching is to transfer knowledge from the fuller vessels to the less full. (1999, p. 152)

In contrast to the objectivist version of the authority of knowledge is the more recent constructivist epistemology, which holds that knowledge about the world is constructed through our perceptions and interaction and discussion within various communities of knowledgeable peers. Bruffee writes:

> The nonfoundational social constructionist understanding of knowledge denies that it lodges in any of the places I have mentioned: the mind of God, touchstones of truth and value, genius, or the grounds of thought, the human mind and reality. If it lodges anywhere, it is in the conversation that goes on among the members of a community of knowledgeable peers and in the "conversation of mankind." (1999, p. 153)

Bates and Poole (2003) note that the two dominant epistemological positions in North American higher education today are objectivism and constructivism:

> Objectivists believe that there exists an objective and reliable set of facts, principles, and theories that either have been or will be discovered and delineated over the course of time. This position is linked to the belief that truth exists outside the human mind, or independently of what an individual may or may not believe. (pp. 27–28)

On the other hand, constructivist epistemologies hold

> that knowledge is essentially subjective in nature, constructed from our perceptions and usually agreed upon conventions. According to this view, we construct new knowledge rather than simply acquire it via memorization or through transmission of those who know to those who did not. (p. 28)

Epistemologies of knowledge are key to how we view and how we practice teaching and learning. An educator operating from an objectivist epistemology is "far more likely to believe that a course must present a body of knowledge to be learned" (Bates and Poole, 2003, p. 28). The objectivist epistemology underlies the didactic approach to teaching, based on the belief that students learn passively by receiving and assimilating knowledge from others. The student is required to generate the correct answer, reflecting back the information first transmitted by the teacher. The teacher must ensure that the information to be transmitted is structured, authoritative and organized in particular ways to enable the student to acquire and repeat it "correctly." Objectivist epistemology underlies two of the major learning theories of the 20th century, behaviorism and cognitivism, discussed in Chapters 3 and 4.

The term "constructivism" refers to both an epistemology and a theory of learning. Constructivist epistemology holds that knowledge is constructed from our perceptions and our interpretations based upon contemporary conventions. Our perceptions are shaped through interactions with others, in particular with more knowledgeable peers and/or the appropriate knowledge community. The constructivist epistemology is reflected in both the constructivist and the online collaborative learning theories, discussed in Chapters 5 and 6.

Theory and Scientific Method

While philosophies of learning have been a recurrent theme and concern since the time of ancient civilizations, theory and scientific methods first emerged in the 19th century under the influence of *positivism*, a term coined in 1847 by the French philosopher, Auguste Comte. Comte (1798–1857) was the first intellectual to systematically articulate positivism and to present empirical method as a replacement for metaphysics or theism in the history of thought. Until then, metaphysics was the dominant view, which emphasized that a divine world lies beyond experience, and transcends the physical or natural world. Theism refers to the belief in the existence of one or several gods who intervene in the lives of humans. Comte rejected metaphysics and theism, arguing that a rational assertion should be scientifically verifiable, that is, demonstrated by empirical evidence or mathematical proof. Theory was an assertion or observation linked to science; the purpose of science, Comte argued, is to observe and measure phenomena that we experience and can directly manipulate. Comte believed that empiricism should be at the core of scientific endeavor and that formal experiment was the key to scientific method. Since emotions and thoughts were not directly observable, they were not accepted as legitimate areas of study and were viewed as irrelevant by positivist science. Positivism holds that theology and metaphysics are imperfect modes of knowledge, whereas positive knowledge is based on natural phenomena with properties and relations verified by empirical science. Theory must therefore be verifiable by empirical science.

The first theories of learning can be traced to the late 19th century, related to the emergence of positivism and scientific inquiry. Whereas "philosophies" of learning deal with values and worldviews, "theories" of learning emphasize an empirical element and a formalized way of study, analysis and conclusion. It is this distinguishing quality of theory, its empirical nature, that remains relevant today, although the rigid aspect of positivism that restricted the study of learning to observable behavior is less accepted by educational researchers.

Theory and Knowledge Communities

Knowledge communities refer to scholarly groups associated with a particular field or related to a discipline. It is the work of the members of a knowledge community to define the state of the

TABLE 1.2 Historical Views on Knowledge

Metaphysical	*Scientific*
• Belief in the sole authority of God and religion • Knowledge is Godliness (proximity to God's mind)	• Belief in the authority of empirical evidence to enable knowing • Knowledge is what we can sense, discuss, study and improve

art and to advance that state in a particular discipline or field of work. Scholarly or knowledge communities are associated with all scientific, cultural and artistic fields of endeavor. Other terms used to describe this concept are knowledge societies, scientific communities, invisible colleges and schools of thought. The concept itself, however, is key because theory building is typically conducted by and within the context of a particular knowledge community. Members collaborate and argue, agree and disagree, and introduce new information and empirical data to contribute to and advance knowledge in the field. Scardamalia and Bereiter (2006) write:

> In every progressive discipline one finds periodic reviews of the state of knowledge or the "state of the art" in the field. Different reviewers will offer different descriptions of the state of knowledge; however, their disagreements are open to argument that may itself contribute to advancing the state of knowledge. (p. 100)

Knowledge creation is a deliberate process of advancing the frontiers in a particular discipline. Knowledge, thus, is viewed as constructed through informed dialogue and conversations conducted among members of a knowledge community.

Academic, cultural, scientific and professional knowledge communities share commonalities or integrative beliefs. Kuhn (1970), whose writings on the structure of scientific revolutions (also called paradigm shifts) are considered to be intellectual landmarks explaining the process of discovery, examined the nature and role of scientific communities. Kuhn asked: "What do its members share that accounts for the relative fullness of their professional communication and the relative unanimity of their professional judgments?... Scientists themselves would say they share a theory or set of theories" (1970, p. 182).

Knowledge communities are scientists or leading thinkers gathered or clustered around a theory and represent the state of the art in that discipline. A particular knowledge community represents the theory of the discipline, how it is defined and articulated in practice, and how it is substantiated.

The concept of knowledge communities is key in this book. The four major learning theories discussed here represent the state of the art as articulated by particular knowledge communities, which flourished at particular points in time. Theories exist in context, and both reflect and illuminate that context. Theories change and improve over time. Knowledge in a field does not merely accumulate, it advances. The next section introduces the theories of learning in the 20th and 21st centuries, and discusses briefly the essence of each theory and how it evolved within the social context of its time.

Learning Theories of the 20th Century

Learning theories emerged in the 20th century, with three major theoretical frameworks shaping the study of learning:

- behaviorist learning theory;
- cognitivist learning theory;
- constructivist learning theory.

This book explores the major aspects of these theories, and the pedagogies and technologies associated with each. The use of a historical approach also illuminates the development of how we understand learning theory and technology, especially with respect to education today.

The major theoretical frameworks are thus viewed along a historical continuum, reflecting how human study and understanding of learning have developed and advanced over the past 100 years. These theories ought not to be considered as distinct silos—independent or autonomous of one another. Indeed, theorists associated with one particular theory may also have contributed to the development of other theoretical frameworks. A particular researcher may have been at the cutting edge; writing at a time of transition and exploration of new ideas and thus, his or her writings may reflect different theoretical perspectives, some of the old and some of the new. For example, Robert Gagné, an educational psychologist widely recognized for his contributions to instructional design, was linked to both behaviorism and cognitivist theories of learning: "Gagné's (1985) conditions for learning underwent development and revision for twenty or more years. With behaviorist roots, it now brings together a cognitive information-processing perspective on learning with empirical findings of what good teachers do in their classrooms" (Driscoll, 2005, p. 352). Nor should a theory be viewed as providing a complete or finite answer to a knowledge problem; it is a step on the path to better understanding. Theoretical frameworks of learning are a dynamic and fluid part of knowledge, improving with new research and also with the new technologies that emerge and transform intellectual, social and economic horizons. Ideas improve and knowledge advances. The development of learning theory in the 20th century can be viewed as evolving, improving upon preceding schools of thought as scholars engaged in discussion, debate, conversation and responded to new information, ideas and technological opportunities.

> If research programs are going well, then occasional challenging results are either quietly ignored, called interesting phenomena to be shelved for later study, or explained away. Only when an alternative view emerges, as cognitive theory emerged in the 1960s to rival behavior theory, do old problems appear significant. (Leahey & Harris, 1997, p. 44)

Change, moreover, is not a smooth process: it represents shifts and breaks in tradition. This is the case with the development of learning theories. Kuhn (1970) referred to the growth of intellectual creativity and progress as paradigmatic shifts and revolutions. Theories are products of their time and the transition from one theory to the next is based on discussion, debate and intellectual struggle as scholars try to make sense of particular knowledge problems with the information available at the time. Intellectual progress is a road of endless conversation and ongoing challenges. New theories are called epistemological breaks but also breakthroughs.

Hence the metaphor of a continuum or evolution (or, in Kuhn's terms, a revolution) of ideas of learning, rather than a "good guy" theory versus a "bad guy" theory, is arguably essential to the study of learning. We continue to study and learn about how people learn; theories should be viewed as building upon (and reacting to) one another, enhancing and advancing our knowledge. We might think of spirals of knowledge, aggregating, advancing and improving over time. At the same time, it is essential to recognize and understand the assumptions that characterize each learning theory, and how learning was understood and organized at that time.

Behaviorist Learning Theory

Behaviorist learning theory focuses on that which is observable: how people behave and especially how to change or elicit particular behaviors. Behaviorism provided a theory of learning that was empirical, observable and measurable.

Developed in the late 19th century, behaviorism was the first major theory of learning and represented a radical leap forward in terms of human science. Scientific method was still in its earliest days. The introduction of Comte's notion of positivism represented a very profound shift in thinking; scientific method challenged and replaced metaphysics in the history of thought.

Hitherto, for millennia, metaphysics and divine intervention had been accepted as the cause of all social, human, physical and biological phenomena.

Behaviorism was one of the first examples of the use of scientific method to explain human action, psychology and learning, offering an explanation that could be empirically verified. Behaviorism introduced a way to study and to shape learning that could be repeated and replicated.

Looking back, we can see that behaviorism was limited and rigid in its perspective. But for its time, behaviorism was hailed as a breakthrough in its ability to study, measure and replicate the same results, time and again. This was a first and by no means modest achievement. Behaviorism, as one of the first positivist approaches to human sciences, was by necessity very narrow in its focus. It was a new approach and sought membership in the positivist scientific community. Behaviorism limited its lens to that which could be observed, emphasizing overt action as being most easily apparent and accessible for study. The term "overt action" refers to behavior; in other words, behaviorism focused on how we act and what impacts upon and changes how we act. Behaviorists limited their consideration to stimulus and response: a particular act stimulated a certain reaction, a response that could be observed, repeated and quantified. In this theory, there is no notion or consideration of thought processes in the mind—the mind is viewed as a black box, largely irrelevant.

Ivan Pavlov (1849–1936) is considered the intellectual founder of behaviorist learning theory. He is famous for his theory of classical conditioning. Burrhus Frederic Skinner (1904–1990) is also famously associated with behaviorist learning theory, but Skinner's work differed from his Pavlovian predecessors in that he focused on what is referred to as voluntary or operant behavioral conditioning, a behaviorist approach different from classical conditioning.

Behavioral learning theory lent itself to instructional design based on very specific and discrete learning steps. And also, very importantly, to the mechanization of this instructional process through new forms of learning technologies such as teaching machines, programmed instruction and computer-assisted instruction (CAI).

Behaviorist learning theory is the focus of Chapter 3 in this book.

Cognitivist Learning Theory

Limitations in the behaviorist framework of learning began to be recognized by the early 1920s. The major problem for researchers was that behaviorism was unable to explain most social behaviors. For behaviorist scientists, what you cannot see or measure does not count. Behaviorists would consider only what they could see and the ability to measure what was seen.

Yet, as researchers and psychologists involved in the scientific study of learning began to realize, the power of the mind to influence or make decisions that are not directly related to an external stimulus was highly significant. The mind did play a tremendous role, even if we could not "see" it.

If behaviorism treated the mind as a black box, cognitive theory recognized the importance of the mind in making sense of the material world. Cognitivism sought to understand what was inside the black box of the mind, in order to emulate it computationally. Emerging as it did during the rise of cognitive science and computer science, cognitivist learning theory absorbed and was influenced by the era. The mind became viewed as a computer: a powerful metaphor that characterized this approach was "mind as computer" (MAC). The model of students mentally processing information (just as computers processed information) is referred to as cognitive information processing (CIPs) and is a major theme in cognitivist learning theory.

Cognitivism was concerned with technology that could model the mind and represent knowledge, and cognitive scientists sought to develop educational technologies such as intelligent tutoring systems (ITS) and artificial intelligence (AI), in an attempt to mimic or replicate the human mind through computer programs. Cognitivism, while a learning theory distinct from behaviorism, nonetheless also presupposes that the primary role of the learner is to assimilate whatever the teacher presents. Cognitive pedagogy, like behaviorist pedagogy, employed a didactic model of teaching: the cognitivist pedagogy was based on objectivist instructional design.

Cognitivist learning theory is the subject of Chapter 4.

Constructivist Learning Theory

Constructivist theory refers to a theory or set of theories about learning that emerged, in part, in reaction to behaviorism and cognitivism. Constructivism emerged during a period of educational reform in the United States and was influenced by new constructivist psychological research and trends emerging in Europe, which emphasized the role of the individual in making sense of the world. Educational researchers and practitioners came to realize that humans could not be programmed, as robots are, to always respond in the same way to a stimulus. In fact, constructivists argued, the mind plays an enormous role in how people act when learning. And that role is not directly comparable to a software program based on discrete steps to consume and process information. Constructivism—particularly in its "social" forms—suggests that the learner is much more actively involved in a joint enterprise with the teacher and peers in creating (constructing) meaning.

Constructivism refers both to a learning theory (an empirical explanation of how people learn) and to an epistemology of learning (a view of the nature of knowledge). They are not identical terms, however. The constructivist learning theory explains how learners construct meaning. The constructivist epistemology refers to a philosophical view that knowledge is constructed through our interactions with one another, the community and the environment, and that knowledge is not something absolute.

The constructivist theory of learning holds that people learn by constructing their own understanding and knowledge of the world through experience and reflecting upon that experience. We are active creators of our own knowledge, reconciling our previous ideas as we encounter new experiences and information. We may change our ideas or discard the new information, based on our investigations, asking questions and assessing and negotiating what we know with others.

In the 20th century, the major psychologists and educators associated with constructivist approaches to teaching and learning were Jean Piaget and Lev Vygotsky.

Constructivist learning theories, pedagogies and technologies are examined in Chapter 5.

Learning Theory for the 21st Century

Online Collaborative Learning Theory

As with learning theories of the 20th century, online collaborative learning (OCL) theory builds upon previous approaches, but presents a new perspective. OCL emerged with the invention of computer networking and the Internet, and the concomitant socio-economic shift from the industrial society to the Knowledge Age.

The three major theories of learning that emerged during the 20th century (behaviorism, constructivism and cognitivism) derived from the field of educational psychology. Robert Calfee's (2006) article, "Educational Psychology in the 21st Century" identifies four key omissions or problems with 20th-century educational psychology that need to be addressed by theory in the 21st century:

First, educational psychology continues to struggle with the most appropriate relation to practice…

Second, the position of adults in educational psychology remains a puzzlement…

Third, neither HBEPI nor HBEPII[1] include "Learning" in a chapter title!…

A fourth and final set of issues centers around <u>methodology</u>. (pp. 30–31)

These four problems with 20th-century educational psychology reflect problems in 20th-century theories of learning, which need to be addressed in contemporary theory development.

In considering education for the 21st century, Calfee (2006) asks: "What should we be doing?" He identifies what he calls RIPs: Really Important Problems, one of which centers on "how best to provide *effective and efficient teaching and learning* for all children" (p. 35). A corollary topic, he writes, is the *role of technology in schooling*, given the incredible impact of technologies elsewhere in society. He writes:

> Other than electrification, today's classroom is remarkably unchanged from the end of the 19th century. The cast of characters and the activities remain virtually unchanged, along with the length of the school day and year and several other parameters. Schools have thwarted numerous innovations; radio, television, and even telephones have minimal presence in today's classrooms. Systems that we take for granted outside the school walls—computers, the Internet, PDAs, handhelds—are either somnolent or prohibited. (p. 35)

These are important issues that call for new learning theories to be linked to practice and to real-world contexts and technologies.

Behaviorist, cognitivist and developmental constructivist theories of learning emphasized learning as an individualistic pursuit. Moreover, the epistemological basis of behaviorism and cognitivism was objectivism: objectivist epistemology holds that knowledge is fixed and finite, and ultimately, knowledge is truth. Knowledge is something that the teacher has mastered, and which students must now similarly master by replicating the knowledge of the teacher. The pedagogies emphasized "transmitting information" by the teacher as a way to "acquire knowledge" by the student, reflected in such didactic approaches as lectures or their mechanized versions in the form of teaching machines, computer-assisted instruction (CAI), intelligent tutoring systems (ITS) and courseware. This was the ethos of the Industrial Age, an era that emphasized the learner's ability to acquire and retain information and associated skills. An implicit educational goal was that the student learn to follow instructions accurately to achieve the desired result.

The 21st-century Knowledge Age has introduced a very new mindset in society. Whereas the Industrial Revolution extended and leveraged our physical capabilities to manipulate objects far beyond muscle power alone, the Internet Revolution and ensuing Knowledge Age emphasizes, extends and leverages our mental capabilities. OCL is proposed as a framework to guide understanding and practice of education in the Knowledge Age. Unlike the behaviorist and cognitivist emphasis on instructions for replicating a textbook answer, OCL focuses on knowledge-building processes. OCL theory differs from constructivist learning theory, by locating active learning within a process of social and conceptual development based on knowledge discourse.

> One important advantage of knowledge building as an educational approach is that it provides a straightforward way to address the contemporary emphasis on knowledge creation and innovation. These lie outside the scope of most constructivist approaches, whereas they are at the heart of knowledge building. (Scardamalia & Bereiter, 2006, p. 99)

OCL provides a learning theory and pedagogy that addresses 21st-century needs and opportunities. As discussed in Chapter 6, OCL theory is grounded in educational practice and focuses on learners of all ages as participants in 21st-century online knowledge communities, whether in formal, nonformal or informal educational settings. Chapters 7, 8 and 9 explore examples of OCL in practice.

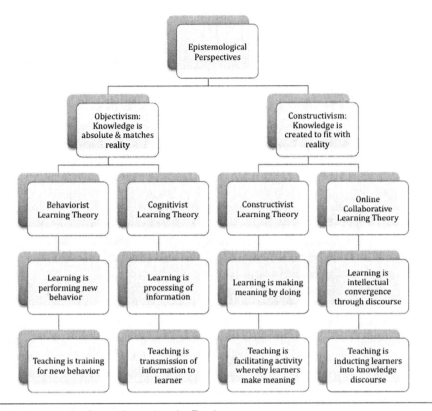

Figure 1.2 Epistemological Perspectives on Learning Theories.

Summary

Chapter 1 addressed the current challenges of teaching and learning in an increasingly online world, in particular the need for learning theories that can speak to and guide education in this context. It explored the definition, importance and role of a theory of learning in general, and discussed how learning theory is based on key concepts such as epistemology, scientific method and knowledge communities.

Chapter 1 revealed that the rise of learning theories was relatively recent; theories of learning, as with most scientific theories, first appeared toward the end of the 19th century and early in the 20th century, as part of the emergence of modern science and scientific method. Learning came under the scrutiny of scientific study around the same time that topics related to human and natural behavior came to be studied and organized within the framework of "theory." During the 20th century, scientific learning theories were articulated, built upon and gained increasing importance in the study and practice of education. Three major learning theories influenced education in the 20th century: behaviorism, cognitivism and constructivism. These learning theories are also each associated with particular learning pedagogies and learning technologies. A theory of learning for the 21st century, Online Collaborative Learning, is also introduced. These four learning theories are each explored in subsequent chapters.

As Chapter 1 has introduced and Chapter 2 will expand on, learning and technology have been intertwined with one another throughout human history. Together, new learning needs and new technologies have contributed to major social and civilizational shifts, as discussed in Chapter 2.

2
Historical Overview of Learning and Technology

We propose that the crucial difference between human cognition and that of other species is the ability to participate with others in collaborative activities with shared goals and intentions.

—**Michael Tomasello et al., 2005**

adjunct arpanet augmenting human intellect case communication technologies cern chapter two collaborative activities collaborative learning approach computer conferencing computer networking computer networking technologies computer system early internet web browser early online learning pioneers email formal education formal learning group discussion group discussions human development human learning human social development information sharing learning technology licklider mass production network technology new developments new learning needs new learning technologies new technologies online collaborative learning online education online technologies personal computers prehistoric ancestors printing press protestant reformation reading materials scientific revolution social web support syllabies tim berners-lee vannevar bush web 2.0 web search engines web site world wide web writing system

Chapter 2 covers the following topics:

- Introduction to history of learning and technology
- Steps in human development

  - Speech
  - Writing
  - Printing
  - Internet

- The invention of the Internet as a meeting of minds
- The Web and its social applications
- Historical overview of online learning

  - Adjunct mode online learning
  - Blended or mixed-mode online learning
  - Totally online learning.

Introduction

Chapter 2 explores the fascinating story of how learning and technology have been integral to human development from our earliest human ancestry. Technology has enabled communication and, linked with our most human characteristic of intentional collaboration, is essential to human learning and development. Chapter 2 explores the role of learning and technology, focusing on specific historical developments that revolutionized our communication and expanded our knowledge-building capacities, from the time of our pre-linguistic and prehistoric ancestors until the present Knowledge Age.

Steps in Human Development: Learning and Technology

Our human ancestors, whether hunters and gatherers eking out survival with family and clans in caves, or members of ancient civilizations who built city states and engaged in commerce, were profoundly different in many ways from today's societies. Nonetheless we all share the need to survive and advance: learning, communication, collaboration and the creation of tools are the fundamental mechanisms that enable human society to survive and progress. Chapters 3, 4, 5 and 6 will each focus on a particular theory of learning and discuss the pedagogy and technology associated with it. Chapter 2 provides a basis for this discussion by providing an overview of how learning and technology have been interconnected throughout human history and are key to social and civilizational advancement.

The need and ability to learn (and hence to educate effectively and efficiently) is at the root of human survival and civilization. Since prehistoric kinships, humans have addressed the need to survive and thrive through learning and teaching their young and one another by inventing new learning technologies.

And we have done so collaboratively and collectively. In fact, evolutionary biologists today propose that the dividing line between humans and other species is the ability to *intentionally* participate in collaborative activities. Traits that anthropologists once believed separated humans from other great apes, such as tool-making, walking, hunting cooperatively and fighting wars, have all been found to exist in other species. Sarah Hrdy, a renowned evolutionary anthropologist, writes that it is intentional collaboration, along with our extra-large brains (relative to our body size and compared to other species) and capacity for language that marks the dividing line for human behavior, separating our nature from that of other apes (2009, p. 9). Michael Tomasello, leader of the Max Planck Institute of Evolutionary Anthropology, writes that "human beings, and only human beings, are biologically adapted for participating in collaborative activities involving shared goals and socially coordinated action plans" (as cited in Hrdy, 2009, p. 9). Collaboration is the key to our survival and to cultural and human development and knowledge.

Hrdy goes on to explore collaboration as the basis for human development:

> Unlike chimpanzees and other apes, almost all humans are naturally eager to collaborate with others. They may prefer engaging with familiar kin but they also easily coordinate with nonkin, even strangers. Given opportunities, humans develop these proclivities into complex enterprises such as collaboratively tracking and hunting prey, processing food, playing cooperative games, building shelters, or designing spacecraft that reach the moon. (2009, p. 10)

Collaboration is a key characteristic of human development, reflected in all our survival and civilizational activities from raising our young to collaboratively gathering food to building spacecraft. The major stages in human development are referred to as paradigmatic shifts: major changes in society, learning, technology and knowledge.

Human social development is the result of key civilizational shifts throughout history. These civilizational shifts (also known as paradigmatic shifts) refer to the major transformations that occurred as technological breakthroughs came together with changing cultural, social and economic conditions to create new contexts, opportunities and challenges.

In both prehistoric and historic periods, technology breakthroughs and new social formations have combined, each influencing the other and thus establishing new lifestyles that, in turn, impacted on each successive generation and society. They are turning points, milestones in human development. Scientists generally identify four major paradigmatic shifts, although the names for these shifts may vary.

A general and condensed chronology of these major socio-technological shifts includes:

- Speech (40,000 BCE): the development of speech and intertribal communication in hunter-gatherer communities produces recognizable civilizations based on informal learning with characteristic crafts and symbolic art;
- Writing (10,000 BCE): agricultural revolution interacts with the massing of populations in fertile regions to produce state structures and cumulative knowledge growth based on the invention of writing and formalization of learning;
- Printing (CE 1600): machine technology and the printing press interact with the development of global trade and communication, to expand the dissemination and the specialization of knowledge and science;
- Internet (CE 2000): advanced network technology interacts with powerful new models of education and training that offer the potential to produce knowledge-based economies and the democratization of knowledge production.

In the 21st century, educators ponder current practice, new technologies and how to address the gap between the two. Scenarios for new learning technologies and practices are explored in

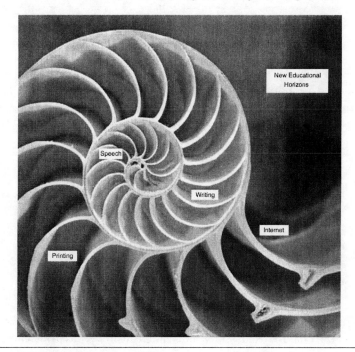

Figure 2.1 Four Communication Paradigms.

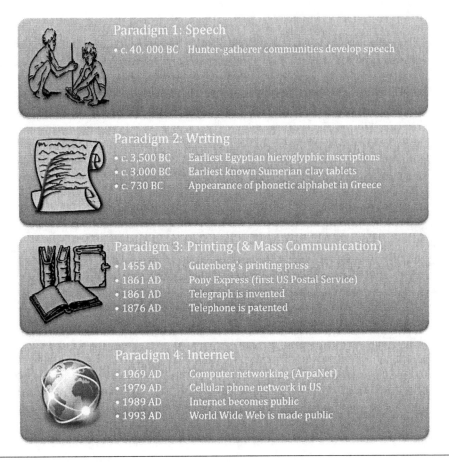

Figure 2.2 Technological Milestones Within the Four Communication Paradigms.

Chapters 6–9. Yet, the history of how we navigated our way to the present is also important. This history tells the story of how human learning has been linked with technology, communication and collaboration. This history is important to our understanding of learning in general and also to frame our study of learning theory in the 20th and 21st centuries.

The next section provides a brief synopsis of this history, exploring the paradigmatic shifts representing major leaps in learning and technology:

Each shift represents an advance to a new level of knowledge.

Paradigm 1: Speech

- 40,000 BCE: the development of speech and intertribal communication in hunter-gatherer clans produces recognizable civilizations with characteristic crafts and symbolic art.

As with children today, the newborn in hunter-gatherer communities began to learn within the context of the mother and the surrounding clan and community. Since earliest prehistory, humans learned from observing and imitating the behavior of others.

Our prehistoric ancestors also developed new technologies to assist in personal and communal survival, in this case communication technologies using the human voice. Speech evolved from grunts, shouts, noises and whistles intended to signal an event or emotion, for example, distress, warning, threat, need, pleasure and pain. Prehistoric speech and language were forms of codified communication: what is good or bad; what to do or not do; who should do it, and when, how and where to do it; and, eventually, why to do it, either for cultural or survival purposes. While this period is often characterized as the Stone Age and it is true that advanced tool-making based on stone is a key characteristic, most importantly this is the age of speech—the most profound technology that mankind has invented.

In prehistoric societies, children learned both by observation and mimicry, as well as from the "technology" of oral education provided by their mothers and the clan. Speech also meant that the communal history of knowledge, beliefs, culture and skills could be passed from one generation to the next. This early stage in the technology of language enabled "oral histories" to pass from one person to another, generation to generation, through stories, legends, rituals and songs. Wall drawings were created to illustrate or instruct, and enhance oral traditions. Language and illustration were important tools for sharing, archiving and transmitting information and knowledge.

Paradigm 2: Writing

10,000 BCE: the agricultural revolution interacts with the massing of populations in fertile regions to produce state structures and cumulative knowledge growth based on the invention of writing and the formalization of learning.

The term "agrarian revolution" refers to the transition from bands or communities of hunters and gatherers that characterized our earliest ancestors to that of an agriculture-based economy and society. Whereas hunters and gathers were constantly on the move to track herds of animals and adapt to the seasons to harvest grain, fruit, nuts and roots, the development of agriculture made human settlement (or semi-settlement) possible. The domestication of animals and cultivation of plants enabled a more stable lifestyle and settled society, as compared to living hand-to-mouth to survive, which required far greater expenditure of time and energy.

The process of producing and harvesting food, the increased yield of crops and the reliability of access to such essentials had an immense social and economic impact on these communities. With more stable living conditions, these early communities had the time and energy to learn new skills: they became more proficient in trading and the structure of their communities became more complex; they established trading economies, privatization and social, economic and political stratification. All of this contributed to a continuous development of culture, knowledge and new technologies.

The technology of writing—numeracy and literacy—evolved during this period. Numeracy (a system of counting and recording numbers) and literacy (a system of writing letters and/or words) developed as a result of the surplus of food and goods derived from domestic production and trade. Storage and trade of goods required a form of recording, and writing solved the need for ways to count and to describe items held, received or distributed, as well as designating ownership. Literacy was, at its most basic, a method for record keeping. It is believed that characters used for communication emerged approximately 3500 BCE in various agrarian civilizations and are linked to the development of surplus yields and private ownership. The original Mesopotamian writing system was derived from a method of account keeping and by the end of the fourth millennium BCE had evolved into a triangular-shaped stylus pressed into soft clay for recording numbers. Around the 26th century BCE cuneiform began to represent syllables of spoken Sumerian and became a general-purpose writing system for logograms, syllables and numbers. The world's oldest alphabet was developed in central Egypt around 2000 BCE from a hieroglyphic prototype (Martin, 1994).

The increased organization and specialization of society required changes in how and what people learned. The majority of the population continued to learn through mimicry and apprenticeship: this included observation, hands-on training and experience by trial and error. Eventually, however, formalized learning emerged among settled populations.

Formalized learning was "invented" as a way to teach a select group of people who had been chosen to serve in matters of importance, such as tasks related to money or religion. These early societies required workers who possessed literary and numerical skills to guarantee accuracy and accountability. Instructors ensured that their curricula were recorded, maintained and updated and that the learning outcomes were assessed. Such formalized education eventually became the basis of schooling as we know it today.

Formal learning in these early societies focused on the skills of writing, reading and counting, but also on civil behavior as appropriate to the students' socio-economic standing. Formal education was based on exclusivity. Only people from privileged backgrounds were allowed to learn the skills to become scribes or officials for political, religious, economic or military service. Through prescribed learning, these people were socialized to be upstanding citizens and followers of the faith.

In 580 BCE, Xenophon, popularly known as the first historian, wrote about learning and Persian laws. He explained that in Persia men are educated to avoid lawless behavior and that formal education served a preventative purpose. In Persian society, special areas of the royal court were set aside for learning. This was a very early form of school.

Formal learning is also traceable back to the Greek philosopher, Plato (427–347 BCE), who founded the Academy in Athens, regarded as the first institute of higher learning in the Western world.

The history of writing is fascinating and of profound interest to understanding communication and human progress throughout the ages and to the present. According to H.J. Martin, "All writing is tied to the form of thought of the civilization that created it and to which its destiny is linked" (1994, p. 15). The history of writing is beyond the scope of this book, however, except to provide the context and framework of the integral links between writing, language, thought and knowledge. Writing enabled knowledge to be communicated. It could be disseminated to others, near and far, and hence not only transmit ideas but contribute to ongoing discussion, debate and knowledge building. Writing also enabled knowledge to be archived and hence disseminated historically: future generations could read the prevailing thoughts and ideas, and thereby learn from and add to the cumulative body of human knowledge. Writing is the basis of formal learning.

The first known writing is believed to have developed around 2300 BCE in Mesopotamia. Writing spread to Crete during the period around 2000 BCE, and by the 9th or 8th century BCE, the

Greek alphabet—the ancestor of modern European alphabets—appeared (Martin, 1994, p. 34). In all of its varieties and instantiations, whether in the ancient Middle East, China or pre-Columbian America, writing emerged and was revered as communication with the deities.

Similarly, Roman Papal doctrines were thought to "hold the word of God"; they were considered divine and sacred and therefore not to be seen by or communicated directly to the common man or woman, but were represented by the church and its few literate priests. Furthermore, all sacred documents were written in Latin, a language not understood by the common person. Reading and writing were skills reserved for a very select few.

However, the power of the written word—4,000 years after its invention—was about to be unleashed. In the 15th century in Europe, the printing press (and related technologies such as paper) was about to be invented.

Paradigm 3: Printing (and Mass Communication)

CE 1600: machine technology and the printing press interact with the development of global trade and communication, creating the specialization of knowledge production and science.

Arguably, the most famous "learning technology" of the third paradigm was the invention of printing. Johannes Gutenberg (1398–1468), a German printer and goldsmith, invented movable type and the mechanical printing press around 1439. He is also known for printing the Gutenberg Bible: approximately 180 copies were published in 1455.

The invention of the printing press was a technological innovation with tremendous implications for Western society, in that it provided a means for disseminating ideas about not only religion, but also science, education and politics. The printing press enabled books, such as the Bible and others, to be printed in larger numbers and for less cost than handwritten, manuscript versions previously available only to the Church and elite. For the first time in history, commercial mass production of books was possible. Printing made books more economical to produce and wider segments of the population could afford them. Publishing allowed people to follow debates, take part in discussions and learn about matters that concerned them. One early example is pamphlets on the plague that taught people how to deal with this illness.

Gutenberg's printing press revolutionized learning and knowledge transmission in Europe to an unprecedented degree: pamphlets, booklets and complete books could now be efficiently and cost-effectively produced and disseminated.

Printing spread widely and rapidly across Europe and by the end of the 15th century, the number of books produced on presses like that designed by Gutenberg reached the hundreds. The rapid spread of publishing was a major factor contributing to the Renaissance, the Scientific Revolution and the Protestant Reformation. Martin Luther's *95 Theses* was nailed to the doors of the Castle Church in Wittenberg, Germany in 1517 (though this claim is debated) and was subsequently printed and widely circulated. The production of more books and the propagation of ideas to a wider audience fueled new ways of understanding, as well as influencing a significant shift in Western thought. Importantly, the broadsheet format of Luther's *95 Theses* and its circulation became a prototype for newspapers and mass media today.

The production of printed books and other reading materials was motivation for the public to learn to read and seek formal education. The availability of reading materials meant more people did learn to read and expand their knowledge on a wide range of topics.

The momentum toward public access of information and knowledge was unstoppable once books became more widely available. By 1465, the printing press in Europe led to the rapid growth of printed materials and the dissemination of information to an eager public.

> There were more than 250 centers of the print trade by 1 January 1501, the fatal moment after books, now out of their cradle, are no longer called incunabula. The estimated 27,000 known publications certainly represent more than ten million copies, circulated in less than two generations in a Europe whose population was under a hundred million. This would give a maximum of some few hundred thousand confirmed readers.[1] (Martin, 1994, p. 227)

The relationship between learning and technology is again illuminated: the base of knowledge created with the development of speech, expanded through writing, is now further advanced as publishing creates and responds to new learning needs. The rise of machine manufacturing and industrialization in the 18th, 19th and 20th centuries is integrally linked with a need for mass literacy techniques and technologies. Mass communication intensifies the need for mass education. With the rise of modern science, new theories of learning emerged in the 20th century to address the industrial age.

Paradigm 4: Internet

CE 2000: advanced information technology interacts with powerful new models of education and training that offer the potential to produce knowledge-based economies and the democratization of knowledge production.

The invention of computer networks in the late 1960s and computer-mediated communication (CMC) in the early 1970s initiated a shift in how we understand our most basic concepts of education, community and society. Our sense of who we are as citizens in the world, how we meet and collaborate with others, and how we learn and contribute to social development was transformed by the telecommunications revolution of the mid 19th century (telegraph, 1861; telephone, 1876) and early 20th century (television, 1925; satellite technology, 1957) and more recently and profoundly with the Internet revolution in the mid 20th century. The developments associated with the Internet, the World Wide Web (known as the Web) and other online technological inventions have introduced profound implications for learning theory and practice.

A look at how quickly and widely computers and the Internet have impacted on work and society worldwide is astounding: Arpanet was invented as recently as 1969, email over packet-switched networks was invented in 1971, computer conferencing/forums were invented in 1972, the public Internet was launched in 1989, and the World Wide Web was invented in 1990 and released to the public in 1993.

It is important to recall that up to the 19th century, communication was almost entirely restricted to one's locality. The first public transatlantic telegraph was sent by Queen Victoria, in 1857. Until then, technologies for communicating at a distance were more or less similar to that of 5,000 years earlier: that is, messages were carried by courier on foot, on beast or by boat. Distance communication was controlled by those with power (royal, military or religious leaders). Throughout history, communication among common people was limited to local, face-to-face conversation, or the use of "distance" technologies—talking drums, smoke signals, carrier pigeons and semaphore (generally, though, these modes of communication were only employed in times of distress). Otherwise information traveled slowly. Even with the introduction of the printing press, important new ideas took years to disseminate from city to city, country to country or between Europe and the New World of the Americas. Until relatively recently, the spread of knowledge was limited.

In the 20th century the invention and adoption of the Internet introduced a great leap forward in communication, both quantitatively and qualitatively. The Internet represents a worldwide knowledge transformation on a global scale.

The invention of computer networking technologies has roots in a vision of concern for collaboration, community, learning and knowledge. One of the earliest technological precursors is hypertext,[2] a concept and technology important as the precursor and inspiration for the World Wide Web.

The history of hypertext began in 1945 with Vannevar Bush's article in the *Atlantic Monthly* entitled "As We May Think," about a futuristic technology that he called Memex, "a device in which an individual stores all his books, records, and communications, and which is mechanized so that it may be consulted with exceeding speed and flexibility. It is an enlarged intimate supplement to his memory" (p. 108).

Bush's groundbreaking vision of a technology to enhance thought pre-dated the computer. Nonetheless, Bush's article and his concept of the Memex directly influenced and inspired the two Americans generally credited with the invention of hypertext—Ted Nelson and Douglas Engelbart.

Nelson coined the words "hypertext" and "hypermedia" in 1965 and worked to develop a computer system that enabled writing and reading that was nonsequential and presented the potential for cross-referencing and annotating (Nelson, 1974). In Project Xanadu, Nelson sought to create a computer networking system that enabled users to view hypertext libraries, create and manipulate text and graphics, send and receive messages and structure information. Such a system allowed users to create linkages among ideas and information resources, to explore the interconnections and generate multiple perspectives on a topic (Nelson, 1987). This vision pre-dates but anticipates the World Wide Web (the Web).

Douglas Engelbart, as with Vannevar Bush two decades earlier, was concerned with enhancing the intellectual capacity of people. In 1962, Engelbart published his seminal work, *Augmenting Human Intellect: A Conceptual Framework*, proposing to use computers to augment training. With his colleagues at the Stanford Research Institute, Engelbart developed a computer system to augment human abilities, including learning. The system was simply called the oNLine System (NLS) debuted in 1968 and later marketed as "Augment." One of the most notable design features of Augment is the emphasis on providing tools to support collaborative knowledge work. The Augment project "placed the greatest emphasis on collaboration among people doing their work in an asynchronous, geographically distributed manner" (Engelbart & Lehtman, 1988, p. 245). Augment enabled idea structuring, as well as idea sharing. While linkages among ideas and authors are supported by Augment, the system employs a hierarchical structure. Xanadu and Augment "were the first systems to articulate the potential of computers to create cognitive and social connectivity: webs of connected information and communication among knowledge workers" (Harasim, 1990a, p. 41).

The initial concept of a global information network came from J.C.R. Licklider in the late 1950s. At a time when computers were viewed as giant calculators, Licklider envisioned the use of networked computers to facilitate an online community, online personal communication and active informed participation in government (Hafner & Lyon, 1996, p. 34). Licklider's 1950s visions were prescient and one of the earliest precursors to the rise of personal computers and computer networking.

In 1960, Licklider published his seminal paper "Man–Computer Symbiosis" in which he proposes the potential of computers to transform society. He put forward a vision that anticipated collaborative learning, emphasizing the potential of the computer to support group discussion, networking, multiple perspectives, active participation and community practice. Although Licklider left the Arpanet project before it was completed, his vision of Arpanet as a knowledge network remained. The actual technological development of Arpanet was the work of Lawrence G. Roberts of the Massachusetts Institute of Technology (MIT).

Another very important technological development related to human communication and collaboration was computer conferencing. Computer conferencing was invented to support group communication and decision-making, and the first system, EMISARI, was developed by Murray Turoff in 1971. In 1974 Turoff founded the Computerized Conferencing and Communications Center at the New Jersey Institute of Technology (NJIT) and developed the EIES computer conferencing system. Other conferencing systems developed in the early–mid 1970s were PLANET, Confer and *Forum. Computer conferencing is important to the history of online education because many of the earliest ventures in online course delivery involved computer conferencing. Over the next 35 years and to the present, Turoff engaged in research and development on CMC with Starr Roxanne Hiltz. Much of their work was and remains directly related to education and one of the most important outcomes was the development and implementation of the "Virtual Classroom," which pioneered the first total delivery of undergraduate education in the world. It was also the first major scientific field trial of online education and, as such, provided an important empirical base for others in the field (Hiltz, 1994).

In 1990, Tim Berners-Lee, a British scientist at CERN (European Organization for Nuclear Research), invented the World Wide Web to meet the demand for information sharing among scientists working in different universities and institutes around the world. In 1992, Lynx was developed as an early Internet web browser. Its ability to provide hypertext links within documents that could reach into other documents anywhere on the Internet is responsible for the creation of the Web, which was released to the public in 1993.

Arpanet and Internet: Meeting of Minds

The origins of the first computer network, Arpanet, are linked to a vision of human collaboration and community. While the term *meeting of minds* was not actually used, this concept suggests a powerful metaphor to help understand computer networking. At one level, "meeting of the minds" (also referred to as mutual assent or *consensus ad idem*) is a phrase in contract law used to describe the intentions of the parties forming the contract. In particular, it refers to the situation where there is a common understanding in the formation of the contract, and Arpanet was essentially that, a mutual agreement to build a network but as networks had not yet been invented, it was a commitment to an intention.

Moreover, computer networks would represent a meeting of minds in both the social and technological aspects. The inventors of Arpanet employed social terms to characterize new tools and technologies. The basic formulation of Arpanet was based on cooperation and negotiation: the network host-to-host communications became facilitated by a "handshake," using the social term to describe a key technical concept of how the most elemental connections between two computers are handled. The term "protocol" was adopted from the ancient Greek *protokollon*, the top of a papyrus scroll that contained the synopsis of the document, its authentication and date (Hafner & Lyon, 1996, p. 144). Protocols also reflect the etiquette of diplomacy, consensus and collective agreement. Network protocols became the technical and social glue of connectivity. A network protocol refers to the address of a packet of information, but, as one of the notable architects of the Internet, Vint Cerf, noted, social protocol also refers to informal consensus: "The other definition of protocol is that it's a handwritten agreement between parties, typically worked out on the back of a lunch bag, which describes pretty accurately how most of the protocol designs were done" (quoted in Hafner & Lyon, 1996, p. 146).

Network technology was socially and technically constructed by an informal group, the Network Working Group (NWG), who worked together in a collaborative and consensual manner. New ideas were sent out to group members and sites as notes called "Request for Comments" (these RFCs were sent via regular post: email had not yet been invented). A spirit of community, openness and collaborative design was invoked. As Hafner and Lyon remark: "For years afterward (and to this day) RFCs have been the principal means of open expression in the computer networking community, the accepted ways of recommending, reviewing, and adopting new technical standards" (1996, p. 145).

Finally, Arpanet represented a meeting of minds not only in the technological design and social construction of computer networking, but also in its applications. Email, computer conferencing, forums, the Internet, virtual communities, online collaborative learning and online collaborative work were products of computer networking and, each in their own way, articulations of a meeting of minds.

Email is the first and most successful social software that has ever been invented. Within four decades, the penetration of the Internet and email by 2010 was 25% of the world's population or 1.8 billion people.

The Web

The World Wide Web (the Web) was invented by Tim Berners-Lee in 1990 as a group work environment to facilitate online collaboration among his fellow scientists at CERN. Based on the concept of hypertext, the project was aimed at facilitating information sharing among researchers. The Web was originally conceived and developed to meet the demand for information sharing between scientists working in different universities and institutes all over the world. CERN is an organization, but it is not a single laboratory; rather, CERN is a focus organization for an extensive community that includes over 8,000 scientists and 60 countries. Although these scientists typically spend time on the CERN site, they usually work at universities and national laboratories in their home countries. Access to online communication was therefore essential to create and maintain the place-independent community.

The basic idea of the Web was to merge the technologies of personal computers, computer networking and hypertext into a powerful and easy-to-use global information system. Berners-Lee developed the protocols underpinning the Web in 1990. The first website went online in 1991. On April 30, 1993, CERN announced that the Web would be free to the public, to enhance interdisciplinary, international and inter-institutional discourse.

The rate of public adoption of the Web has been astronomical and the implications transformational. Within a few months of its public appearance, the Web was adopted worldwide as a means of facilitating ease of access to the Internet and enabling vaster graphic capabilities. Within 15 years, the Web accumulated one billion users. By 2011, it had 2.2 billion users. The Web thus became central to public access to the Internet and also enabled the creation of a global knowledge network.

The rise of the Web was a major catalyst in public use of online technologies: it made access to the Internet easy; it also made the production of online graphics accessible to basic users, making the Web a hospitable and valuable communication space. The Web helped to popularize the term "online." "Online" was no longer a remote or obscure territory: even the next-door neighbors were "online." Communication activities such as email, forums and texting came to expand or replace postal mail, telephone calls and memos.

Having an email identity and online presence is today not only common but expected. An online presence is both a social and an economic phenomenon. We use it increasingly for social communication and work activities. In the early 21st century, the Web underwent a technological maturation and a shift that emphasized social interaction and new interactive tools. Whereas the original Web was based on static Web pages, Web 2.0 focused on dynamic sharable content.

Web 2.0 (the Collaboration Web)

Web 2.0 has come to be associated with, even defined as, the social Web, or the collaborative Web. While social communication, interaction and collaboration, as well as user-generated content, characterized learning networks, online education and virtual communities in the pre-Web decades of Arpanet and the Internet, the emphasis of Web 2.0 was on new or better tools for social interaction, community and collaboration and content construction. Web 2.0 marks an evolution in the tools available to create and support online communities, as well as new developments such as social networking sites, wikis, blogs and communities based on sharing of social objects, such as photos, videos, music, products, encyclopedia topics and classified ads.

Social Networks

The original social software of email and group forums remain major activities on the Web, but it is the invention and adoption of social networks that marks the keystone for Web 2.0. Online social networks, renowned for social discourse and relationship building, were first launched in 2004 with MySpace and Friendster. They have become the major online application. By 2012, Facebook had 1 billion users, and there are 15 social network sites (excluding dating sites) which each have more than 100 million active users. Social network sites in 2012 have over 4.5 billion active users..

Figure 2.3 Web 2.0 the Collaboration Web.

Blogs

The term "blog" derives from weblog, which refers to a personal journal or diary that is available on the Web. The person who maintains and updates the blog is called a blogger. The term originated as a website devoted to a chronological publication of personal thoughts with associated web links, with the postings organized according to the most recent entry. Blog technology enabled the organization of text postings, images and hypertextual linkages. Blogs gained popularity during the 2004 US elections when they were used to report on or discuss political events. Blogs are written in a conversational manner, and a blog today will include comments from readers of the blog that can give rise to a discussion. Nonetheless, a blog is not intended to be a group discussion forum. Blogs were not developed to support social discourse and do not provide technological support for group discussions that evolve and deepen over time, unlike threaded discussion forums or computer conferences.

Social Objects

Web 2.0 is characterized by social networks that are built around the sharing and discussion of particular social objects. Social networks such as Facebook are built principally around posting of messages, while other social networks have emerged based on sharing of photos, videos or other products or media. Many of these networks are associated with the concept of user-generated content because the members create and post content that is public and can be shared with anyone on the Web.

Examples of social networks that have formed around social objects include:

- Flickr: group discussion related to posting and sharing of photos;
- Amazon: group discussion related to posting and sharing of products;
- YouTube: group discussion related to posting and sharing of videos;
- Wikipedia: group discussion related to posting and sharing of encyclopedia topics.

Search Engines

A search engine is a computer program that searches and retrieves files or information from a computer database or computer network. A web search engine is a computer program or tool to search the entire Web. Due to the vast quantity of information available on the Web, search engines have become an essential feature and tool for "surfing." Google.com, for example, is not only the leading web search engine, but the most visited website in the world. It was registered on September 15, 1997, and by 2010 the site had received well over 10 billion hits. The field of web search engines is urgent given the exponential growth of the Web and its content. New search engines are being developed with new ways to search for, analyze and visualize information. While Google remains the leader in terms of market share, new developments such as visualization, the semantic web and cloud computing continually advance our ability to store and retrieve information and organize it for building knowledge. The capacity and scope of Web-based applications has grown exponentially.

The Web has also introduced remarkable opportunities for transforming teaching and learning and advancing online learning. However, the history of online learning began long before the Web; it was one of the earliest applications of the Net. Within a few years of the invention of Arpanet, the beginnings of online education took shape.

Historical Overview of Online Learning

Online learning (or online education) refers to the use of online communication networks for educational applications, such as: course delivery and support of educational projects, research,

TABLE 2.1 Brief History of Online Learning

Year	Technology	Online Educational Applications
1861	Telegraph is invented	
1876	Telephone is invented	
1969	Arpanet is invented	
1971	Email is invented	
1972	Computer conferencing is invented	
Mid-1970s		First adjunct mode online courses
Mid-1970s		Online communities of practice (OCoP)
1981		First totally online courses (adult education)
1982		First online program (executive education)
1983		Blended classroom model emerges (schools)
1984		First totally online undergraduate courses
1985		First totally online graduate courses
1989	Internet launched	
1989		First large-scale online courses
1993	World Wide Web is made public	
1995		First state university adoption
1996		First large-scale online education field trials
1997		First industry-wide adoption
2004		Online education mainstreams

access to resources and group collaboration. Online learning is mediated by the Web. The implications of the Internet and Web technologies for education are still unfolding—providing new experiences to generate understanding of how to benefit from and improve learning online. The need to understand how this major technological revolution is influencing education and transforming our discipline is critical, from the smallest to the most dramatic changes.

The earliest form of online education was invented in the mid-1970s by academics who were also engaged as Arpanet researchers. These were academics working on Arpanet developments, and introduced the innovations they were encountering as topics in their university courses, thereby introducing students to email (then known as electronic mail) and computer conferencing as course content. Educational experimentation and student interest in these new communication technologies ignited exploration, and, as a result, computer-mediated communication (CMC) became not only course content but pedagogical process. Students began to use email to send questions to their professors and comments to one another, while faculty explored applications of email and computer conferencing for providing additional information to students, clarifying questions and expanding opportunities for time- and place-independent group discussion in their courses.

Soon educators from a wider set of disciplines within universities and eventually from the school system began to experiment with educational CMC, and the "adjunct" or enhanced mode of online learning was born.

Adjunct Mode Online Learning

The adjunct or enhanced mode of online education refers to the use of network communication to enhance traditional face-to-face (or f2f) distance education. In adjunct mode, the use of the Internet is an add-on that complements the existing curriculum. The online activities do not replace the traditional techniques nor do they represent a significant portion of the course grade. They are used to enhance the class activities. Examples of this pedagogical approach include the use of email to contact a professor or submit assignments, the distribution of course material by the instructor, as well as the administering of quizzes or distribution of course grades. Adjunct mode also involves student use of the Internet to search for course resources and undertake course-related research. It provides a new approach for extending group discussion: the use of computer conferences or forums enables the continuation of discussion initiated in class or the inclusion of guest experts or peers from other locations. Originating in the 1970s, adjunct mode was the first major educational application on the Internet. Today, adjunct mode is ubiquitous in the use of the Internet for learning throughout the world.

Mixed-mode or Blended-mode Learning

By the early 1980s, new online educational applications emerged, expanding adjunct mode into "mixed mode" or "blended mode," in which a significant portion of the traditional face-to-face classroom or distance education course was conducted online (Harasim, 2006a). Typically about 50% of course activities and of the overall grade is based on online activities in blended mode. Today the term blended mode is used in many ways: it typically refers to a mix of face-to-face and online course activities. However, blended learning can also be used to describe a pedagogical mix of distance education or courseware applications with online collaborative activities such as group discussions, seminars, debates, research or group projects. Blending may also be institutional, as in the case of a degree program offered by two or more institutions, or instructional, to refer to a course with team teaching.

Totally Online Learning

The earliest totally online courses were developed and offered in the mid-1980s at post-secondary levels. The courses were based on online collaborative learning approaches such as seminars and group discussion (Harasim et al., 1995; Mason & Kaye, 1989; Harasim, 1990b, 2006a).

As educators and researchers adopted this new domain in their work, they also wrote about it and presented their experiences to scholarly and professional venues; interest in online learning was generated and the field began to grow. However, in its early manifestations in the 1980s, it remained limited to a relatively small group of early advocates.

Most of the early online learning pioneers came from the face-to-face classroom context. The earliest users and adopters emphasized pedagogies involving student collaboration, interaction and knowledge building. In the decade before the public launch of the Internet and the World Wide Web, distance education did not identify with online education, nor were courseware providers able to easily offer their individualized multimedia pedagogy online. The collaborative learning approach was largely the norm for online education in the 1980s.

Summary

Chapter 2 discussed how from mankind's earliest days, learning and technology have been profoundly linked; they are kindred spirits, consonant and interconnected. And, linked to collaboration, they enhance the essence of what it means to be human. The four major paradigmatic shifts associated with speech, writing, printing and the Internet illuminate how technology and learning formed the basis for civilizational advances. The invention of the Internet and the Web are transforming our contemporary society, thereby introducing opportunities and motivation for transforming the conditions of learning: how we view learning, and how we can shape our educational practice to better support learning.

Chapter 2 provided an introduction for Chapters 3, 4 and 5 which examine key learning theories and technologies in the 20th century. These chapters also build a framework for considering new theoretical approaches for teaching and learning online.

3
Behaviorist Learning Theory

The science of education can and will itself contribute abundantly to psychology. Not only do the laws derived by psychology from simple, specially arranged experiments help us to interpret and control mental action under the conditions of schoolroom life. Schoolroom life itself is a vast laboratory in which are made thousands of experiments of utmost interest to "pure" psychology.

Edward L. Thorndike, 1910

abstract relationships sample behavior abstractions automatic behavior behavior specialists behavioral instructional theory behaviorism behaviorist learning theory behavioural instructional design taxonomies bloom cognitive domain conditional stimulus conditioned stimulus correct answer correct behavior educational psychology field sample behavior human behavior human behaviors instructional design instructional stimuli interpretation extrapolation sample behavior learning theory negative reinforcement new behavior observable behavior operant behavior organism behavior organizational principles sample behavior particular behaviors particular stimulus pavlov pavlov watson thorndike skinner behaviorist positive behavior positive reinforcement programmed instruction repetitious behavior reward punishment scientific theory skinner stimulus student behavior subjectivity taxonomies taxonomy teaching machine teaching machines unconditioned stimulus undesired behavior verbal behavior voluntary behavior

Chapter 3 presents the following topics:

- Context of behaviorist theory
- Behaviorist learning theory and major thinkers

    - Pavlov
    - Watson
    - Thorndike
    - Skinner

- Behaviorist learning pedagogy

    - Reward and punishment
    - Behavioral instructional design
    - Taxonomies of learning

- Behaviorist learning technology

    - Teaching machines
    - Computer-assisted instruction (CAI).

Context of Behaviorist Theory

The 20th century marks the period when theories of learning and academic scholarship in education emerged and flourished. Given the 1,000-year history of formalized learning, it may be surprising to discover that a science or theory of learning emerged only in the past 100 years. However, as Chapter 1 explained, while discussions of learning have been ongoing for millennia, these discussions were rooted in philosophy and religious thought, not theory.

Positivism and the rise of scientific method had a strong influence on the emerging field of education in the early 20th century. In particular, the discipline of psychology had an impact on education because psychology studied human behavior and had already established empirical research methods based on a positivist framework. In general, learning theories of the 20th century were derived from educational psychology. Educational researchers and psychologists sought to better understand learning by collecting and analyzing empirical data generated through clinical experimentation. The nature of learning, how learning occurs, what influences learning (positively and negatively), how to structure and support learning and what we believe learning to be were largely based on interpretations of experiments with laboratory animals. The resultant perspectives were influential, but also issues of significant debate.

In the early 20th century, with the rise of modern science and new communication technologies, the speed of change increased: ideas were more easily communicated, disseminated and debated. Freud, together with his colleagues, had contributed to the rise of psychology as an empirical field and discipline. Moreover, to some degree it was Freudian theory that influenced and led to the first theory of learning: behaviorism. Behaviorism emerged as a reaction *against* the Freudian emphasis on the unconscious mind and the Freudian use of introspective analysis and self-reports to study the mind. Behaviorism was a counterargument to this position. Behaviorism distrusted self-reports as a source of reliable data and instead emphasized that which was strictly observable. Under behaviorism, the definition of learning was reduced and simplified to simple conditioning: the stimulus and the response. The motto of behaviorism might well be expressed as "behavior, not mind!"

Behaviorist Learning Theory

Behaviorist learning theory focuses on that which is observable: how people behave and especially how to change or elicit particular behaviors. In the early 20th century, behaviorism introduced a theory of learning that was empirical, observable and measurable.

This earliest theory of learning emphasized overt action: that which was most easily apparent and accessible for study, behavior. The term "overt action" means behavior and behaviorists studied how we act and what impacts upon and changes how we act. Based on clinical experiments with animals, behaviorist thinkers discovered that a response to certain stimuli would be repeated, and could be observed, controlled and quantified.

Behaviorist theory could not account for subjectivity and, given its historical context, it would not. The early rise of scientific theory was set in the context of positivism. To be considered a "science," behaviorism had to adhere to rigid positivist principles, which were based upon rigorous "objectivity" and ignored or dismissed "subjectivity" and anything to do with introspection or mental states (called mentalism at the time). To be considered scientific, research must employ the experimental method, which involves manipulating one variable to determine if changes in one variable cause changes in another variable. This method relies on controlled methods, random assignment and the manipulation of variables to test a hypothesis.

> [B]ehaviorism embodies two of the key principles of positivism: that our knowledge of the world can only evolve from the observation of objective facts and phenomena; and that theory can only be built by applying this observation in experiments where only one or two

factors are allowed to vary as a function of an experimenter's manipulation or control of other related factors. (Winn & Snyder, 1996, p. 114)

In behaviorist theory, what is in the mind is not accessible for study, and hence irrelevant and should not be considered in research. The mind is viewed as a black box that is largely irrelevant, and, therefore, by extension educational practice based on behaviorist terms would not take the mind into account. The emphasis is on environmental stimulus and observed response.

Behaviorist learning theory emphasizes two major types of conditioning:

- *classical conditioning*: for example, Pavlov's dog experiments in which behavior becomes a reflex response to a stimulus; and
- *operant conditioning*: the example of Skinner's rat experiments, which refer to the reinforcement of a behavior by a reward or punishment.

Pavlov: Classical Conditioning

The development of behaviorism is associated with many scientists, but most famously with the Russian physiologist, Ivan Pavlov (1849–1936), who is considered the intellectual founder of behaviorist learning theory. He is famous for his theory of classical conditioning and his experiments with a dog, food and a bell. Pavlov was a physiologist involved in medical research, with special interest in reflexes. Reflexes are automatic behavior caused by stimulus in the environment: the smell of food cooking causes us to salivate. In 1904 Pavlov won the Nobel Prize in Medicine (Physiology) in recognition of his work on the physiology of digestion. It was his pioneering work in digestion that led him to serendipitously discover what he subsequently called conditioned reflexes. Pavlov was studying the physiology of digestion in dogs, when he discovered that in addition to salivating in the presence of meat powder, dogs had begun to salivate in the presence of the lab technician who fed them, even if there was no meat powder around. The dogs had learned to associate food with the person who fed them; this person became the stimulus for the food and his presence would cause salivation on its own. Pavlov began to study the stimulus and response in dog salivation, using a bell (a neutral stimulus), which became associated with feeding time, and thus became a conditioned stimulus as a result of consistent pairing with the unconditioned stimulus, meat powder in this example. Pavlov referred to a relationship that can be learned as conditional reflex, as opposed to unconditioned reflexes that are natural. This became the theory of classical conditioning. Pavlov manipulated the situation of stimulus–response, by linking a conditional stimulus (the bell) to the unconditional stimulus (the food), and eventually took the unconditional stimulus away. The dog now salivated to the bell. This demonstrated that behavior could be manipulated through conditioning: responses could be manipulated or learned. Pavlov proved that a conditional stimulus could cause a response on its own, demonstrating that classical conditioning succeeded. Classical conditioning refers to a theory about how behavior is learned and was first applied to animals and then to humans.

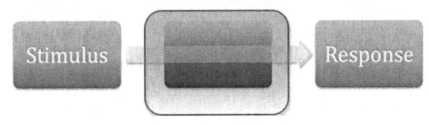

Figure 3.1 Behaviorist "Black Box."

Here is a simple description of Pavlov's experiment:

- before conditioning: the dog is a normal canine; placing food in front of the dog stimulates the dog to salivate;
- during conditioning: a bell rings a few seconds before food is presented in front of the dog;
- after conditioning: the ringing bell is enough to cause the dog to salivate, even when food is absent.

The above experiment may seem simplistic but the results are widely regarded as representing the first major theory of learning; that is, a theory based on scientific evidence that is replicable and observable. Behaviorism emphasized that the repetition of a certain behavioral pattern makes that pattern automatic. If it is replicable and observable, then it is real. This is the underlying behaviorist theory of learning. Behaviorism was based upon empirical evidence and arguably, therefore, part of the emerging stream of scientific processes, reflecting modern science.

Watson

Many psychology researchers expressed interest in Pavlov's ideas, and as his research was shifted to human behavior, these other researchers also contributed their ideas on human psychology and learning theory to build a school of thought. John B. Watson (1878–1958) was the first American psychologist to use Pavlov's ideas and is credited with coining the term "behaviorism." In 1913, Watson published *Psychology as the Behaviorist Views It.* "Psychology as the behaviorist views it," wrote Watson,

> is a purely objective experimental branch of natural science. Its theoretical goal is the prediction and control of behavior. Introspection forms no essential part of its methods, nor is the scientific value of its data dependent upon the readiness with which they lend themselves to interpretation in terms of consciousness. (1913, p. 158)

He subsequently wrote many other works on the subject. Watson was very firmly a behaviorist and was a significant force in establishing behaviorism in the United States. He describes

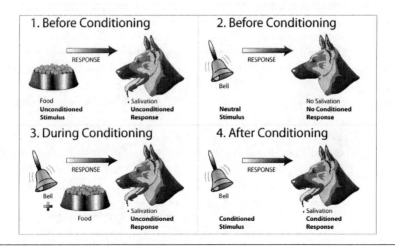

Figure 3.2 Classical Conditioning: Pavlov's Dog Experiment.

psychology as the process where behavior is predictable and controlled, and he argues that terms such as *consciousness, mind* or *images* do not have a place in psychology:

> I believe we can write a psychology ... and ... never use the terms consciousness, mental states, mind, content, introspectively verifiable imagery, and the like.... It can be done in terms of stimulus and response, in terms of habit formation, habit integrations and the like.... In a system of psychology completely worked out, given the response the stimuli can be predicted; given the stimuli the response can be predicted. (1913, p. 167)

Thorndike

Edward L. Thorndike (1874–1949) was interested in the association or connection between sensation and impulse, and studied learning connected to action. His work is referred to as *connectionism* within the behaviorist school. Thorndike's experiments with a "puzzle box" measured the amount of time it took an animal to operate the latch of the box and to escape. The animal was repeatedly returned to the puzzle box and would again escape. The amount of time taken to escape decreased with exposure, however, as the animal associated the inside of the box with the impulse to escape. These experiments supported the view that learning is the result of associations forming between stimuli (S) and responses (R). According to Thorndike, such associations or "habits" become strengthened or weakened by the nature and frequency of the S–R pairings. Thorndike's S–R theory was based on the concept of trial-and-error learning in which certain responses come to dominate others due to rewards. Thorndike's experiments also led him to question the existence of the animal's mental states, suggesting that the animals act without thinking or feeling. Connectionism (like all behavioral theory) posited that learning could be adequately explained without referring to any unobservable internal states.

Skinner: Operant Conditioning

The American psychologist, Burrhus Frederic Skinner (1904–1990), is also famously associated with behaviorist learning theory. However, Skinner's work differed from his Pavlovian predecessors in that Skinner focused on voluntary or operant behavioral conditioning, whereas Pavlov focused on what is known as classical conditioning.

Operant conditioning was introduced by Skinner as an alternative to Pavlov's classical conditioning. Pavlov's work focused on how a neutral stimulus, such as a bell, affected a result, whereas Skinner explored how a direct stimulus led to a positive response that created a behavioral change. Skinner's work is known as operant conditioning, and emphasizes the use of positive and negative reinforcement to manipulate or teach new behavior. Operant conditioning is related to voluntary behavior rather than involuntary reflexive responses.

Through experimentation Skinner discovered that behavior can be conditioned by using both positive and negative reinforcement. One well-known example is that of a laboratory rat learning to find the cheese in a maze. Positive reinforcement conditions the rat to find the end of the maze through successive approximations, or steps. First, the rat is placed in a maze with the cheese located nearby. The rat is rewarded with the cheese when it reaches the first turn (A). Once the first kind of behavior becomes ingrained, the rat is not rewarded until it makes the second turn (B). After many times through the maze, the rat must reach the end of the maze to receive its reward (C). Skinner's research on operant conditioning led him to conclude that simply rewarding small acts can condition complex forms of behavior.

Operant refers to the process of operating on the environment. The subject, in this case a rat, is doing whatever it does in the box shaped like a maze. While so doing (operating), the rat encounters a special stimulus, cheese. The cheese is called a reinforcing stimulus. This special stimulus has the effect of changing or modifying the behavior of the subject, tending to reinforce the tendency to repeat the behavior in future. The stimulus will cause the rat to make the correct turn in the maze to find the cheese. If the cheese is moved, the rat must learn to follow the pathway until another reward is discovered (by taking another turn in the maze), and so on. If the cheese disappears, the operant behavior is extinguished. A behavior followed by the reinforcing stimulus results in increased probability of that behavior occurring in the future, whereas a behavior no longer followed by the reinforcing stimulus results in a decreased probability of that behavior.

However, experiments also demonstrated that many repetitions were required before laboratory animals (mice, rats) learned that certain responses resulted in a reward of food (stimulus). Skinner found that such changes in behavior took considerable time and required many successive approximations of behavior. This meant that any changes in behavior required many repetitions before they were learned. Often a big change would be reduced to many smaller acts or components repeated over a long period.

Skinner was a strong adherent of behaviorism and focused on changes in observable behavior, ignoring the possibility of any processes in the mind. He dismissed mentalism or processes of the mind as "fiction." Skinner concentrated on science as empirical observation and viewed psychology as part of the scientific revolution (he excluded biology and the social sciences). Psychology need not consider fictional concepts such as "subjectivity," because psychology was a science.

> Psychology, alone among the biological and social sciences, passed through a revolution comparable in many respects to that which was taking place at the same time in physics. This was, of course, behaviorism. The first step, like that in physics, was a reexamination of the observational bases of certain important concepts.... Most of the early behaviorists, as well as those of us just coming along who claimed some systematic continuity, had begun to see that psychology did not require the redefinition of subjective concepts. The reinterpretation of an established set of fictions was not the way to secure the tools then needed for a scientific description of behavior.... There was no more reason to make a permanent place for "consciousness," "will," "feeling," and so on, than to make a permanent place for "phlogiston" or "vis anima."[1] (Skinner, 1964, p. 292)

In 1948, Skinner published the book *Walden Two*, about a utopian society based on operant conditioning. *Walden Two* is science fiction novel that presents an experimental community based on a planned economy, critical of inefficient capitalism. The community's government is not democratic and is governed by Planners and Managers. The code of conduct is based on

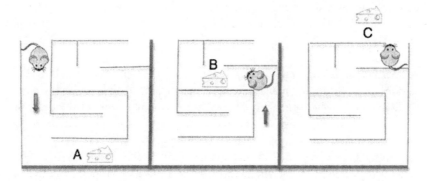

Figure 3.3 Operant Conditioning: Skinner's Rat and Cheese Maze.

behaviorism. Work is limited to four hours of work daily from each person and engaging in the arts and applied scientific research is promoted. Children are educated communally by trained behavior specialists, outside the nuclear family, and loyal to the community.

Skinner's 1953 book, *Science and Human Behavior*, was a nonfiction consideration of how operant behavior could function in reality, in such social institutions as education, economics, law, religion and government. Operant conditioning would shape behavior through such mechanisms as positive reinforcement (reward), negative reinforcement, non-reinforcement and punishment.

However, there were some significant problems with Skinner's own science, in particular a disturbing disjuncture between his model and the empirical results of his experiments. Some researchers argued that his claims exceeded his evidence and that he could not prove or demonstrate empirically that the responses were the result of a particular stimulus. Skinner responded to these criticisms, the "psychologist's fallacy" attributed to the stimulus–response model, by creating a set of highly controlled conditions in which a discriminating stimulus could be defined and linked to a specific and particular response. But Skinner's approach to creating a positivistic and interpretation-free psychology resulted in a model that was testable only under very limited and limiting conditions. And this too was critiqued. Skinner's work on verbal behavior was criticized, for example, by Noam Chomsky (1959), who argued that Skinner's claims exceeded what was "lawfully" demonstrated by his research, and wrote that Skinner either had to reduce his claims or admit that they were not based on scientific evidence. Most behavior could not be explained by Skinner's research, wrote Chomsky:

> If he (a behaviorist) accepts the broad definitions, characterizing any physical event imping-ing on the organism as a stimulus and any part of the organism's behavior as a response, he must conclude that most behavior has not been demonstrated to be lawful.... If we accept the narrower definitions, then behavior is lawful by definition (if it consists of responses); but this fact is of limited significance, since most of what the animal does will simply not be considered behavior. Hence the psychologist either must admit that behavior is not lawful, or must restrict his attention to those highly limited arenas in which it is lawful.... Skinner does not consistently adopt either course. (1959, p. 30)

Eric Bredo's (2006) article "Conceptual Confusion and Educational Psychology" addressed issues where learning theorists demonstrated psychological fallacies and limitations in their positions. Bredo writes of behaviorism:

> In effect, the doctrinaire behaviorist has to choose between being "scientific" in a narrow positivistic sense only under highly controlled conditions, or generalizing to less controlled conditions in a merely metaphorical or interpretive way. Chomsky argued that Skinner could not have it both ways. (2006, p. 49)

Moreover, Bredo suggests the stimulus–response model of the organism tends toward notions of mechanization of education and management of learning, in which a "real science" of psychology would be based on what was essentially an "input-output model of the organism. It also seemed as though a positivistic psychology might make it possible to mechanize education and perhaps even create a scientifically managed social utopia" (Bredo, 2006, pp. 47–48). The S–R model was criticized as narrow, conceptually confused and mechanistic.

As early as 1896, John Dewey had already criticized the stimulus–response model as deterministic and wrong because it succumbed to the psychologist's fallacy. He wrote:

The fallacy that arises when this is done is virtually the psychological or historical fallacy. A set of considerations which hold good only because of a completed process, is read into the content of the process which conditions this completed result. A state of things characterizing an outcome is regarded as a true description of the event which led up to this outcome; when as a matter of fact, if this outcome had already been in existence, there would have been no necessity for the process. (1896, p. 367)

Behaviorist learning theory has been most successful or relevant in contexts where the learning objectives to be attained are unambiguous and where their attainment can be judged according to commonly agreed upon criteria of successful performance in task-oriented learning. Examples might be learning accountancy procedures, learning to swim or learning to operate a sophisticated machine.

Behaviorist Learning Pedagogy

Behaviorist pedagogy aims to promote and modify observable behavior in people. Learning is considered a behavior that demonstrates acquisition of knowledge or skills. To understand behaviorist learning pedagogy, we look at the following three techniques and models:

- Reward and punishment;
- Behavioral instructional design;
- Taxonomies of learning.

Reward and Punishment

Behaviorist techniques are employed in education to promote behavior that is desirable and to discourage that which is not. The most common is the behaviorist technique of reward (positive reinforcement) and punishment (negative reinforcement). A number of classroom practices find their roots in this technique. Some examples are outlined below.

- *Contracts* are established between a student and a teacher or a counselor regarding behavior change. If a student is not completing homework, the student and teacher might design a contract outlining agreed-upon changes: for example, the student agrees to request extra help and the teacher agrees to be available after school to provide additional assistance.
- *Consequences* occur immediately after a behavior, and may be positive or negative, short or long term. Consequences occur after the "target" behavior occurs, and, whether positive or negative, reinforcement may be applied.
- *Positive reinforcement* (reward) is the presentation of a stimulus that increases the likelihood of a response. For example, a teacher provides positive reinforcement by smiling at students after they provide a correct response or commending students for their good work.
- *Negative reinforcement* increases the likelihood of a positive behavior by withdrawing or removing a consequence that the student finds unpleasant. For example, achieving an 80% score on a test makes the final exam optional.
- *Positive punishment* refers to adding something that decreases the undesired behavior. For example, after-school detention for coming late to school.
- *Negative punishment* refers to removing something that decreases the undesired behavior. An example is missing recess as a consequence of misbehaving in class. (Standridge, 2002)

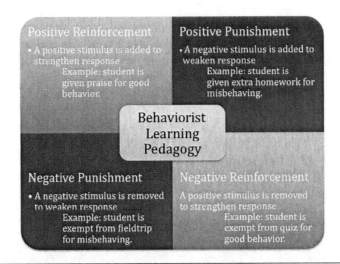

Figure 3.4 Examples of Behaviorist Pedagogy: Punishment and Reinforcement.

The prevailing pedagogy of behaviorist learning theory is aimed at achieving the correct (intended) behavior. Behaviorist learning theory focuses significantly on predictability: that is, ensuring that what is intended is achieved, and that the link between a stimulus and the response it evokes is reliable. The response to a particular stimulus should be consistent, automatic and replicable, time after time.

A correct response to a stimulus would receive a positive reward. An incorrect response to a stimulus would yield a negative response (punishment). Behavioral pedagogies were rigidly adopted in some quarters within the field of learning theory. Memorization, repetition, reinforcement of correct answers, examinations and the organization of the curriculum content into specific behavioral objectives resulted.

Behavioral Instructional Design

Behaviorism was prominent in the origins of instructional design. Instructional design is the systematic planning and presenting of instructional sequences, based on a theory of learning. Behavioral instructional theory therefore consists of prescriptions for what stimuli to employ if a particular response is intended. "The instructional designer can be reasonably certain that with the right set of instructional stimuli all manner of learning outcomes can be attained" (Winn & Snyder, 1996, p. 133).

As Watson (1919) argued, the focus of instructional design is precision, prediction and replication:

> We want to predict with reasonable certainty what people will do in specific situations. Given a stimulus, defined as an object of inner or outer experience, what response may be expected? A stimulus could be a blow to the knee or an architect's education; a response could be a knee jerk or the building of a bridge. Similarly, we want to know, given a response, what situation produced it…. In all such situations the discovery of the stimuli that call out one or another behavior should allow us to influence the occurrence of behaviors: prediction, which comes from such discoveries, allows control. (Quoted in Burton et al., 1996, p. 47)

Behavioral instructional design was also influenced by its context. In addition to the emphasis on predictable change in student behavior, behavioral instructional design was also influenced by World War II military trainers (and psychologists) who emphasized practice and reinforcement in military training. They determined the learning outcomes necessary for "performance" and identified the specific "tasks" required to perform a job. "Based on training in the military during the Second World War, a commitment to achieve practice and reinforcement became major components to the behaviorist-developed instructional design model (as well as nonbehavioristic models)" (Burton et al., 1996, p. 58). This definition of education and learning as control and predictability of behavior became increasingly controversial: while Bertrand Russell claimed that Watson made "the greatest contribution to scientific psychology since Aristotle," others referred to Watson as the "simpleton or archfiend ... who denied the very existence of mind and consciousness [and] reduced us to the status of robots" (Malone, 1990, as quoted by Burton et al., 1996, p. 47).

Taxonomies of Learning

Behaviorism emphasized the ability to analyze and deconstruct the elements or steps of learning into instructional design, by breaking down a task into smaller steps or chunks and by specifying behavioral objectives. To develop behavioral objectives, it is necessary to identify and specify quantifiable behaviors or outcomes: for example, *95% of the learners will correctly answer all questions on this post-test, after completing the assigned educational unit.* Learning success was assessed by tests developed to measure performance in relation to each objective.

Taxonomies or classifications of learning behaviors were therefore considered to be important, in order to design and test instruction. Benjamin Bloom's 1956 taxonomy of learning (cognitive, affective and psychomotor domains) is a classic in this field. Benjamin Bloom (1913–1999) was an American educational psychologist recognized for his significant contributions to the classification of educational objectives. He worked on the problem of how to develop specifications so that educational objectives could be organized according to their cognitive complexity. Such a classification or hierarchy would be the basis for assessing student outcomes and provide professors with more reliable procedures for setting and assessing instructional objectives. It could also serve as means for formulating instructional objectives.

Developed in fact by a committee of college and university examiners, Bloom was the editor and principal author of *Taxonomy of Educational Objectives: The Classification of Educational Goals*. The purpose of a taxonomy, as Bloom noted in his Foreword, was to permit classification of educational objectives just as biological taxonomies classified plants and animals into such categories as phylum, class, order, family and genus. Bloom "intended to provide for classification of the goals of our educational system. It is expected to be of general help to all teachers, administrators, professional specialists, and research workers who deal with curricular and evaluation problems" (Bloom et al., 1956, p. 1). The taxonomy could help teachers specify curricular objectives and ensure that the educational plans cover the range of behaviors required to be taught.

The taxonomy was to comprise three handbooks: Handbook I addressed the cognitive domain and was published in 1956. It is the text commonly referred to as Bloom's taxonomy of learning. Handbook II, on the affective domain, and Handbook III, on the manipulative or motor-skill area, were produced by other writers. Handbook I focused on the cognitive domain, which involves knowledge and the development of intellectual skills including recall or recognition of specific facts, procedural patterns and concepts that serve in the development of intellectual abilities and skills. The six categories set out as learning objectives for students were listed according to level of difficulty, in that the first must be mastered before the next. Bloom describes these as follows:

a. *Knowledge*:

Knowledge, as defined here, involves the recall of specifics and universals, the recall of methods and processes, or the recall of a pattern, structure or setting. For measurement purposes, the recall situation involves little more than bringing to mind the appropriate materials. Although some alteration of the material may be required, this is a relatively minor part of the task. The knowledge objectives emphasize most the psychological processes of remembering. (Bloom et al., 1956, p. 201)

Knowledge is further structured into subcategories:
- Knowledge of Specifics
- Knowledge of Ways and Means
- Knowledge of the Universals and Abstractions in a Field
- *Sample behavior: The student will recall the three subcategories of Bloom's definition of knowledge.*

b. *Comprehension*:

This represents the lowest level of understanding. It refers to a type of understanding or apprehension such that the individual knows what is being communicated and can make use of the materials or idea being communicated without necessarily relating it to other materials or seeing its fullest implications. (Bloom et al., 1956, p. 204)

Subcategories include:
- Translation
- Interpretation
- Extrapolation
- *Sample behavior: The student will explain the purpose of Bloom's taxonomy of the cognitive domain.*

c. *Application*:

The use of abstractions in particular and concrete situations. The abstractions may be in a form of general ideas, rules of procedures, or generalized methods. The abstractions may also be technical principles, ideas, and theories which must be remembered and applied. (Bloom et al., 1956, p. 205)
- *Sample behavior: The student will write an instructional objective for each level of Bloom's taxonomy of the cognitive domain.*

d. *Analysis*:

The breakdown of a communication into its constituent elements or parts such that the relative hierarchy of ideas is made clear and/or the relations between ideas expressed are made explicit. Such analyses are intended to clarify the communication, to indicate how the communication is organized and the way in which it manages to convey its effects, as well as its basis and arrangement. (Bloom et al., 1956, p. 205)

Analysis is divided into:
- Analysis of Elements

- Analysis of Relationships
- Analysis of Organizational Principles
- *Sample behavior: The student will compare and contrast the cognitive and affective domains.*

e. *Synthesis:*

The putting together of elements and parts so as to form a whole. This involves the process of working with pieces, parts, elements, etc., and arranging and combining them in such a way as to constitute a pattern or structure not clearly there before. (Bloom et al., 1956, pp. 205–206)

Subsections are:
- Production of a Unique Communication
- Production of a Plan, or Proposed Set of Operations
- Derivation of a Set of Abstract Relationships
- *Sample behavior: The student will design a classification scheme for writing educational objectives that combines the cognitive, affective and psychomotor domains.*

f. *Evaluation:*

Judgments about the value of materials and methods for given purposes. Quantitative and qualitative judgments about the extent to which material and methods satisfy criteria. The criteria may be those determined by the student or those which are given to him. (Bloom et al., 1956, p. 207)
- Judgments in terms of internal evidence
- Judgments in terms of external criteria
- *Sample behavior: The student will judge the effectiveness of writing objectives using Bloom's taxonomy of the cognitive domain.*

Learning taxonomies assisted instructional designers in identifying behaviors that could be deconstructed and programmed as learning objectives and tasks, as well as in quantifying and assessing the outcomes. Learning taxonomies provided a kind of framework or template for describing and categorizing human behavior, although trying to identify the immense range of all human behaviors soon proved to be unrealistic and impossible. In 1962, Robert Gagné developed a taxonomy of learning that comprised five domains. Gagné's taxonomy became the basis for cognitivist instructional design and technology and is discussed in greater detail in Chapter 4.

Behaviorist Learning Technology

Instructional technology has its roots in behaviorism. The rise of scientific methodology and the study of how people learn coincided with mechanization in the labor force and demands for an increasingly educated population.

Industrialization required workers who could read and follow instructions. They should be able to perform their tasks repeatedly and reliably. Education must be able to teach literacy and to instill the discipline for repetitious behavior and predictable performance at work. Mass schooling and compulsory education were developed to meet these needs. These needs were also fueled by World War II and the need for highly skilled workers, which required major training initiatives.

Behavioral learning theory lent itself not only to instructional design based on very specific and discrete learning steps, but also to mechanization of this process through new forms of learning technologies. Learning technologies that were intended to encourage practice and reinforcement of specific tasks were developed. Mechanization also appealed to the need for efficiency and to making instruction more methodical. Two major examples of technologies based on behaviorist learning theory emerged:

- Teaching machines and programmed instruction;
- Computer-assisted instruction (CAI).

Teaching Machines and Programmed Instruction

Teaching machines were first developed in the mid-1920s as self-scoring testing devices. The teaching machine housed a list of questions and a mechanism through which the learner responded to questions. Upon delivering a correct answer, the learner is rewarded. The earliest examples of teaching machines included automatic (chemically treated) scoring cards used for self-checking by students while studying the reading assignment. A similar form of individualized learning and immediate feedback was achieved with the use of punch cards.

Another early example is the testing device developed by Sidney Pressey, an educational psychology professor at Ohio State University. He developed a machine to provide drill-and-practice items to students in his introductory courses. Pressey (1926, p. 374) stated, "the procedures in mastery of drill and informational material were in many instances simple and definite enough to permit handling of much routine teaching by mechanical means." The teaching machine that

Figure 3.5 Pressey's Testing Machine.

Pressey developed, shown in Figure 3.5, resembled a typewriter carriage with a window that revealed a question with four possible answers. On one side of the carriage were four keys. The user pressed the key that corresponded to the correct answer. When the user pressed a key, the machine recorded the answer on a counter to the back of the machine and revealed the next question. After the user was finished, the person scoring the test slipped the test sheet back into the device and noted the score on the counter.

Skinner updated the teaching machine in the 1950s, shown in Figure 3.6, under the name of programmed instruction (PI). PI derived from teaching machines by linking self-instruction of the content with self-testing. This approach dominated the field in the 1960s and 1970s. Whereas earlier forms of teaching/testing devices employed multiple-choice approaches, Skinner required students to form composed responses (words, terms) and he sought totally correct answers; PI would reinforce a response that was close to the correct answer/behavior and through successive approximations would seek to achieve the desired behavior and avoid any wrong answers.

PI was based on Skinner's theory of "verbal behavior" as a means to accelerate and increase conventional educational learning. It consisted of self-teaching with the aid of a specialized textbook or teaching machine that presented material structured in a logical and empirically developed sequence or set of sequences. PI allowed students to progress through a unit of study at their own rate, checking their own answers and advancing only after answering correctly. In one simplified form of PI, after each step, students are presented with a question to test their comprehension, then immediately shown the correct answer or given additional information. The main objective of instructional programming is to present the material in small increments so that students could approximate and eventually achieve total accuracy in their responses.

Figure 3.6 Skinner's Teaching Machine.

Teaching machines and PI emphasized the development of hardware rather than software (or content). Even though PI eventually moved to focus more on content and analysis of instruction, it soon disappeared from educational consideration and use.

Computer-Assisted Instruction (CAI)

Computer-assisted instruction (CAI) was developed during the 1950s for teaching and training. CAI is essentially a drill-and-practice approach to learning, and the control is with the program designer and not the learner (although small levels of individual customization were implemented). It is the earliest example of educational applications of a computer. Computing in the 1950s and 1960s was very complex but educational applications were already being envisioned and implemented. Due to significant technical problems, lack of quality software and high costs, this approach did not initially flourish. However, the US Department of Defense became a major, and occasionally the major, player in funding CAI developments during the 1950s and until today (Fletcher, 2009). Two early projects were PLATO and TICCIT. PLATO (Programmed Logic for Automated Teaching Operations) was specifically designed for developing and presenting instruction. PLATO was one of several projects at the University of Illinois Coordinated Science Laboratory funded by the military in the 1950s. Its major impact is considered to be in "encouraging individuals to develop and use CAI" (Fletcher, 2009, p. 72). TICCIT (Time-shared Interactive Computer-controlled Television) was developed at the University of Texas, and later Brigham Young University, as a computer system designed to implement formal principles of instructional design. Many of the techniques developed for PLATO and TICCIT found their way into K-12 and university education.

In the 1980s, with the rise of personal computing and its appearance in the school system, CAI approaches flourished in the public sector. There were as yet no competing educational computing options. Personal computers were in their initial stages, and educational adoption of computers was at its most primitive. Drill and practice, and "electronic page turning," both associated with CAI, were the earliest forms of educational software. These approaches were relatively easy to program on a computer; they required little computer memory and reflected the low level of understanding of educational computing of the time.

The military, however, found CAI approaches to be highly efficient. While the costs of anticipating responses to all learner states and interactions were a problem, a growing body of data indicated success.

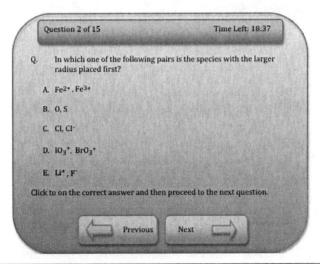

Figure 3.7 Example of a CAI Chemistry Exam Question.

Figure 3.8 Students Using CAI.

Among the findings from comparisons of CAI with standard classroom learning in military, academic and industry sectors were reductions of 24 to 54% in the time taken to learn. Technology costs aside, a 30% reduction in the time needed to learn would save the DOD 15 to 25% of the $4 to 5 billion it spends annually for specialized skill training (from novice to journeyman). (Fletcher, 2009, p. 72)

Today, the military continues to support CAI development and applications, in the form of intelligent tutoring systems (ITS), and also through the development of digital learning objects.

Summary

Chapter 3 introduced behaviorism, the earliest theory of learning developed. Behaviorism also offers the simplest explanation of learning theories to date. It focuses exclusively on behavior and posits that a stimulus leads to a response: S — R.

The chapter explored the two major types of conditioning the characterize behaviorism. Classical conditioning, associated with Ivan Pavlov and his famous "dog experiments," held that behavior is conditioned to become a reflex response to a stimulus. Operant conditioning, the theory of B. F. Skinner, refers to the reinforcement of a behavior by a reward or a punishment.

There have been many critiques of behaviorism's rigid focus on behavior and its extreme rejection of the mind. Critiques of Skinner's research methods and the fact that his claims were based on very limited and restricted evidence also fueled the debate.

Pedagogical approaches associated with behaviorist learning theory were explored under three categories: reward and punishment, behavioral instructional design, and taxonomies of learning. Behaviorism marks a time in American history in which efficiencies of learning and mass education were being emphasized. Industrialization required a huge labor force that was literate and able to follow instructions accurately. The two world wars also emphasized military training that must be conducted quickly and intensely, with strict protocols and controlled behavior. Behaviorist pedagogies such as instructional design emphasized efficient behavioral control.

The rise of education technologies occurred within the behaviorist school of thought. Teaching machines, programmed instruction and computer-assisted learning (CAI) were invented within this context.

4
Cognitivist Learning Theory

I believe that at the end of the [20th] century the use of words and general educated opinion will have altered so much that one will be able to speak of machines thinking without expecting to be contradicted.

—**Alan Turing, 1950**

artificial intelligence **behaviorism** behaviorist behaviorist learning theorists behaviorist theory cognitive learning theory cognitivism cognitivist learning theory cognitive cognitivist cognitivist learning theorists cognitivist theory computer intelligence computer-assisted learning computer-based learning environments conditions of constructivist learning critical influence on curriculum different learning conditions different learning outcomes gagné instructional theory good learning experiences good learning machines human learning id theory individualized learning information processing information processing schema theory gagné theory instruction cognitivist learning pedagogy gagné instructional design schema techniques cognitivist learning technology intelligent tutoring systems artificial intelligence limitations instructional design instructional design theory instructional designer intelligent tutoring systems interactive learning environments its to tutor students key learning technology learning events learning stimuli learning theory model students new theory predictability psychological theory real classroom learning relevant prior knowledge schema theory schemata stimuli stimulus student model tutor

Chapter 4 covers the following topics:

- Context of cognitivism
- Cognitivist learning theory

  - Cognitive information processing
  - Schema theory
  - Gagné's theory of instruction

- Cognitivist learning pedagogy

  - Gagné's instructional design
  - Schema techniques

- Cognitivist learning technology

  - Intelligent tutoring systems
  - Artificial intelligence.

Context of Cognitivism

Limitations in the behaviorist theory of learning began to be recognized by the early 1920s. The major problem for researchers was that behaviorism was unable to explain most social behaviors. For behaviorist scientists, what one cannot see or measure does not count. Believing was based "only" on seeing and the ability to measure what was seen. Anything else was not considered to be scientific or worthy of consideration.

Yet, as researchers and psychologists involved in the scientific study of learning began to realize, the power of the mind to influence or make decisions that are not directly related to an external stimulus was highly significant. It began to become clear that the mind did play a tremendous role.

Cognitivist Learning Theory

Cognitive theory emerged as an extension of and a reaction to behaviorist theory (although aspects of behaviorist theory remain evident in cognitivist theory). The rise of cognitivist learning theory was a response to behaviorism's rigid emphasis on the direct link between "stimulus and response." Cognitivist psychologists argued that the link between stimulus and response was not straightforward and that there were a number of other factors that intervened to mitigate or reduce the "predictability" of a *response* to a *stimulus* (Winn & Snyder, 1996). Nonetheless, cognitivism did not reject behaviorist science altogether but shifted the emphasis from external behavior to a focus on the internal mental processes and to understanding how cognitive processes could promote effective learning. Elements from the behaviorist tradition were reshaped and incorporated into the cognitivist model of learning: stimuli became inputs and behaviors were the outputs.

Cognitivist theory was concerned with what comes between stimulus and response, seeking to understand the processes of the mind, the processes that the behaviorists had rejected. If behaviorism treated the organism as a black box, cognitive theory recognized the importance of the mind in making sense of the material with which it is presented. Cognitive learning theory was concerned with the mental processes that operated on the *stimulus*, and which intervened to determine whether or not a *response* was made and, if so, which *response*? Behaviorists believed that these mental processes could not be studied because they were neither observable nor measurable. However, despite its very strong influence on psychology and education, behaviorism could not eliminate consideration of mental states and such words as "thinking," "imagining," "conceptualizing" and others. Cognitivists argued that these processes were what constituted human learning and determined how we think and act, and hence must be studied. Hence, as shown in Figure 4.1, the key difference between behaviorist and cognitivist theories of learning was the importance accorded to what goes on between the stimulus or input and the resultant behavior. Cognitivists were interested in modeling the mental structures and processes that operated in the mind in order to explain behavior.

The rise of cognitive learning theory in the mid 20th century was influenced by developments in such fields as linguistics, neurology, psychology, education and the nascent field of computer science. Very soon cognitive theory replaced behaviorism as the major school of thought and experimental paradigm. In particular this was accomplished because of, or in the context of, the invention of the computer. The computer had a powerful impact on cognitive theory. Metaphors such as "mind as computer" and "human information processing" came to dominate cognitivist research as related to educational practice.

A number of schools of thought are associated with cognitivist learning theory and are described below:

- Cognitive information processing (CIP)
- Schema theory
- Gagné's theory of instruction.

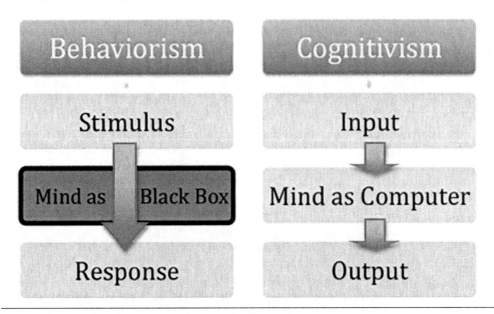

Figure 4.1 A General Overview of the Behaviorist and Cognitivist Foci.

Cognitive Information Processing (CIP)

Emerging as it did during the rise of cognitive science and computing, cognitivist learning theory absorbed and was influenced by the era. The model of computerized information processing (CIP) is commonly associated with cognitivism. As noted earlier, cognitivism viewed the mind as a processor of information, much like a computer. Indeed, a powerful metaphor that has been used to characterize this approach is that of the "mind as computer." More infamous is the quotation by a founder of computer science, the MIT professor Marvin Minsky, who once described the human brain as "a meat machine—no more, no less."

Clark (2001, p. 7) notes that while Minsky's phrase was "ugly," it also offered

> a striking image, a compact expression of both the genuine scientific excitement and the rather gung-ho materialism that tended to characterize the early years of cognitive science research. Mindware—our thoughts, feelings, hopes, fears, beliefs, and intellect—is cast as nothing but the operation of the biological brain, the meat machine in our head.

As a machine, the mind is made available for study and experimentation. In fact, according to this point of view, the mind is best studied from a kind of engineering perspective:

> This notion of the brain as a meat machine is interesting, for it immediately invites us to focus not so much on the material (the meat) as on the machine: the way the material is organized and the kinds of operations it supports.... What we confront is thus both a rejection of the idea of mind as immaterial spirit-stuff and an affirmation that mind is best studied from a kind of engineering perspective that reveals the nature of the machine that all that wet, white, gray, and sticky stuff happens to build. (Clark, 2001, p. 7)

According to the CIP perspective, the human learner is a processor of information. The CIP model or metaphor holds that just as computers encode data and programs using memory and

CPU, so too the mind encodes information as symbols and procedures. The mind processes information; it works by cognitive information processing.

> Like the traditional cognitive view, the CIP model portrays the mind possessing a structure consisting of components for processing (storing, retrieving, transforming, using) information and procedures for using the components. Like the behavioral view, the CIP model holds that learning consists partially of the formation of associations. (Andre & Phye, 1986, p. 3)

Hence, the focus of CIP was to understand how the mind processes information. The CIP model influenced instructional design and hence had significant implications for cognitivist pedagogy. Moreover, CIP and MAC (mind-as-computer models) had a strong influence on cognitivist educational technologies such as intelligent tutoring systems (ITS) and artificial intelligence (AI) technologies.

Schema Theory

The concept of schema in cognitivist learning theory is related to mental representation and structural knowledge. Schema theory or schema perspectives hold that learning is easier if new subject matter is compared to existing knowledge and is structured or representational. Schema theory considers how our thinking uses various symbol systems, such as concept maps or graphic organizers, to help us learn and develop skills. Jonassen et al. (1993, p. 6) write that schema theory

> contends that knowledge is stored in information packets, or schema that comprise our mental constructs for ideas. A schema for an object, event, or idea is comprised of a set of attributes or slots that describe and therefore help us to recognize that object or event. These slots contain relationships to other schema. It is the interrelationships between schema that give them meaning.

While there are many descriptions of what schemata are, Winn and Snyder (1996) note that all descriptions concur with the following characteristics:

1. schema as memory structure: "It is an organized structure that exists in memory and, in aggregate with all other schemata, contains the sum of our knowledge of the world" (p. 118). For example, we recall certain structures in a book of fiction, such as plots. And our memory of a book is typically based on this structure (what happened? When? To whom? By whom?), even when we cannot recall exact details or make errors in our recall.
2. schema as abstraction: "It exists at a higher level of generality, or abstraction, than our immediate experience with the world" (p. 118). We know that a cat is a mammal with four legs, two eyes, a tail, and certain habits. The specific color or size of a particular cat is at a different level.
3. schema as network: "It consists of concepts that are linked together in propositions" (p. 118). The network consists of nodes and links. An example cited by Winn and Snyder is the schema of a face. Not a particular or specific face. But a human face in general, in which the head (a sort of oval) is the central node, eyes (different smaller ovals) are linked to one another and to a nose and mouth, which are described by their relationships of size, location and shape. A mouth is always below the nose and is bigger than the eyes. A nose is always below the eyes and above the mouth. These nodes are linked and together form a face.

4. schema as dynamic structure: A schema is not immutable and changes as we learn new information through instruction or through life experience.

Schema theory proposes that our knowledge of the world is constantly interpreting new experience and adapting to it. These processes, which Piaget (1968) has called *assimilation* and *accommodation*, and which Thorndyke and Hayes-Roth (1979) have called *bottom-up* and *top-down* processing, interact dynamically in an attempt to achieve cognitive equilibrium without which the world would be a tangled blur of meaningless experiences. (p. 118)

5. schema as context: "It provides a context for interpreting new knowledge as well as a structure to hold it" (p. 119). Schemata determine how we interpret new information, and even influence how we explore our environment. Anticipatory schemata direct our exploration of the environment and which sources of information we select.

Gagné's Instructional Design

Robert M. Gagné (1916–2002) was an American instructional psychologist best known for his 1965 book, *The Conditions of Learning*, and for his contributions to instructional design theory. Gagné's theory of instruction evolved from behaviorist roots to embrace the cognitivist information processing model. *The Conditions of Learning* reflected behaviorist theory; the fourth edition of this book, published in 1985, is associated with cognitivist theory in general and CIP in particular. Gagné's ideas and his writings were revised based on his research and instructional practice. In 1996, Gagné (with Karen Medsker) published *The Conditions of Learning: Training Applications*.

Gagné's theory extended beyond CIP to a certain degree, in that he incorporated empirical data on how teachers behave in the classroom. His early work was predominantly as a psychologist with the US military, training air force personnel. Overall he spent about 50 years engaged in military research on training. The issues that he addressed were how to determine what skills and knowledge are required for someone to perform effectively at a particular task or job. And how to determine how these requirements might best be learned. Gagné's work centered on instructional design and the prescription of a didactic pedagogy based on individualized learning. Instruction was viewed as the transmission of information. The role of the student was to respond to the stimuli effectively. The role of the instructor was to design and present the correct and appropriate stimuli to elicit the appropriate student behavior.

Gagné's taxonomy of learning outcomes has similarities to Bloom's taxonomy of cognitive, affective and psychomotor outcomes, in that both focused on learning outcomes. A taxonomy is a systematic classification of something. Taxonomies were being developed in the sciences, such as taxonomies of mammals, fossils, birds, living fauna or flora. Creating a taxonomy of learning outcomes was in keeping with this scientific ethos. Instructional design required a way of identifying and organizing learning outcomes, in order to be able to specify the behaviors required to achieve these outcomes. Both Bloom and Gagné believed that it was important to create a classification system of learning into categories of domains.

Gagné's theory of instruction comprises three major components, each with subcomponents:

1. a taxonomy of learning outcomes:

    a. verbal information
    b. intellectual skills

TABLE 4.1 Gagné's Theory of Instruction

Learning Outcomes:	*Specific Conditions for Learning:*	*Events of Instruction:*
• Verbal information	• Verbal information	• Gaining attention
• Intellectual skills	• Intellectual skills	• Informing learner of objective
• Cognitive strategies	• Cognitive strategies	• Presenting stimulus
• Attitudes	• Attitudes	• Providing guidance
• Motor skills	• Motor skills	• Eliciting performance
		• Assessing performance
		• Enhancing retention and transfer

      c. cognitive strategies
      d. attitudes
      e. motor skills

2. specific conditions for learning each outcome:

      a. conditions for learning verbal information
      b. conditions for learning intellectual skills
      c. conditions for learning cognitive strategies
      d. conditions for learning attitudes
      e. conditions for learning motor skills

3. nine events of instruction (methods and procedures to facilitate specific learning processes):

      a. gaining attention
      b. informing the learner of the objective
      c. stimulating recall of prior learning
      d. presenting the stimulus
      e. providing learning guidance
      f. eliciting performance
      g. providing feedback
      h. assessing performance
      i. enhancing retention and transfer.

Gagné identified five categories of learning outcomes, each category leading to a different type or class of human performance. Gagné's intent was to specify the learning outcomes in order to design the instructional activities that could achieve those outcomes.

Gagné's "conditions of learning" are a key aspect of his instructional design theory. Gagné and Driscoll (1988) refer to them as the building blocks for instruction, because of their critical influence on learning the various outcomes. Each of the five learning outcomes has associated conditions of learning: different learning outcomes call for different learning conditions. These are discussed in more detail in the Cognitivist Learning Pedagogy section that follows.

Gagné's nine events of instruction tie his instructional theory together. These events are intended to promote the transfer of knowledge or information through the stages of memory. Gagné's events of instruction are based on the CIP perspective of learning.

Cognitivist Learning Pedagogy

Winn and Snyder (1996) provide a thoughtful and important reminder about theory and practice in general, and in particular with respect to cognitivism:

History teaches us that theories change more readily than practice. Therefore when research-ers started to develop cognitive theories that compensated for the inadequacy of behavior-ism to explain many aspects of human behavior, the technologies and practices by means of which psychological theory is applied changed more slowly, and in some cases not at all. The practices recommended by some schools of thought in instructional design are still exclu-sively behavioral. (p. 112)

There are many theoretical and pedagogical links between behaviorism and cognitivist learning theory, and many key theoreticians and researchers can be associated with both schools. This is especially true of instructional design. As noted in Chapter 1, Robert Gagné, the major name associated with instructional design theory, was initially a member of the behaviorist learning school of thought before his association with cognitivism.

Cognitivist Instructional Design

Cognitivist instructional design proceeded from a premise of the predictability of human behav-ior, similar to the behaviorist perspective. Hence, instruction was designed to be prescriptive. And given the belief in predictability, it was assumed that if a certain stimulus resulted in a particular response or outcome, it would do so again and again. The role of the instructional designer was to identify the learning stimuli that would lead to certain outcomes. By identifying and prescrib-ing the appropriate stimulus and related pedagogical strategies, the instructional designer could ensure that students would learn the intended skills or set of subskills that would result in overall mastery of the skill. This, of course, implied a huge requirement, given the very diverse and exten-sive range of skills that exist in the real world. It required listing and classifying *all* human tasks.

As noted above, Gagné's theory of instruction identified a taxonomy of learning outcomes, specific conditions for learning each outcome and nine events of instruction (methods and pro-cedures to facilitate specific learning processes). Gagné subdivided the nine events of instruction into the following procedures:

1. gaining attention: this involves some form of stimulus change to get the attention of the student, such the teacher calling the students to attention, the computer software flashing a message;
2. informing the learner of the objective: the instructor tells the students what they will be able to do after learning;
3. stimulating recall of prior learning: the instructor assists the student in recalling relevant prior knowledge to apply to new situations by reminding them;
4. presenting the stimulus: the instructor will provide an example, a model, a reading or give directions as stimulus for student information acquisition or motor skills to facilitate pattern recognition;
5. providing learning guidance: the instructional activities promote the encoding of the learning into long-term memory in a meaningful way;
6. eliciting performance: this step has students demonstrate their learning;
7. providing feedback: feedback can relate to helping students correct any incorrect answers or helping them to improve their current skill;
8. assessing performance: formal assessment can be conducted through various techniques such as testing, portfolios, performances or projects;
9. enhancing retention and transfer: this can be facilitated through mechanisms such as repeat-ing or iterating event 5 or 6 and 7 as appropriate. Software simulations also assist by demon-strating the consequences of students' problem solving or decision making. (Gagné, 1985)

Gagné's instructional theory has had significant influence and prominence in educational practice, primarily in the field of adult and military training. The specificity of the analyses and classification has provided instructional designers with explicit steps to incorporate into the training procedures.

Gagné's instructional theory, nonetheless, was the most linked to educational practice among cognitivist theorists.

Schema Techniques

Schemata, as discussed earlier in this chapter, are a hypothetical construct, which is a metaphor for describing the ways that humans construct and store knowledge. "Because structural knowledge has been tied to memory processes and problem solving, it seems useful to prescribe instructional and learning strategies for fostering the acquisition of structural knowledge" (Jonassen et al., 1993, p. 12). The authors suggest a number of explicit methods to convey structural knowledge that can improve learning and performance of higher-order mental operations like problem solving. Many of these techniques are included in Table 4.2.

Cognitivist Learning Technology

The field of "educational technology" emerged during the behaviorist period and gained increased importance and influence for cognitivist researchers and instructional designers. Computers were the key learning technology for cognitivist learning theorists. Key examples include:

- intelligent tutoring systems
- artificial intelligence.

Intelligent Tutoring Systems (ITS)

Intelligent tutoring systems (ITS) refer to a didactic, content-specific instructional technology. ITS have been in existence since the 1970s. Precursors of ITS were early mechanical systems such as Charles Babbage's vision of a multipurpose computer which he developed in principle in 1834 as the *analytic engine*, as well as Pressey's mid-1920s *teaching machines* or "intelligent" machines which used multiple-choice questions submitted by the instructor. In the 1970s, computer-assisted instruction (CAI) emerged as an instructional method based on a systematic instructional approach administered on a computer. In CAI the computer evaluates whether the student's response is right or wrong, and then branches the student into either moving ahead (with appropriate feedback) or into corrective action such as reviewing the earlier material or presenting a simpler question. Branching is designed (coded) by the instructional designer into the program: if the student's answer is correct, then the student advances to the next question. If the student's response is incorrect, then remediation is invoked. This is the behaviorist instructional design.

Hardware and software have evolved at tremendous rates since the 1970s. As computers developed in sophistication, so too did instructional applications. Shute and Psotka (1996, p. 571) write that increasingly complex branching capabilities in CAI led to what became known as ICAI

TABLE 4.2 Schema Pedagogies

- Semantic maps
- Causal interaction maps
- Concept maps
- Semantic features analysis
- Cross-classification tables
- Advance organizers
- Graphic organizers

(or Intelligent CAI) and eventually to ITS. It is a continuum from linear CAI to the more complex branching of ICAI and then ITS, although the authors note that this does not mean that the continuum represents a worst-to-better progression.

Branching is a common and key characteristic of CAI and ITS, and reflects the complexity of knowledge and multiple pathways of curriculum. However, the quality of branching, and its complexity, does distinguish ITS from CAI. Whereas CAI is content-free, ITS are based on specific knowledge domains that are taught to the individual students by the computerized tutor.

Shute and Psotka (1996, p. 574) provide a generic depiction of the process:

> A student learns from an ITS primarily by solving problems—ones that are appropriately selected or tailormade—that serve as good learning experiences for that student. The system starts by assessing what the student already knows, the *student model*. The system must concurrently consider what the student needs to know, the *curriculum* (also known as the *domain expert*). Finally the system must decide which curriculum element (unit of instruction) ought to be instructed next and how it shall be presented, the *tutor* or inherent teaching strategy. From all of these considerations, the system selects, or generates, a problem, then either works out a solution to the problem (via the domain expert) or retrieves a prepared solution. The ITS then compares its solution, in real time, to the one the student has prepared and performs a diagnosis based on differences between the two.

Key constructs that guide ITS design are thus:

- knowledge of the domain (domain expert)
- knowledge of the learner (student model)
- knowledge of teaching strategies (tutor).

However, there are many challenges to the cognitivist views of learning and learning technologies.

Figure 4.2 ITS Training (Photo Courtesy of the US Army).

One reason that ITS may disappear in the future is that, while many researchers agree that intelligence in an ITS is directly a function of the presence of a student model, the student model may, in fact, be the wrong framework around which to build good learning machines. (Shute & Psotka, 1996, p. 591)

Second, there are problems with the concept of machine "intelligence." Intelligence is associated with awareness; the term "intelligent tutoring system" can be viewed as misleading or inappropriate and promising far more than it can or has delivered. Shute and Psotka cite Gugerty (1993) that ITS may promise too much, deliver too little and constitute too restrictive a construct:

There is a sense in which the goals of traditional intelligent tutoring systems are both too ambitious and too narrow. Most traditional ITS ... are designed to provide tutoring in a stand-alone setting.... This ambitious goal requires that the ITS handle all aspects of the very difficult task of tutoring, including expert problem solving, student diagnosis, tailoring instruction to changing student needs, and providing an instructional environment.... On the other hand, the goal of developing very intelligent stand-alone ITS is narrow in the sense that it limits our conception of how intelligence can be incorporated into computer-based training and education. (Shute & Psotka, 1996, p. 591)

Other researchers in ITS began to critically reconsider their own work. One extensive research program (the Highly Interactive Computing Environment [HiCE] group at University of Michigan) involved using ITS to tutor students who were learning to program. Studies were conducted on student modeling, categorizing bugs and helping students to identify and fix the bugs. However, after ten years, the researchers began to question their assumptions about learning, and began to shift from an objectivist to a constructivist perspective. Rather than continue to view computer bugs as deviations from the expert's correct solution, and to try to bring the student's view into congruence or accord with that of the expert, the HiCE group began to view learning as a process of enculturation into a knowledge community. And to reconsider their definition of a student model to that of a community: "Instead of trying to model students, we are now trying to provide students with the tools, facilities and communities they need to support the development of models for their own uses" (Sack, Soloway and Weingrad, 1994, p. 373).

Other challenges to ITS were on the horizon by the 1980s and 1990s. The rise of the Internet and the Web foreshadowed a huge paradigmatic shift. ITS developers had not anticipated nor prepared for this technological revolution. The problem was solved temporarily by posting ITS computer-based training and courseware online, on the Web. This resulted in what is known as online computer-based training, or online courses (discussed in Chapter 6). Online course-authoring tools enable instructional designers to create their own courseware. Traditional courseware requires computer programmers to code the software; course-authoring tools attempt to simplify the programming requirements so that content experts can author their own courseware.

However, ITS technology has not been adopted within the larger educational market, and even within the smaller training market the field of ITS has experienced profound problems as Shute and Psotka (1996), among others, have noted:

We can see the seeds of discontent growing. Go to any ITS-related conference and notice how researchers in the field have begun to discontinue using the term "ITS." Instead, in a show of semantic squirming, they refer to advanced automatic instructional systems (formerly, ITS) as: interactive learning environments, cognitive tutors, individualized teaching systems, computer-assisted learning, automated instructional support systems, computer-based learning environments, immersive tutoring systems, knowledge communication systems, computer tools, and so on.

Not only is the ITS construct too ambitious, but there is no universally accepted definition of what comprises computer intelligence. (p. 595)

A significant concern with the development of learning theory, pedagogy and technologies by both behaviorists and cognitivists was that the researchers and scholars had little contact with educational practice or practitioners. Pavlov was a medical physiologist who focused on reflexes related to digestive systems while Skinner worked with animals in research laboratories. While behaviorist approaches based on the carrot and the stick dominated (and still do) classrooms at all levels of education, nonetheless, these are very broad interpretations of the stimulus–response activities of classical behaviorism or operative conditioning. Behaviorist learning theorists did not take real classroom learning or educational practice into consideration.

Cognitivist learning theorists were similarly divorced from educational practice, with the exception of Gagné, who spent 50 years working with military training as a psychologist and was subsequently involved with military training research. His instructional design theory and processes have particularly influenced the field of training. Classroom applications in K-12 or higher education were not, however, significantly influenced by Gagné's instructional design model.

The technologies developed by cognitivist researchers and developers were similarly isolated from classroom realities. Nor were they ever adopted or considered for classroom applications. Shute and Psotka (1996) observe: "There are actually very few ITS in place in schools, yet they exist in abundance in research laboratories. We need to move on" (p. 595).

Artificial Intelligence (AI)

The invention of computers after World War II generated anticipation of astounding possibilities for computer programs to be capable of human-like intelligence. In 1950, Alan Turing reflected on the potential of computer programs to simulate the human mind. Turing is known as the inventor of the first computer, in 1936, although his computer was on paper only. The Turing computer was a tape that could store a symbol or simple instructions and a head that could read the instructions and perform very simple operations (read the symbol, select a new symbol, move it left or right). Despite its simple capabilities, Turing argued that his machine could realize anything that can be realized from operations. In 1950, he argued that the mind itself was the result of similar operations (at the neural level). He is thus viewed as the creator of artificial intelligence studies. Turing (1950) wrote:

Instead of trying to produce a programme to simulate the adult mind, why not rather try to produce one which simulates the child's? If this were then subjected to an appropriate course of education one would obtain the adult brain. Presumably the child-brain is something like a note-book as one buys it from the stationers. Rather little mechanism, and lots of blank sheets. (Mechanism and writing are from our point of view almost synonymous.) Our hope is that there is so little mechanism in the child-brain that something like it can be easily programmed. The amount of work in the education we can assume, as a first approximation, to be much the same as for the human child. (p. 436)

The AI movement originated with such scholars as Alan Turing, Marvin Minsky and Allen Newell, who all believed that the development of computers that could "think" like humans was just around the corner. The major constraint, they believed, was the size of current computing power. Bigger

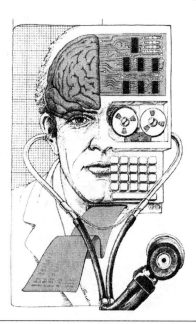

Figure 4.3 Artificial Intelligence as Conceptualized in Mid 20th Century.

and faster computers should be able to solve the problem and achieve human-like cognitive performance. Computers would be able to think, and they would thus be able to instruct.

The AI movement had emerged in the 1950s, in the early post-war period. Thousands of American GIs had returned home from World War II and were going to college on the GI Bill. The impact on educational institutions was unprecedented growth. New ways to meet the demand for education were a high priority. The use of computers for instruction seemed like one obvious solution. Efficient instruction could be met by using computing machines. It could also be facilitated through efficient instructional pedagogies.

During the period of the 1970s and 1980s AI researchers continued to optimistically believe in the imminent viability of computer intelligence. The rapid growth in computing power and capabilities seemed to promise that the goal of thinking computers was nigh. However, the problems began to prove far greater than simply the need for more computer memory or speed. A crisis in the movement was triggered not only by the technological problems but in the very definition and implementation of computer intelligence. As noted earlier in the chapter, there was no universal definition of what constitutes computer intelligence. The AI movement lost its impetus for the moment, although research continued with ITS.

Brent Wilson (1997b) acknowledged a growing disaffection with theories of AI as well as with instructional design (ID). As a scholar engaged in ID studies, he found a similar sense of chaos and lack of direction among adherents and researchers. Writing about ID, Wilson states: "Artificial intelligence right now is facing some of the same crises we are confronting.... A growing number of AI researchers have lost faith in traditional views of the representability of knowledge" (1997b, p. 77). He concludes: "In summary, ID theory, with its prescriptive orientation toward both procedure and product, lies in conceptual limbo" (1997b, p. 70).

In the 1960s and 1970s, social reform movements were impacting society and education in the United States. New perspectives on learning based on constructivist epistemology and theory were coming from Europe and began to strongly influence American education. It was a time of change and of changing perceptions on the role of the student and of the citizen. Theories of constructivist learning generated significant researcher as well as teacher interest. Piaget's theories were taking hold and at the same time Bruner was introducing the ideas and writings of Lev Vygotsky, who presented an approach to social constructivism, perspectives related to active learning and student-centered models of learning.

Summary

Cognitivism emerged as a reaction to what had become viewed as simplistic and rigid emphasis by behaviorists on predictive stimulus-response. Cognitivism recognized that reinforcement did impact on the probability of certain behaviors but was in general interested in theorizing and modeling the mental structures and processes that could explain human behavior. The emphasis was on the mental or cognitive models. The rationale was that if it were possible to devise accurate models, then it would be possible to create and/or prescribe learning events to address more complex behaviors, such as problem solving and decision making.

Nonetheless, cognitivists shared certain fundamental views and pedagogies with behaviorists. Cognitivist learning theory was instructor-centered: the focus was on the instructor and instructional design. Knowledge was to be transmitted to the learner, either by the instructor or by the instructional software. Cognitivism presupposed that the primary role of the learner is to assimilate what the teacher presents, and thus it retained a didactic model. Both behaviorism and cognitivism shared a similar epistemology: objectivism. This epistemology held that knowledge was known by the instructor who would predigest and then transmit it to the student. Cognitivism, like behaviorism, focused on individualized learning perspectives and procedures.

There is some blurring between the behaviorist theoretical school and the cognitivist theory of learning, because some transitions were initiated or led by those who were participants in the previous school of thought. Still, cognitivism was a very strong field in educational psychology, and remains so.

Nonetheless, a new theory of learning was about to challenge this school of thought: constructivism.

5
Constructivist Learning Theory

In hindsight, the reason for my students' poor performance is simple. The traditional approach to teaching reduces education to a transfer of information … However, education is so much more than just information transfer, especially in science. New information needs to be connected to pre-existing knowledge in the student's mind. Students need to develop models to see how science works. Instead, my students were relying on rote memorization. Reflecting on my own education, I believe that I also often relied on rote memorization. Information transmitted in lectures stayed in my brain until I had to draw upon it for an exam. I once heard somebody describe the lecture method as a process whereby the lecture notes of the instructor get transferred to the notebooks of the students without passing through the brains of either. That is essentially what is happening in classrooms around the globe.

—Eric Mazur, 2009

cognitivist learning theory collaborative learning environment computer-based constructivist learning environments computer-supported collaborative computer-supported intentional learning environment constructivism constructivist constructivist learning theory intentional learning environments learner learners learning circle network learning environments learning network projects learning process learning theories learning theory local area network logico-mathematical knowledge microworlds intentional learning environments online collaborative learning theory online learning environment online learning networks other knowledge building interactions other learning theories other social constructivist pedagogical approaches own knowledge pedagogies perspective piaget pre-digital knowledge technologies pre-digital learning technologies preexisting knowledge project-based learning communities scaffold scaffold knowledge building activities scaffold particular learning strategies social constructivism social knowledge society practical knowledge student prior knowledge successive knowledge building activities term twentieth century view knowledge views virtual learning environments von glasersfeld vygotsky zpd

Chapter 5 will cover the following topics:

- Context of constructivism
- Constructivist learning theory and major thinkers

  - Piaget: developmental constructivism
  - Vygotsky: social constructivism

- Constructivist learning pedagogy

  - Active and authentic learning
  - Learning-by-doing

- Scaffolded learning
- Collaboration
- Constructivist learning technology
  - Construction kits and microworlds
  - Scaffolded knowledge-building environments
  - Telecollaboration
  - Online course delivery.

Context of Constructivism

Constructivism refers to a theory or set of theories about learning that emerged in Europe and were introduced to the United States around the 1970s, during a period of social reform and civil rights movements and challenges to the "old" order and its hierarchies. The social movements had a strong impact on education. Moreover, cognitivist views came under criticism. Educational researchers and practitioners began to reject the notion that humans could be programmed like robots, to always respond in the same way to a stimulus. In fact, it became recognized that the mind plays an enormous role in how people act when learning. But that role is not directly comparable to a software program based on discrete steps to consume and process information as put forward by cognitivist theorists. Constructivism—particularly in its "social" forms—suggests that the learner is much more actively involved in a joint enterprise with the teacher and peers in creating (constructing) knowledge.

Constructivist Learning Theory

Constructivism refers both to a learning theory (how people learn) and to an epistemology of learning (what is the nature of knowledge). Both the constructivist theory of learning and constructivist epistemology are generally quite distinct from behaviorism and cognitivist theories of learning, although some theorists are associated with more than one of these theories. Moreover, the constructivist epistemology is reflected in other learning theories, not only constructivist theory. Thus it is important to keep in mind that the term constructivism is used in two distinct ways, to refer to a theory and to an epistemology.

Constructivist theory posits that people construct their own understanding and knowledge of the world through experiencing the world, and reflecting on those experiences. Our encounters with new ideas, new things and new perspectives require that we reconcile the new with our prior understanding: does the new fit with our previous understanding and if not, do we discard it, integrate it with our existing views or change our existing beliefs? This process is one of asking questions, exploring, engaging in dialogue with others and reassessing what we know. As such we are active creators and constructors of our own knowledge.

Moreover, as discussed in Chapter 1, the constructivist epistemology, regarding what is knowledge, is very distinct from the objectivist epistemology that underlies behaviorist and cognitivist theory. In the constructivist perspective, knowledge is constructed by the individual through his or her interactions with the community and the environment. Knowledge is thus viewed as dynamic and changing, constructed and negotiated socially, rather than something absolute and finite. This has important implications for teaching and learning, and will be explored further in the section on Constructivist Pedagogy.

Constructivist learning theory, like behaviorist and cognitive learning theories, is not one unified entity. Rather it is an umbrella term representing a range of perspectives based on two or more rather distinct positions while sharing some common denominators. Duffy and Cunningham (1996) clarify the basis of constructivism, noting that despite the diversity of views encompassed in the concept of constructivist learning theory, there seems to be a general consensus to the general view that "learning is an active process of constructing rather than acquiring knowledge," and that "instruction is a process of supporting that construction rather than communicating knowledge" (p. 177).

In the 20th century, the major theorists associated with constructivist approaches were Jean Piaget and Lev Semyonovich Vygotsky. Two major camps or perspectives are associated with constructivism, one with each theorist:

- "cognitive constructivism" is how the individual learner understands the world, in terms of biological developmental stages; and
- "social constructivism" emphasizes how meanings and understandings grow out of social encounters.

Cognitive constructivism focuses on the individual learner and emerged from the thinking and research by Piaget. Social constructivism emerged from the work of Vygotsky and emphasizes the social essence of knowledge construction.

Piaget

Jean Piaget (1896–1980), a Swiss-born professor of psychology and student of biology, devoted his life to the question of cognitive development, and particularly to classifying the stages of human development. Piaget posited that humans learn through the construction of progressively complex logical structures, from infancy through to adulthood. Humans, in his view, learn through the construction of one logical structure after another. Piaget also concluded that the logic of children and their modes of thinking are initially entirely different from those of adults, and that successive knowledge-building activities increase in depth and complexity as humans move from one stage to another in their development: age-based stages. Learning followed development: it occurred according to the child's age and stage of development. Development ceases as the child reaches early adulthood, according to Piaget's four stages of development, and Piaget did not discuss adult learning.

Piaget was not only a psychologist but also a biologist. He strongly defended and promoted the scientific method, and he believed that the scientific approach was the only valid way of gaining access to knowledge. This conviction influenced Piaget's perspectives on psychology, and led him to declare: "This made me decide to devote my life to the biological explanation of knowledge" (Munari, 1994). Munari, who collaborated with Piaget from 1964 to 1974, wrote of Piaget that

> With regard to his work as a researcher and university teacher, the constant concern influencing and guiding his work and, indeed, his entire life was that of winning recognition, especially by his colleagues in physics and the natural sciences, for the equally *scientific* nature of the human sciences and, more specifically, of psychology and epistemology. His attitude and his involvement in the field of education led him quite naturally to champion the pupil's active participation as the royal road to the scientific approach in school. (Munari, 1994)

Piaget is also identified with genetic epistemology or genetic constructivism, what he referred to as "a kind of embryology of intelligence" (cited in Munari, 1994). As Munari notes,

> In particular, the basic postulate of genetic psycho-epistemology whereby the explanation of all phenomena, whether physical or social, is to be sought in one's own mental development and nowhere else, helped to give the historical dimension a new role, in teaching methods as well as in general debate on education. Every theory, concept or object created by a person was once a strategy, an action, an act.

Piaget's concept of genetic epistemology reflects the span of his interest in the areas of biology, philosophy and child psychology, all related to how the child comes to know his or her world. Genetic epistemology reflects Piaget's work in studying knowledge and, in particular, the origins or genesis of knowledge, and reflects his interest in both the philosophy (epistemology) and psychology of knowledge.

George Bodner, professor of chemistry, whose 1986 article "Constructivism: A Theory of Knowledge" examines the use of constructivism in the classroom, noted:

> Piaget believed that knowledge is acquired as the result of a life-long constructive process in which we try to organize, structure, and restructure our experiences in light of existing schemes of thought, and thereby gradually modify and expand these schemes. (p. 875)

Bodner quotes a passage from Piaget (1968) in which Piaget describes the period between birth and the acquisition of language as a mini-revolution; a Copernican revolution in our personal universe, as our understanding develops from total self-centeredness to being a participant in a social universe.

> At eighteen months or two years this "sensorimotor assimilation" of the immediate external world effects a miniature Copernican Revolution. At a starting point of this development the neonate grasps everything to himself—or, in more precise terms, to his own body—whereas at the termination of this period, i.e., when language and thought begin, he is for all practical purposes but one element or entity among others in a *universe that he has gradually constructed himself*, and which hereafter he will experience as external to himself. (Piaget, quoted in Bodner, 1986, p. 875; emphasis added)

All humans pass through the same stages of cognitive development at around the same age, according to Piaget. Piaget believed that children pass through a largely invariable and universal sequence of four stages:

1. *Sensorimotor* (birth to approximately 2 years of age): a period in which infants begin to construct an understanding of the world through the senses and through movement. Sensory experiences (seeing, hearing) are coordinated with physical, motor actions. Reflexes become intentional actions such as grasping. The infant begins to develop an understanding that objects can exist externally, even if they cannot be seen. The infant also begins to demonstrate goal-directed behavior, such as kicking a ball.
2. *Preoperational* (2 to 7 years): by observing children at play Piaget was able to demonstrate that around the age of 2 years, the child exhibits a qualitatively new stage of development, which he termed preoperational. At the preoperational stage of development the child is able to mentally act on objects and to represent objects using words and drawings, but is not yet able to think through actions. The child also engages in collective monologue with other children, each child is talking but not interacting with other children. Children are considered egocentric at this stage, assuming that others share their point of view.
3. *Concrete operational* (7 to 11 years): by around the age of 7, a child is able to use logic appropriately and to solve actual problems, although not abstract problems. This is the stage of concrete operations, best learned through hands-on learning and discovery while working with tangible objects.
4. *Formal operational* (12+ years): This stage commences at around 12 years of age (puberty) and continues into adulthood. In this stage, individuals move beyond concrete experiences

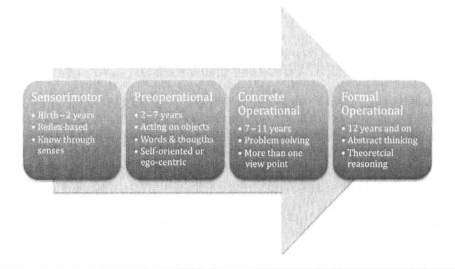

Figure 5.1 Piaget's Stages of Cognitive Development.

and begin to think abstractly, reason logically and draw conclusions from the information available, as well as apply all these processes to hypothetical situations. During this stage the young adult is able to understand such things as love, entertain possibilities for the future and become more aware of social issues. (Santrock, 2008, pp. 221–223)

These four stages of development are posited by Piaget as the psychological states that children pass through as they grow up. Related to these four stages is the mechanism by which children move from one stage to the next. Piaget's concept of constructivism relates to his studies of how knowledge is internalized and how people learn. Humans, according to Piaget, internalize knowledge through experience and make sense of these experiences through adaptation involving processes of: *assimilation, accommodation* and *equilibration/disequilibration.* It is through these three processes that we learn, outgrow some ideas and adopt new ones. These concepts reflect both Piaget's model of intellectual development and his constructivist theory of knowledge.

Assimilation occurs when a child or person comes across a new object or event and makes sense of it by assimilating the information about the object (for example, learning a new word). Assimilation involves applying a pre-existing mental structure to interpreting sensory data. This is true for the reflex action of a newborn to suck, and is a constant process throughout life. Disequilibration occurs when an action cannot be assimilated into pre-existing structures or when we cannot achieve the goals we seek (sucking a thumb not a nipple does not lead to food or when what we learned does not accomplish our goal). Accommodation occurs when the person realizes that the activity does not achieve the expected result, and that existing schemes or operations must be modified. We must accommodate new ways of making sense of an object or event. Constructivism is meaning-making through activity, according to one's age and stage of development.

An instructor, for example, seeks to stimulate conceptual change by challenging a student's existing concepts in order to create cognitive disequilibration. The student will try to restore equilibrium or resolve the problem. Through a process of disequilibration and requilibration, the student constructs new cognitive structures.

Piaget was concerned with epistemology and the question of how knowledge is acquired. Rather than view knowledge as matching reality, as in the objectivist epistemology, Piaget held that knowledge is constructed as the learner seeks to find an equilibrium between the biological processes of assimilation and accommodation, through the cognitive functions of organization and adaptation (internal self-regulating mechanisms).

The basic tenet of Piaget's constructivism is that knowledge is constructed in the mind of the learner. Whereas the traditional (objectivist) view of knowledge is that of a *match with reality*, Piaget's constructivist view is that knowledge is a *fit with reality*. The learner is not an empty vessel to be filled with the knowledge of the teacher, but is an active organism creating meaning through contact and interaction with the external world.

Piaget distinguished among three types of knowledge that children acquire: physical, logico-mathematical and social knowledge (Piaget, 1969).

1. Physical knowledge is associated with empirical knowledge, which is knowledge about physical objects available from the perceptual properties of objects: size, color, thickness, texture, taste and sound. For example, a ball bounces whereas glass breaks when dropped on the floor.
2. Logico-mathematical knowledge is related to abstract knowledge about objects, such as number, volume, mass, weight, time, speed and size. Comparing the different rate of bouncing between a basketball and a baseball dropped on the floor is an example of logico-mathematical knowledge.
3. Social knowledge is culture-specific and can only be learned in one's own culture, through actions on or interactions with people. Examples include cultural symbol systems, music, history and language. Playing in a basketball competition on a day called Saturday exemplifies social conventions about dates and sports.

Understanding the types of knowledge that Piaget identified is important but not easy. As Ernest von Glasersfeld, also a Piagetian scholar, writes:

> Any serious attempt to come to terms with Piaget's epistemological beliefs runs into three formidable obstacles. First, the simple fact that during his productive lifetime—well over 60 years—he wrote more than any one person could keep up with; and his ideas, of course, developed, interacted, and changed in more and less subtle ways. Second, as Piaget himself is reputed to have said, he spoke one language to biologists, another to psychologists, and yet another to philosophers; and one could add that, apart from these, he invented a private one to speak about mathematics. Third, although he never ceased to praise the virtue of "decentration"—the ability to shift perspective—as a writer, it seems, he did not often try to put himself into his readers' shoes. His passionate effort to express his thoughts in the greatest possible detail impedes understanding as often as it helps it. Even the best intentioned reader is sometimes reduced to a state of exhausted despondence. Yet, I have not the slightest doubt that it is worth struggling to overcome these obstacles, because it can lead to an interpretation that provides a view of human knowledge and the process of knowing which, it seems to me, is more coherent and more plausible than any other. (Von Glasersfeld, 1982, p. 612)

Von Glasersfeld explains what he considers to be the key point of cognitive constructivism: "For a constructivist," he writes,

> that is how it has to be. From that perspective there is no way of transferring knowledge—every knower has to build it up for himself. The cognitive organism is first and foremost an

organizer who interprets experience and, by interpretation, shapes it into a structured world. That goes for experiencing what we call sensory objects and events, experiencing language and others; and it goes no less for experiencing oneself. (Von Glasersfeld, 1982, p. 612)

As with any major school of thought there are many critiques of Piaget. Von Glasersfeld referred to the obstacles of understanding Piaget, given his vast number of publications. In addition, as von Glasersfeld also noted, Piaget spoke many disciplinary languages and studied and wrote about many fields, and this in itself causes confusion and obstacles for readers.

Seymour Papert, who introduced constructivist computing to school children, notes that Piaget's real interests and contributions were epistemology, an area overlooked by educators. Papert wrote about Piaget in *Time* magazine's 1999 special issue on the "Century's Greatest Minds":

> Although every teacher in training memorizes Piaget's four stages of childhood development, the better part of Piaget is less well known, perhaps because schools of education regard it as "too deep" for teachers. Piaget never thought of himself as a child psychologist. His real interest was epistemology—the theory of knowledge...
>
> The core of Piaget is his belief that looking carefully at how knowledge develops in children will elucidate the nature of knowledge in general. Whether this has in fact led to deeper understanding remains, like everything about Piaget, controversial. (p. 105)

However, more fundamental theoretical arguments have also been raised. One such critique comes from Howard Gardner, a psychologist at Harvard University and author of many books about multiple intelligences. In response to the question put to many well-known scholars and public figures in 2008: "What did you change your mind about?," Gardner wrote that he changed his mind about Piaget's theory of learning. The focus of Gardner's thought piece "Wrestling with Jean Piaget, My Paragon," is presented below.

> I thought that Piaget had identified the most important question in cognitive psychology— how does the mind develop; developed brilliant methods of observation and experimentation; and put forth a convincing picture of development—a set of general cognitive operations that unfold in the course of essentially lockstep, universally occurring stages. I wrote my first books about Piaget; saw myself as carrying on the Piagetian tradition in my own studies of artistic and symbolic development (two areas that he had not focused on); and even defended Piaget vigorously in print against those who would critique his approach and claims.
>
> Yet, now forty years later, I have come to realize that the bulk of my scholarly career has been a critique of the principal claims that Piaget put forth. As to the specifics of how I changed my mind:
>
> Piaget believed in general stages of development that cut across contents (space, time, number); I now believe that each area of content has its own rules and operations and I am dubious about the existence of general stages and structures.
>
> Piaget believed that intelligence was a single general capacity that developed pretty much in the same way across individuals: I now believe that humans possess a number of relatively independent intelligences and these can function and interact in idiosyncratic ways...
>
> ...Finally, Piaget saw language and other symbols systems (graphic, musical, bodily etc) as manifestations, almost epiphenomena, of a single cognitive motor; I see each of these systems as having its own origins and being heavily colored by the particular uses to which a system is put in one's own culture and one's own time.

Why I changed my mind is an issue principally of biography: some of the change has to do with my own choices (I worked for 20 years with brain damaged patients); and some with the Zeitgeist (I was strongly influenced by the ideas of Noam Chomsky and Jerry Fodor, on the one hand, and by empirical discoveries in psychology and biology on the other). (Gardner, 2008)

Vygotsky

Lev Semyonovich Vygotsky (1896–1934), a Russian psychologist, is the scholar today most prominently associated with constructivism. He proposed a theory of cognitive development that emphasized the underlying process rather than the ultimate stage of human development and he focused on the social rather than individual context of human cognitive development. Vygotsky's view of constructivism was a reaction against that of Piaget. Vygotsky focused on the relationship between the cognitive process and a subject's social activities. Whereas Piaget focused on what is biological human development, i.e., individual development, Vygotsky emphasized the social context of human development and learning. Piaget placed the developmental stage before learning, whereas Vygotsky placed learning before development. Piaget emphasized biological development (the theory of stages); learning, for Vygotsky, preceded and led to development.

Vygotsky's theories are most famously presented in his book *Thought and Language*, written shortly before his early death. The title of the book illuminates Vygotsky's position that thought and language are integral to one another. Vygotsky argued that humans, even as infants, engage in internal dialogue, and it is the internalization of this dialogue that leads to speech and thought. All humans are taught language by adults and others, who speak to the child, point at and name things and introduce language to make meaning of the child's experiences. Jerome Bruner, the American psychologist who brought Vygotsky to the notice of American educators, notes that Vygotsky used the epigraph "*Natura parendo vincitur.*"

For it is the internalization of overt action that makes thought, and particularly the internationalization of external dialogue that brings the powerful tool of language to bear on the stream of thought. Man, if you will, is shaped by the tools and instruments that he comes to use, and neither the mind nor the hand alone can amount to much…. And if neither hand nor intellect alone prevails, the tools and aids that do are the developing streams of internalized language and conceptual thought that sometimes run parallel and sometimes merge, each affecting the other. (Bruner, 1962, vi–vii)

Vygotsky's approach to human development was fundamentally different from that of other developmental psychologists. Rather than focusing on a particular period of development, most commonly how a child becomes an adult, Vygotsky posed research questions with a broader perspective: what is the process of intellectual development from birth to death.

Vygotsky studied the processes of how a child developed, rather than how well the child performed: what did the child do under various task conditions and how did the child respond to the task. Vygotsky also considered the importance of tool invention and use as a prerequisite but not sufficient condition for the evolution of cognitive functioning. What was of key importance, for Vygotsky, was the role of social and cultural factors: biological development does not occur in isolation. Thus the basic human condition is based on social use of tools. The development of culture was the internalization of the tools of the culture. Vygotsky offered a socio-historical perspective: tools emerge and change, as do cultures. Tools are part of our cultural and cognitive development.

Social interactions are an essential part of human cognitive development, Vygotsky argued. Thus while other animals may also use tools, humans went beyond that to develop social speech.

Whereas other theories of human development focused on the individual, Vygotsky focused on social activity. Rather than viewing development as the progress from the individual into social relations, Vygotsky posited the opposite: he viewed socialization as leading to higher (individual) cognitive functions. Moreover, the process of conversion from social relations to psychological function is mediated by some kind of link or tools. A tool is something that extends our abilities in the service of something else, while a sign signifies something else.

Human speech is a key example: Vygotsky emphasized both egocentric speech and social speech. He wrote that whereas Piaget viewed egocentric speech as reflecting egocentric thought and reasoning in a preoperational child, a pattern which then disappears as the logical operations of the next stage are acquired, Vygotsky himself believed that egocentric speech evolves into inner speech. It does not disappear, but "denotes a developing abstraction from sound, the child's new faculty to 'think words' instead of pronouncing them" (1962, p. 135). All known facts of egocentric speech, writes Vygotsky, point to one thing: "It develops in the direction of inner speech … egocentric speech is not yet separated from social speech" (1962, pp. 135–136). Based on his experiments, Vygotsky concluded that as children become more aware of themselves as individuals within a social world, their egocentric speech becomes subvocal and inner-directed. Egocentric speech leads to inner-directed thought; thought then leads to social speech.

Vygotsky's theory of intellectual development is also a theory of learning; he studied the behavior of young children where there is a "prelinguistic phase in the use of thought and a pre-intellectual phase in the use of speech" (Bruner, 1962, vii).

The title of Vygotsky's 1962 book was translated from Russian as "thought and language." It could also be translated as "thinking and speaking." Thought and speech are highly interrelated in Vygotsky's theory.

Vygotsky's theory of learning emphasizes the role of the social and cultural influences on our thoughts and language. Vygotsky created the concept of ZPD, the "zone of proximal development" (proximal is a term meaning nearest). According to ZPD, learning takes place when learners solve problems beyond their actual developmental level—but within their level of potential development—under adult guidance or in collaboration with more capable peers. What this means is guided or supported learning. This does not suggest that the instructor guides the learner to the instructor's

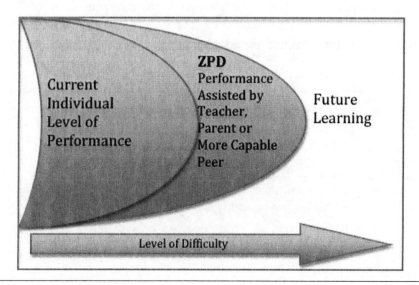

Figure 5.2 Zone of Proximal Development.

intended goal through successive approximations (as in Skinner's behaviorism), but on the contrary, that the more advanced peer or teacher (or parent) supports the learner by providing the tools (language, concepts) needed to advance and eventually independently achieve the learner's intended goal.

Although Vygotsky never used the term scaffolding as a metaphor, it has become closely associated with ZPD, in which the peer or adult supports the learner in constructing knowledge. Scaffolds in learning can be compared with the use of scaffolds in the construction of buildings.

> The scaffold, as it is known in building construction, has five characteristics: It provides a support; it functions as a tool; it extends the range of the worker; it allows the worker to accomplish a task not otherwise possible; and it is used selectively to aid the worker where needed … a scaffold would not be used, for example, when a carpenter is working five feet from the ground. (Greenfield, 1984, p. 118)

In the classroom, a scaffold is a set of activities designed by the teacher to assist the learner move through increasingly difficult tasks to master a new skill. The teacher designs the classroom activities based on the student's prior knowledge, that is, for example, what they learned previously in the classroom or perhaps through other life experience. Classroom activities are designed to help move students from point A to point B, to progress from what they know to what they need to know to complete the course or the class unit—to bring them through the zone of proximal development to achieve their potential.

Constructivist Learning Pedagogy

How we perceive knowledge and the process of "coming to know" shapes our educational practice. If we believe that learners passively receive information, then priority in instruction will be on transmission of knowledge to the learner. If, on the other hand, we believe that learners actively construct knowledge in their attempts to make sense of their world, then instruction is likely to emphasize the development of meaning and understanding.

Constructivist pedagogies focus on the learner or group of learners, while pedagogies associated with behaviorist and cognitivist theories focus on the instructional designer or instructor rather than the learner in the organization of learning. Constructivist learning theory focuses on the role of the learner in making meaning and constructing understanding. Both Piaget and Vygotsky emphasized the active role of the learner, but whereas Piaget emphasized stages of behavior and the child's accomplishment according to preceding developmental stages, Vygotsky emphasized the importance of social interaction. Children, according to Vygotsky, build new concepts by interacting with others and receiving feedback on their hypotheses or the task that they are seeking to accomplish. This is the zone of proximal development, in which a child discusses a problem, a task or a concept with an adult or competent peer who can assist the child by providing the language needed to solve the problem or accomplish the task. The child internalizes the language until she or he is able to complete the task independently.

The constructivist view of learning has generated a number of teaching approaches, based on the following four key principles or values:

1. Active learning
2. Learning-by-doing
3. Scaffolded learning, and
4. Collaborative learning.

Active Learning

In the most general sense, active learning means encouraging students to participate and act, such as conduct a real experiment, rather than passive learning (listening to a lecture, reading a book). Active learning is typically student-centered, and the role of the student is to engage in an activity, such as constructing and testing a theory, hypothesis or strategy. Students then reflect on and discuss what they are doing and how their understanding is changing. The teacher must understand the students' pre-existing conceptions and guide the activity to address, build on and refine pre-existing conceptions.

Contrary to criticisms by some educators, constructivism does not dismiss the active role of the teacher or the value of a parent or a knowledge expert. Rather than transmit information or knowledge to the student, however, the constructivist teacher encourages and assists students in constructing their knowledge about a subject rather than reproducing a series of facts about it. The constructivist teacher introduces techniques such as problem-solving and inquiry-based learning activities whereby students formulate and test their ideas, and draw conclusions and inferences. They may do this individually or pool and convey their knowledge in a collaborative learning environment. The learner is viewed as an active participant in the learning process. Guided by the teacher, students actively construct their knowledge rather than mechanically ingest knowledge from the teacher or the textbook. The teacher thus plays an active and essential role, assisting in identifying a knowledge problem, providing guidance in how to understand it and suggesting resources. The problem (or question) should be interesting, relevant, appropriate and engaging to the learner, so that the student feels that it is her or his knowledge problem. In addition, the problem should be what educators refer to as "ill-defined" or "ill-structured," meaning that it is not just an easy problem, but one that is like problems in the real-world. It should be complex. And authentic, in that it reflects what practitioners do. Authentic activities focus on active learning in real-world contexts, and typically involve production, rather than activities that are abstract or remote from practice.

Constructivism seeks to tap into and trigger the student's innate curiosity about the world and how things work. Students are not expected to reinvent the wheel but to attempt to understand how it turns, how it functions. They are engaged by applying their existing knowledge and real-world experience to the problem, learning to hypothesize, test their theories and ultimately draw conclusions from their findings.

Pedagogies designed in the tradition of active and authentic learning problems may involve individual or collaborative approaches. Bodner, a professor of chemistry, writes about the role of the constructivist teacher in shifting from someone who teaches to someone who *facilitates* learning, teaching by *negotiation* rather than imposition (1986). Bodner notes that social knowledge such as the days of the week or symbols for chemical elements can be taught by rote or direct instruction. And probably should be. "But physical and logico-mathematical knowledge cannot be transferred intact from the mind of the teacher to the mind of the learner" (1986, p. 876). This kind of knowledge benefits from active constructivist learning. Bodner describes a constructivist dialogue between a professor and his students:

> This dialog shows many of the signs of a constructivist teacher who questions students' answers whether they are right or wrong, insists that students explain their answers, focuses the students' attention on the language they are using, does not allow the students to use words or equations without explaining them, and encourages the student to reflect on his or her knowledge, which is an essential part of the learning process. (1986, p. 876)

Learning-by-doing

In *Time* magazine's 1999 special issue on "The Century's Greatest Minds," Seymour Papert cites Albert Einstein as using the words "so simple only a genius could have thought about it" to describe the theory advanced by Piaget that children don't think like adults (p. 105). Papert writes that Piaget

> is revered by generations of teachers inspired by the belief that children are not empty vessels to be filled with knowledge (as traditional pedagogical theory has it), but active builders of knowledge—little scientists who are constantly creating and testing their own theories of the world.

Papert notes that

> Piaget was not an educator and never enunciated rules about how to intervene ... But his work strongly suggests that the automatic reaction of putting the child right may well be abusive. Practicing the art of making theories may be more valuable for children. (1999, p. 105)

Papert emphasized "doing something" and "getting something done."

Seymour Papert was a co-founder with Marvin Minsky of the Artificial Intelligence Lab at MIT and a founding faculty member of the MIT Media Lab. Papert collaborated with Piaget at the University of Geneva in the late 1950s and early 1960s. He created the Logo computer programming language used as an educational tool for children. In 1981, he founded Logo Computer Systems Inc. (LCSI) as a publisher of constructivist educational software for K-12 schools around the world. The LCSI website states that: "The constructivist philosophy believes that students excel by building and constructing for themselves the specific knowledge that they need rather than having a teacher dictate numerous facts. Teachers play a role as knowledge facilitators" (Logo Computer Systems Inc., 2002).

Papert is well-known for developing the Logo programming language and applying it in education based on constructivist pedagogy. However, Papert writes, there is more to it than that: what is important is not the programming language but a certain spirit, a "Logo spirit." This spirit or philosophy is based on "doing something," "getting something done." Papert adapted the term "constructivist" to "constructionist," to signify a philosophy of life, a philosophy of learning by doing and especially learning by making.

> The frame of mind behind the Logo culture's attitude to "getting it to happen" is much more than an "educational" or "pedagogic" principle. It is better described as reflecting a "philosophy of life" than a "philosophy of education." But insofar as it can be seen as an aspect of education, it is about something far more specific than constructivism in the usual sense of the word. The principle of getting things done, of making things—and of making them work—is important enough, and different enough from any prevalent ideas about education, that it really needs another name. To cover it and a number of related principles (some of which will be mentioned below) I have adapted the word constructionism to refer to everything that has to do with making things and especially to do with learning by making, an idea that includes but goes far beyond the idea of learning by doing. (Papert, 1999)

Papert writes that education has two wings: one is informational, while the other is constructional. Public perception of technology in general, and educational technology in particular, is a distortion, a one-sidedness that emphasizes the informational and ignores the constructional. It is a one-sidedness that characterizes as well public views of education, which emphasizes the informational over its constructional role.

> There's education as putting out information; teacher lecturing, reading the book. There's learning by doing, which is the constructional side versus the informational side. And, unfortunately, in our schools the informational side is the one that gets the emphasis, and so there's this line-up between one-sided emphasis in the thinking about school, and the one-sided emphasis in thinking about technology. Both of them emphasizing the informational side, and they reinforce one another. So in many ways, through this, the wrong image we have of what digital technology is about reinforces instead of undermining some of the weaknesses and narrowness of traditional education. (Papert, quoted in Schwartz, 1999)

Papert's constructionism describes an educational philosophy that teaches children to *do* something rather than teaching them *about* something. Some of his early work involved teaching children to be mathematicians rather than teaching them about mathematics in the traditional way.

This led to the Logo language, which is a form of LISP programming language. The Logo language was developed in conjunction with a device called a turtle, which was a small robot holding a pen which could be programmed to draw geometric shapes.

Other constructivist pedagogical approaches include the following:

- *Problem-based learning* (PBL) is the use of a convincing scenario based on a realistic problem presented to a student. Various aspects of the problem may be presented from different perspectives.
- *Distributed problem-based learning* brings together a group of learners working together to solve a problem.
- *Case-based learning* engages students in discussion of specific situations, typically real-world examples. This method is learner-centered, and involves group engagement in building of knowledge and analysis of the case. Much of case-based learning involves learners striving to resolve questions that have no single correct answer; this approach is widely used in such disciplines as medicine, business and education.
- *Inquiry-based learning* is a form of self-directed learning. Students take more responsibility for: determining what they need to know; identifying the appropriate resources; using the resources in their learning; assessing and reporting their learning.
- *Role-play simulation* and *game-based learning*: these are learning processes in which participants act out the roles of specific individuals or organizations in order to develop particular skills and or to assume different perspectives in order to gain a deeper appreciation of the problem being addressed. A simulation or a game involves an artificial environment or plausible scenario that supports the roles, processes and structures of active and authentic learning.

Scaffolded Learning

Vygotsky created the concept of the zone of proximal development (ZPD), which, as noted earlier in this chapter, has also come to be known as scaffolding. With ZPD or scaffolding a more knowledgeable peer or adult supports the learner in constructing knowledge, until the learner no longer needs this support. Scaffolding refers to specialized teaching strategies or tools designed to support learning when students are first introduced to a new subject. Scaffolding gives students a context, motivation and foundation from which to understand the new information. In order for learning to progress, scaffolds should be gradually removed as the learner progresses, so that students will eventually be able to demonstrate comprehension independently. The premise is that scaffolding is not instruction but a form of collaboration between the teacher and the learner as part of the process of learning, something that the learner could not previously conduct on his or her own but now becomes able to achieve independently. As noted earlier, the term scaffolding derives from the tools that support the construction of buildings. It also refers to the activities of a teacher or mentor or parent to support the child in progressing from his or her actual level of development to achieving the potential level of development.

Collaboration

A key principle of social constructivism is the pedagogical emphasis on the role of "collaboration," particularly among the learners but it can also include collaboration between children and adults, such as teachers, parents or practitioners. Unlike "cooperative learning" in which each group member contributes an independent piece to the whole as a division of labor, in collaborative learning the members participate and interact throughout the process to co-produce a finished artifact or product. However, collaboration does not guarantee the use of constructivist approaches.

> The use of groups may simply be used as an alternative instructional strategy, with little change in the learning goals from traditional didactic instruction ... From this perspective, groups are used for reasons that include providing variation in the classroom activity, teaching students how to cooperate and work together, sharing work loads and hence permitting larger projects, and to promote peer tutoring. (Duffy & Cunningham, 1996, pp. 186–187)

Constructivist collaboration, on the other hand, argue Duffy and Cunningham, emphasizes the sharing of alternative viewpoints and challenging or developing each alternative point of view. "Hence, our reason for using groups is to promote the dialogical interchange and reflexivity" (1996, p. 187).

Typically, collaboration refers to a small group (of perhaps three to five students) for a team project or up to 20 students in a group discussion, debate or seminar. Students work together to discuss the topic or to conduct the project.

Collaborative approaches such as scaffolding or cognitive apprenticeship are most often based on interaction between the learner and the teacher. As noted above in the discussion of scaffolding, the support of the teacher is slowly taken away as the learner gains proficiency and learns the topic and becomes able to independently understand and use the concept or tool. This is also the case with ZPD, in which the learner is able to achieve his or her potential through the support of a more knowledgeable other or a teacher.

Lave and Wenger (1991) point to the importance of society's practical knowledge and the learning that goes on among practitioners in communities of practice. Other social constructivist pedagogical approaches include peer collaboration, learning networks or communities: methods that involve group interaction and learning with others.

Constructivist pedagogies have developed outside the learning theories developed by Piaget or Vygotsky. Neither Piaget nor Vygotsky were linked to education during their lifetimes. Piaget was devoted to a tremendous range of interests, but these did not include educational practice. Vygotsky died at a very early age. Educators have nonetheless actively engaged with the notions of constructivist learning, albeit with little theoretical guidance. Concepts of social democracy stemming from the 1970s had strongly influenced education. Hence there has been a strong focus on principles such as active learning, learning by doing and collaboration, but without theoretical clarity on how these techniques contribute to learning and hence how to implement them. The role of the teacher has been unsettled. As noted earlier in this chapter, Papert wrote that: "Piaget was not an educator and never enunciated rules about how to intervene ... But his work strongly suggests that the automatic reaction of putting the child right may well be abusive" (1999, p. 105). Hence, the teacher should not correct the student. Moreover, the teacher should be a participant in the classroom, as the LCSI notes: "We believe that there is such a thing as becoming a good learner and therefore that teachers should do a lot of learning in the presence of the children and in collaboration with them." Popular slogans have emphasized that the role of the constructivist teacher is as "guide on the side" not "sage on the stage." The role of the teacher has been marked by the reactions against instruction, yet without clear alternatives.

Constructivist Learning Technology

The technologies specifically associated with constructivist learning were often referred to as learning environments or microworlds. The term learning environment was primarily associated with computer-based software that is open-ended to enable and require user input, action and agency. It was primarily related to computer-based software, rather than online or web-based environments.

David Jonassen (1994, p. 35) summarized several characteristics as distinguishing constructivist learning environments, such as:

1. provide multiple representations of reality, to avoid oversimplification;
2. "represent the natural complexity of the real world";
3. emphasize knowledge construction instead of knowledge reproduction;
4. emphasize authentic tasks in a meaningful context rather than abstract instruction out of context;
5. provide learning environments such as real-world settings or case-based learning instead of predetermined sequences of instruction;
6. foster thoughtful reflection on experience;
7. "enable context- and content-dependent knowledge construction";
8. support "collaborative construction of knowledge through social negotiation," not competition among learners for recognition.

Jonassen's list has been accepted by both social and cognitivist constructivists, albeit with some differences in emphasis.

Computers are viewed as the optimal medium for applying constructivist principles to educational practice, because computer software can support various strategies and approaches more easily and effectively than other media. Computer software can also link to resources necessary in simulations and microworlds. Computer-based constructivist learning environments such as construction kits, microworlds, scaffolded intentional learning environments, learning networks (telecollaboration) and computer-supported collaborative learning environments were developed in the 1980s and 1990s, and are discussed below.

Construction Kits and Microworlds

In the late 1980s and 1990s educational computer software development sought to support the variety of ways learners construct their own understanding—both as independent work and in collaboration with other learners. Microworlds were designed to provide students with opportunities to connect prior learning with current experience, and they were often created by learners using computer tools as construction kits.

Papert was an early contributor to the computing and the educational world. In fact, he writes that in the 1960s people laughed at him when he talked about children using computers as instruments for learning and for enhancing creativity: the idea of an inexpensive personal computer seemed like science fiction at the time (www.papert.org). But, he notes, it was in his MIT laboratory that children first had the chance to use the computer to write and to make graphics. The Logo programming language was created there, as were the first children's toys with built-in computation. Logo could be used by students of various ages and computer experience to construct and engage in microworlds.

Logo enabled young learners to experiment in a geometry microworld, creating or constructing objects such as houses, buildings and cities. Logo also enabled students to create objects with motors controlled by the computer, similar to Papert's original turtle robot. Today Logo is linked with the Lego Company, and involves robotics for school children.

Papert viewed programming as key to the constructivist culture. He acknowledges that Logo may not be the solution, but argues that it expresses the liberation of learning from pre-digital learning technologies.

> The Logo programming language is far from all there is to it and in principle we could imagine using a different language, but programming itself is a key element of this culture…
>
> But one can be sure that an alternative culture of educational programming will not emerge soon, or ever … This claim is not based on an arrogant belief that we the inventors of the Logo philosophy are smarter than everyone else. It is based on the belief that the Logo philosophy was not invented at all, but is the expression of the liberation of learning from the artificial constraints of pre-digital knowledge technologies. (Papert, 2002, p. xvi)

Another early contribution to constructivist learning technologies was Apple Computer's Hyper-Card software. HyperCard was a multimedia database that enabled users to create linkages among multiple objects on a personal computer. Learners used HyperCard to construct presentations on different subjects, selecting and linking a wide range of resources to organize and display information, reports, projects and presentations. One simple example is a classroom postcard project: each student created a HyperCard postcard comprising a message and a graphic. Postcards were bundled and sent as a file online by a teacher in one school to a project classroom elsewhere—where students would read the postcards and respond. In the late 1980s the ability to link graphics with text was a major technological advance, a limited skill among teachers and students.

Mind tools refers to computer tools intended to serve as extensions of the mind. Examples of mind tools are: databases, spreadsheets, emails or concept maps. Jonassen created a software called Mindtools as "a way of using a computer application program to engage learners in constructive, higher-order, critical thinking about the subjects they are studying" (Jonassen, 1996). The learner enters an intellectual partnership with the computer to access and interpret information and organize personal knowledge in new ways, using a database or spreadsheet tool.

Scaffolded Intentional Learning Environments

Computer-based constructivist learning environments were developed during the 1980s and 1990s, and some of these went online using local area networks, mainframe computers or the Internet. CSILE (computer-supported intentional learning environment) was developed by Carl Bereiter and Marlene Scardamalia in 1983, initially at York University, Toronto, and then at the Ontario Institute for Studies in Education, University of Toronto. Scardamalia, Bereiter, McLean, Swallow and Woodruff (1989) wrote:

> There has been a history of attempts in computer-assisted instruction to give students more autonomy or more control over the course of instruction. Usually these attempts presupposed a well-developed repertoire of learning strategies, skills, and goals, without providing means to foster them. (p. 51)

Scardamalia and Bereiter envisioned an environment in which students could learn and practice these metacognitive skills. Their software, called computer-supported intentional learning environments (CSILE), aimed to foster rather than presuppose a student's metacognitive abilities. CSILE software was designed to scaffold knowledge-building activities, using a communal database constructed by learners and their teachers. Students would enter text and/or graphic notes into the database on any topic created by the teacher. All students in the project read one another's notes and could contribute to or comment on them, using computers linked together on a local area network. Authors would be notified when comments were made. In 1983, CSILE was prototyped in a university course and in 1986 it was used for the first time in an elementary school, as a full version. In 1995, the software was redesigned in accordance with the World Wide Web and renamed Knowledge Forum (discussed in Chapter 6).

Learning Networks or Telecollaboration

Another category of constructivist learning environments in the 1980s and 1990s is referred to as telecollaboration or online learning networks (Harasim et al., 1995). Learning network projects began with the use of email running on mainframe computers. The development of the Internet led to a vast number of class–class or school–school network learning activities. One of the earliest examples of online learning networks or telecollaboration was the work by Margaret Riel who created the pedagogical approach of Learning Circles. Learning Circles were student-centered learning projects that began as cross-classroom projects, in which classrooms in different schools and countries communicated by email; by the 1990s, the AT&T telecommunications corporation and then the National Geographic Society offered learners and teachers the opportunity to work with leading scientists. Students also had access to online curriculum units in the sciences in which they collected data and ran and shared their results with others in the network. Riel continues to design, research and direct Learning Circles, a program that brings student/teacher teams from different counties into project-based learning communities over electronic networks. The Learning Circle network is now part of the International Education and Resource Network (iEARN). Riel also helped design the model for Passport to Knowledge, an National Science Foundation-funded "electronic travel" socio-technical network.

Another telecollaboration model is the JASON project founded in 1989 by Robert D. Ballard following his discovery of the shipwreck of the *RMS Titanic*. Given the large interest in this discovery expressed by children, Ballard and his team dedicated themselves to developing ways to enable teachers and students around the world to participate in global explorations using interactive telecommunications such as email. Since then, JASON has connected more than 10 million students and teachers with real scientific exploration and discovery. Participants engage in community-based partnerships related to scientific exploration and analyses. Teacher professional-development programs are also included. For example, "Operation: Resilient Planet" is an ecology curriculum unit based on National Science Education Standards including Science as Inquiry, Physical Science, Life Science, Earth and Space Science, Science in Personal and Social Perspectives and History and Nature of Science. The complete curriculum includes print, video, online games, online labs and fieldwork-based on an interactive website, the JASON Mission Center, where students from across the globe can put their knowledge to work and take the Argonaut Challenge. The JASON Foundation for Education was founded in 1990 as a nonprofit organization to administer the project. The Foundation became a subsidiary of the National Geographic Society in 2005.

MayaQuest is a similar project that enables students to follow and connect with a team of scientists trekking by bicycle through the jungles to remote archeological sites. Students ask questions of the scientists and of the local peoples, and engage in scientific activities using the Internet.

The online learning environment provides access to social/contextual support. Computers are used to assist active experiences—gathering data and resources, conversing with colleagues, struggling through a challenging puzzle or application—or they assist in reflection. For example, while an online conversation through email is an active event, such discussions usually prompt reflection. Teachers can also employ computers as authoring tools for such pedagogies as students' journals and portfolios, to encourage learner examination of experience.

The use of real-world tools, relevant experiences and meaningful data seeks to inject a sense of purpose to classroom activity. Students learn, among other things, to manipulate and analyze raw data, critically evaluate information and operate hardware and software. This technological literacy imparts a very important set of intellectual and technical skills intended to serve students as well in the working world.

The depth and breadth of online information poses its own challenge. Internet content is less structured and manageable than material outlined by a textbook. Information from the Internet is more dynamic than the printed word. Students need to learn to question and evaluate the information they find. There are many Internet sites that offer raw data—pictures from space, numbers from the census and text from court testimony. These resources need context to provide meaning, and lessons should include components that help students use the information wisely and productively, bearing in mind the need to always ascertain the currency and authenticity of the data.

Online Learning and Course Delivery Platforms

The need for online platforms to support the delivery of online courses or educational activities became recognized and in the 1990s a variety of software began to emerge to address this important issue. These platforms were known under various names such as learning management systems, course management tools, virtual learning environments and computer-supported collaborative learning software. Generally, they were not especially customized to scaffold particular learning strategies, but rather provided generic tools such as discussion-forum software bundled with other tools such as a quiz tool, gradebook or calendar. While the field of online education was first based on the use of computer conferencing (and in some cases, email) in the 1980s, in the late 1990s "learning" platforms consisted of a conferencing or forum system, quiz tool, gradebook and other administrative tools. Together, these generic tools could be accessed by the teacher and the learner to support educational projects or courses. Examples of asynchronous learning platforms in the 1990s and 2000s include Blackboard, WebCT, Desire2Learn and Moodle.

Online learning platforms or environments are constructivist in that they facilitate user-generated content; they can be structured by the user (teacher or learner) to support online discussion, discourse and work projects. The environments most used today are generic asynchronous discussion forums with additional tools. The discussion forum can be structured to support subforums (such as seminars with related role plays or small-group discussions), to open or close forums at specific times or dates, to facilitate specific pedagogical activities (a lecture, a podcast, a question-and-answer forum) and other forms of discourse. However, many educators typically use only one or two online tools and ignore the discussion-forum software. For example, teachers may use only the quiz tool and perhaps the gradebook. Or only post the course material online, for students to download. The examples of online quizzes, gradebooks, podcasts or posting of course materials do not engage the learner in constructivist interactions such as discussions, debates or other knowledge-building interactions. Unfortunately, developers of constructivist learning environments could not ensure that teachers would use constructivist pedagogies when using their technologies. As Driscoll notes, the developer of the constructivist computer conferencing software, Construe, acknowledged that the software could also be "used to support very traditional instructional strategies" (2005, p. 406). Driscoll disagrees. She writes:

> However, as one who has herself employed Construe in a graduate course, I am convinced that the use of all the software's features as an integrated system guarantees a very powerful learning environment that will yield learning outcomes consistent with constructivism. (2005, p. 406)

Nonetheless, the word "guarantees" is likely over-optimistic. The availability of constructivist features does not compel their effective use or their use at all. The lack of educational frameworks and guidelines has held back progress in this area, because teachers do not understand the underlying pedagogies or theory, may not know how to use the various features or do not choose to use them in their classroom or online courses.

Nonetheless, many tools and platforms developed in the 1990s are maturing in the sense of incorporating scaffolds, new pedagogical supports and other features to more explicitly facilitate knowledge building and collaborative learning. Research, field experience and, in the case of open-source software, new environments are emerging to address improvements in the field of online learning and knowledge building, and are discussed in Chapter 6.

Summary

Chapter 5 focused on constructivist learning theory, constructivist pedagogy and associated technologies. As we have seen, there has been an evolution in the nature and focus of learning theories in the 20th century. Behaviorism emphasized stimulus–response, and the need to tightly control the learning through pedagogies and technologies associated with instructional design. Cognitivist learning theory was a reaction to, but also, in certain ways, an extension of, behaviorism. Cognitivism rejected the black-box metaphor of behaviorism and focused instead on the black box, seeking to understand what happens in the mind between the stimulus and response or inputs and outputs. In cognitivism, the mind is primarily represented by computational metaphors such as a cognitive information processing unit or mind as computer. The mind of a student, for example, acquires information sent by a knowledge transmitter, the teacher. The pedagogies and technologies associated with cognitivism emphasize the nature of cognition in order to be able to transfer or transmit the message accurately.

Constructivism introduced a new perspective to 20th-century learning theory, both in terms of theory and epistemology. It offered a perspective that views knowledge as constructed by the learner, either through physical development and maturation as posited by Piaget, or primarily influenced by the socio-cultural context, as theorized by Vygotsky, whereby the mind generates thought, language and knowledge.

Constructivism resonated with practicing teachers and became a highly popular concept in the field. However, neither Piaget nor Vygotsky had ever written about the implications of their theories for the classroom, and hence the resulting constructivist pedagogies and technologies were primarily attempts by practitioners to implement notions of active learning. Constructivist pedagogies were characterized by such broad principles as active learning, learning-by-doing or learning-by-making, scaffolded learning and collaboration. Constructivism also stimulated the development of a variety of technologies and their application. The use of the computer, and eventually computers linked by local area networks and then the Internet, was a powerful catalyst that contributed significantly to the rise of online learning networks and similar applications.

The advance of online technologies in education has, moreover, matured in terms of the potential for knowledge construction. The wealth of experimentation and experience associated with constructivism in the 1990s has generated new perspectives and advances sharpened by the current paradigmatic changes associated with the rise of the 21st-century Knowledge Age.

In Chapter 6, we focus in particular on the emergence of the Web and the role of collaborative learning in knowledge construction. A theory of Online Collaborative Learning is proposed and delineated.

6
Online Collaborative Learning (OCL) Theory

In education, most of the 20th Century was occupied with efforts to shift from a didactic approach focused on the transmission of knowledge and skills to what is popularly called "active learning," where the focus is on students' interest-driven activities that are generative of knowledge and competence. We believe a shift of equal if not greater magnitude will come to dominate educational dialogue in the present [21st] century.

—**Scardamalia and Bereiter, 2006**

active learning brainstorming collaborative learning conceptual change convergence detail online different online learning models discipline effective online learning group discussion idea generating k-12 online learning knowledge age knowledge building knowledge community knowledge construction knowledge creation knowledge work learner learners learning environments learning theory online collaborative learning online discussions online education while online educational discourse environments online educational discussion forums online educational growth online forum online learning activities online learning conditions online learning environments online learning program online learning quality online learning systems online learning theory online learning today online learning tools other online tools pedagogical approaches pedagogies realities seaman semantic web similar online environments sloan term online theoretical framework traditional classroom united states

Chapter 6 introduces online collaborative learning and explores:

- The context of online collaborative learning (OCL)
  - History of online learning
  - Definitions of online learning
    - Online collaborative learning (OCL)
    - Online distance education (ODE)
    - Online courseware (OC)

- OCL theory
  - Discourse, collaboration and knowledge building
  - OCL processes

- OCL pedagogy
  - Three phases of collaborative discourse

        1 Idea Generating
        2 Idea Organizing
        3 Intellectual Convergence

- OCL technology
  - Online learning tools
  - Online learning environments
  - Attributes of OCL
    1. Place-independent discourse
    2. Time-independent (asynchronous) discourse
    3. Many-to-many discourse
    4. Text-based discourse
    5. Internet-mediated discourse.

Introduction

Chapter 6 focuses on the new field of online learning that has emerged with the invention of computer networking and the concomitant emphasis on collaboration and knowledge building that distinguishes the 21st-century "Knowledge Age." In particular, Chapter 6 introduces online collaborative learning as a framework to guide learning theory and practice within this context. Theories of learning first arose in the 20th century and, as discussed in Chapters 3–5, were primarily linked to didactic pedagogies and use of mechanical and computational technologies of the time. To a significant degree, these learning approaches were based on "right" and "wrong" answers, emphasizing student repetition and replication of the course content. Educational reform in the latter part of the 20th century shifted the emphasis from passive didactic learning approaches toward active learning techniques. The major drivers for educational transformation, however, were yet to come as computer networking, the Internet and the Web were just being invented.

The invention and widespread adoption of the Internet introduced a paradigmatic shift—a major socio-economic leap in human development, with profound implications for learning. The Internet revolution is the fourth and most recent shift in human development (see Chapter 2) and is the basis for the 21st-century Knowledge Age. The Knowledge Age introduces new and unprecedented learning needs and opportunities that will impact how we view and practice learning. The growth of the Internet has been exponential (becoming increasingly rapid) rather than incremental, and has accelerated the speed and value of knowledge creation today. These changes have set the stage for a new theory of learning that can take into account the ubiquity of the Internet and the societal shift toward collaborative learning emphasizing the building, rather than the transmission, of knowledge.

Knowledge has become the principal component of today's economy, both as a process and as a product. To create knowledge, people need free exchange of information and ideas, free access to accumulated knowledge bases, and opportunities for communication and collaboration. The Internet has provided this access, not just to a select few but worldwide. Together with the transformation of work through the digitalization of labor, the Internet has given rise to a new economy, one based on knowledge work, and has created the need for a society able to understand and create knowledge. Knowledge products are inventions created to solve a problem, whether in the form of a new tool, a new process, or an innovation of an existing technique. The implications for education and for learning are profound and as yet unmapped; they are not, however, unknown or untraveled. As Chapter 6 will examine, the use of the Internet for collaborative knowledge creation is the basis of the Knowledge Age and a new theory of learning with relevant pedagogies and technologies must respond to this new reality. There is also a significant body of field research to ground new theoretical frameworks. Scardamalia and Bereiter (2006, p. 98) write that:

> Ours is a knowledge-creating civilization…. Sustained knowledge advancement is seen as essential for social progress of all kinds and for the solution of societal problems. From this standpoint the fundamental task of education is to enculturate youth into this knowledge-creating civilization and to help them find a place in it.

In addition to the focus on youth, it is equally urgent to emphasize education of adults, professional development, and lifelong learning as part of 21st-century educational change. New theories and pedagogies of learning are required for all learners in the Knowledge Age. Twentieth-century models, even constructivist learning theory, have, moreover, been found inadequate in addressing the importance of conceptual change and knowledge building. Active learning as it is defined and practiced falls short in addressing social issues and real problems. The motivation of interest-centered learning can become ad hoc and self-centered or limited. Scardamalia and Bereiter (2006, p. 98) note: "In light of this challenge, traditional educational practice—with its emphasis on knowledge transmission—as well as the newer constructivist methods both appear to be limited in scope if not entirely missing the point."

Online Collaborative Learning (OCL) is proposed here as a new theory of learning that focuses on collaborative learning, knowledge building, and Internet use as a means to reshape formal, nonformal and informal education for the Knowledge Age. OCL responds to 21st-century Knowledge Age requirements and provides a theoretical framework to guide the transformations in instructional design. Moreover, decades of research and practice from around the world indicate that OCL has the potential not only to enhance conventional classroom and distance education but to enable entirely new and better learning options. OCL theory, pedagogies and technologies are presented and explored in this chapter while Chapters 7, 8 and 9 provide case examples and scenarios of OCL in practice.

Chapter 6 is composed of four main sections:

- *Context of Online Collaborative Learning*: This section introduces the context, history and major definitions of online learning. The context provides an overview of the implications for learning of the Knowledge Age. Whereas theories of learning in the 20th-century industrial society emphasized didactic approaches to teaching and learning based on memorization and replication of the curriculum, this section argues that the 21st-century Knowledge Age requires learning that emphasizes collaborative discourse, knowledge creation and use of online communication technologies. Online learning emerged in the late 20th century, but there is a need for sharper definitions of the term: some online approaches echo 20th-century models of knowledge transmission while others, such as OCL, initiate 21st-century approaches to knowledge creation.
- *Online Collaborative Learning Theory* is presented as a theoretical framework to guide learning in the Knowledge Age. Key to OCL is collaborative discourse that supports and advances knowledge-construction activities. Conceptual learning is emphasized along with active engagement. A theoretical framework for OCL is presented, comprising three phases of discourse for intellectual change and knowledge creation: idea generating, idea organizing and intellectual convergence.
- *Online Collaborative Learning Pedagogy* discusses a variety of online pedagogies that can facilitate knowledge building in educational settings, particularly group discussions,

seminars, debates, problem-solving activities and teamwork related to invention and innovation. The OCL theoretical framework and its three phases provide a guideline for curriculum design, implementation and assessment.

• *Online Collaborative Learning Technology* focuses on two distinct but complementary components: OCL tools and OCL environments. Each component has a critical role to play, and educators should be aware of the differences and their implications. OCL technological environments, moreover, have distinct attributes that shape and affect the affordances of online educational discourse. Five attributes are identified and explored in relation to their implications for collaborative learning and knowledge-building discourse.

Context of Online Collaborative Learning

The Knowledge Age both requires and enables knowledge advancement, as a process and a product at a global level. Socio-economic transformations today emphasize processes of innovation over repetition, collaboration over individualistic approaches and knowledge creation over information transmission in how we work and, concomitantly, in how we learn. Knowledge products can be characterized as inventions and innovations: new ideas, solutions, tools and technologies, as well as new applications of these inventions; new ways of doing things as well as doing new things. The current generation of youth has grown up collaborating using online technologies. Tapscott and Williams, authors of the 2006 book *Wikinomics: How Mass Collaboration Changes Everything*, note that the current generation is larger than the baby-boom generation and "through sheer demographic muscle they will dominate the twenty-first century" (p. 46). What the authors call the Net Generation (Net Gen), born since the 1980s, numbers over two billion people. Moreover, the Net Gen is a collaboration generation.

> This is the first generation to grow up in the digital age, and that makes them a force for collaboration … The vast majority of North American adolescents know how to use a computer, and almost 90 percent of teenagers in America say they use the Net. The same is true in a growing number of countries around the world…. This is the collaboration generation for one main reason: Unlike their parents in the United States, who watched twenty-four hours of television per week, these youngsters are growing up interacting.
>
> Rather than being passive recipients of mass consumer culture, the Net Gen spends time searching, reading, scrutinizing, authenticating, collaborating and organizing… (Tapscott & Williams, 2006, p. 47)

The Net Gen also expends tremendous time and effort in solving problems, creating new ideas and tools and generating intellectual property online. Digital youth are already proficient and prolific in working and interacting online. They do so not for classroom activities but as participants in online multiplayer games and generators of content for social networks.

This is profoundly important because as the 2009 US National Online Survey exploring school district use of Internet and Web 2.0 use in K-12 education noted: "There is a serious and persistent gap between how the digital youth of today learn in school and how they interact and work outside of school" (IESD, 2009). Educators, meanwhile, are confounded and unsure of how to proceed. Students are adepts of online group work yet classroom work from the school to the university is not significantly predicated on online work or collaboration. Traditional classroom work treats online activities as secondary to the "real" curriculum. Most classwork and homework is individual. And here lies the paradox. Despite the rise of the Internet in the real world, teachers are reluctant to adopt it into the educational world. National studies in the United States have demonstrated that educator attitudes are critical to the growth of any online learning program and key to acceptance of online learning theory and pedagogy (Allen & Seaman, 2008). Teacher and faculty support is critical to effecting substantive educational transformation and adoption of online learning, but many teachers are resisting. "More than six years of data from the national Sloan survey of online learning have shown that faculty acceptance of online education has consistently been seen as a critical barrier to its wide-spread adoption" (Allen & Seaman, 2008, p. 1). This is a major conundrum for society. But the solution is not to advocate educational adoption of the Internet without a theory or strategy to guide the pedagogical transformations required. Teachers, trainers and faculty need to understand the educational paradigmatic changes occurring, how educational transformation can address the needs of a Knowledge Age, and how they can develop and implement new pedagogies that are consonant with these realities. This is where a contemporary theory of learning is critical. The educational conundrum cannot be addressed until educators identify with new learning theories and pedagogies that address Knowledge Age realities that they can confidently apply in their classes.

The Need for a New Learning Theory

Twentieth-century education was based on behaviorist, cognitivist and developmental constructivist theories of learning that emphasized learning as an individualistic pursuit. Moreover, the epistemological basis of behaviorism and cognitivism was objectivism. The view of knowledge as unchanging, finite and absolute has implications for teaching: the pedagogies emphasize "transmitting information" as a way to "acquire knowledge," reflected in such approaches as lectures or their mechanized versions in the form of teaching machines, computer-assisted instruction, intelligent tutoring systems and courseware. This was the ethos of the Industrial Age, an era that emphasized the learner's ability to acquire and retain information and skills. Teaching students to follow instructions accurately to achieve the desired result was a principal educational goal.

The 21st-century Knowledge Age has introduced an entirely new mindset. Whereas the Industrial Revolution extended and leveraged our physical capabilities to manipulate objects far beyond muscle power alone, the Internet revolution and ensuing Knowledge Age emphasize, extend and leverage our mental capabilities. The Knowledge Age mindset seeks the better or best way to solve a problem, rather than merely following instructions or replicating a textbook answer. This may well require redesign or the new design of a solution. Knowledge is viewed as dynamic and evolving, not static and finite. As global communication has become ubiquitous, our knowledge communities have globalized—becoming more diverse. The speed of intellectual change and knowledge construction has increased—becoming more dynamic. And knowledge has become the marker for the new age—the Knowledge Age. Knowledge, in the form of innovating and creating "know how," rather than "know to do," is the basis of today's society and economy. Knowledge is embedded in software to control machines, modern factories, robotic production, transportation, telecommunications and other wealth-generating enterprises. Production today uses far less physical labor; it uses mental labor. The concept of the knowledge worker has emerged to reflect the nature of work in today's world. The term "knowledge worker" was coined by Peter Drucker in *c.*1959 to refer to someone who performs intellectual rather than manual labor. A knowledge worker incorporates his/her education and experience (know-how) to transform information into knowledge. The category of knowledge worker includes those who work in the IT industry, but it is also applied to professionals outside the field of IT, such as scientists, engineers, doctors, lawyers, teachers and students.

The 21st-century Knowledge Age signals the need for a theory of learning that emphasizes knowledge work, knowledge creation and knowledge community. Whereas the 20th-century Industrial-Age learning theories and pedagogies focused on narrow individualistic tasks with simple sets of rules and clear destinations, the 21st-century Knowledge Age emphasizes creative, conceptual work where there is no clear right or wrong answer, or where there may be many right answers, requiring the knowledge workers to collaborate to identify or create the best option. The role of the instructor or moderator becomes defined as mediating between the learners and the knowledge community, which serves as the state of the art in that discipline.

The educational challenge is not how to create sweeter carrots or sharper sticks, but how to engage learners in creative work with intrinsic rewards, within the context of the Internet and the Knowledge Age, and how to bridge the gap between 21st-century environments and 20th-century pedagogies. New educational designs and pedagogies based on new theories such as OCL provide a basis for addressing Knowledge-Age realities that educators can apply in their work. We begin by considering the history of online learning, in the next section.

History of Online Learning

Educational adoption of computer networking, now referred to as online education or online learning, can be traced to the late 1970s and early 1980s. Online education was developed by a few educational innovators: professors in post-secondary education (in the late 1970s and early 1980s); teachers in public schools (early 1980s); and by the mid to late 1980s by educators in the training sector (Harasim, 2002). A variety of online pedagogical approaches were implemented and many were studied. It was, within the small circle of those who adopted this technology for teaching, a time of creativity, but also of research. Most of the early pioneers came from classroom contexts, where they were already exploring new pedagogies such as collaborative learning and knowledge work. They saw opportunities in computer networking and they designed online pedagogies based on a reconceptualization of collaborative classroom learning approaches such as group discussions, seminars and group projects. These efforts were OCL in its infancy or earliest articulation. The opportunity for time- and place-independent group discussion was a powerful catalyst for envisioning dialogue and debate unfettered by access constraints. In the extract below, Starr Roxanne Hiltz, one of the most highly recognized pioneers of online learning, tells how she came to envision a Virtual Classroom:

> The term Virtual Classroom™ and the concept was first a gleam in its creator's eye during a graduate seminar on the Sociology of Architecture, led by Professor Suzanne Keller at Princeton University in 1977. The final assignment was to design "an ideal classroom" for the 21st century. First I sat down and started sketching a set of inter-connected physical spaces for different forms of interaction among people and knowledge resources. In this imagined learning environment there was a multi-media lecture hall, where the Professor pronounces words of Truth and Knowledge, and the students try to absorb this and take notes. In a sumptuously furnished circular "conversation pit" with leather couches and marble coffee tables, the Professor as Discussion Leader and Socrates would conduct seminar-type sessions, moderating discussions and presentations in which the majority of the talking was done by the students. There was also a "learning resources" area, with reference materials, computer hardware and software, and perhaps laboratory equipment, where individuals and small groups of students might do research and prepare their assignments. There were obvious problems. How could you create a comfortable, upholstered discussion space for say, 30 people, without having to put in microphones so that participants could be heard across the huge circle without shouting? How could you possibly provide an adequate amount of computer and other resources, so that they would always be available to students for use in assignments, whenever they wanted them, without the endowment of a Princeton or Harvard?
>
> Suddenly it came to me. A teaching and learning environment did not have to be built of bricks and boards. It could be constructed in software. It could be Virtual! In an era when

many teachers and students have their own microcomputers, it was no longer necessary for them to travel to a classroom ... the classroom could come to them, over their telephone lines and through their computer. (Hiltz, 1999, p. 31)

Online education in the 1980s was viewed (if at all) as an educational outsider, certainly not a contender for status quo or mainstream acceptance. By the early to mid-1990s, the scene began to change as the public release of the Internet and the Web increased access. The late 1990s represented a dramatic shift in public recognition and perception of online education: online learning began to be viewed as valid and beneficial, and became increasingly accepted, adopted and mainstreamed.

The shift toward increasing acceptance and adoption of online education has been documented in a series of public reports sponsored by the Alfred P. Sloan Foundation. These reports act as significant barometers of online educational growth and acceptance in the United States. The first report, *Sizing the Opportunity: The Quality and Extent of Online Education in the United States, 2002 and 2003* (Allen & Seaman, 2003), examined the importance of online education at more than 1,000 universities in the United States. When asked to compare the online learning outcomes with those of face-to-face instruction a majority of the respondents (academic leaders and administrators) said that they believed that learning online would soon be better than face-to-face. Two out of every three also responded that online learning was critical to their long-term strategy. The survey also revealed that students were clearly willing to sign up for online courses: over 1.6 million students (11% of all US higher education students) took at least one online course during the fall of 2002. This report marked the beginning of a sea change in the acceptance of online learning. Within a decade, attitudes toward online education had shifted; the perception of online education by academic leaders went from almost zero (or negative) in the early 1990s to acknowledging it as a field with important potential by 2002.

The 2004 Sloan report, entitled *Entering the Mainstream: The Quality and Extent of Online Education in the United States, 2003 and 2004* (Allen & Seaman, 2004) continued to illuminate the changing state of the art in online learning. The report concluded that the two major problems that complicated online learning's progress for over a decade had been solved. First, the study found that three-fourths of academic leaders at public colleges and universities now believed that online learning quality equals or surpasses face-to-face instruction. The larger the school, the more positive the belief in the quality of online learning compared with face-to-face instruction. And second, that schools of higher education viewed online education as critical to their long-term strategy.

Online learning, according to these reports, came to be viewed as critical to the mission of educational institutions and educators. Allen and Seaman's (2010) report, *Class Difference: Online Education in the United States, 2010*, represented the eighth annual Sloan report on the state of online learning in US higher education. This study, like those for the previous seven years, was aimed at answering key questions about the nature and extent of online education. The results of the study were based on responses from more than 2,500 colleges and universities. The study found that over 5.6 million students (more than 30% of higher education students) were taking at least one online course during the fall 2009 term. Moreover, for the past several years, online enrollments had been growing substantially faster than overall higher education enrollments: the 2008 figures represented a 20% increase on the number reported the previous year, and far exceeded the 2% growth of the overall higher education student population. Growth of online education was, moreover, not concentrated on a few program offerings but was distributed across almost all disciplines (Allen & Seaman, 2010).

Studies also demonstrate that a significant number of public school students are taking online courses. While the number of students and the growth rate is less than that of students in post-secondary education, growth is taking off. A 2008 survey of K-12 online learning found "that in 2007–2008 approximately 1,030,000 students were enrolled in fully online and blended courses" (Picciano & Seaman, 2009, p. 5). This figure represented an increase of 47% since 2005–2006.

Online learning has mainstreamed, become recognized and valued by the public and has been adopted by educators around the world. The prevailing view as reported by the Sloan studies is that online learning can be as good as or better than classroom education. These reports primarily represent the views of academic leaders and administrators, but nonetheless the number of online courses and students is impressive. Moreover, increasingly, studies are reporting empirical benefits of online learning. A 2009 report on online education prepared for the US Department of Education concluded that: "On average, students in online learning conditions performed better than those receiving face-to-face instruction" (Means et al., 2009). The report examined comparative studies of online versus face-to-face classroom teaching from 1996 to 2008, some of which was conducted in K-12 settings but also in colleges and in adult continuing education programs, such as medical training and the military. The report was a meta-analysis of 99 studies that had conducted quantitative comparisons of online and classroom performance for the same courses. The report for the Department of Education found that, on average, students doing some or all of the course online would rank higher than the average classroom student. Barbara Means, the study's lead author and an educational psychologist at Stanford Research Institute (SRI), was quoted in the *New York Times* (August 19, 2009): "The study's major significance lies in demonstrating that online learning today is not just better than nothing—it actually tends to be better than conventional instruction."

These data are intriguing and important. The report provides powerful data and evidence of the value of learning online. However, the report was not able to link results with pedagogical approaches, since most research studies did not include pedagogical information. The results arguably point to the promise of online learning, and demonstrate that this potential can be met. The challenge is that it is not clear how best to realize the potential of online education. Current benchmarks of traditional face-to-face classroom education are themselves under attack. The big question is what is the bar that education should set for online learning? How and why is online better? And at what? Is it enough that online education is better than traditional classroom education? This might suggest that education's goals are to better accomplish traditional objectives. Yet, the more pressing and profound challenge is to shape online learning to meet the collaborative knowledge needs of the 21st-century Knowledge Age. This creates a new and different set of expectations and perspectives on learning, and drives the development of new designs and objectives for formal and nonformal education.

Teacher training and professional development are essential to help educators gain confidence in adopting online learning; more profound is the need for learning theory to address the new realities and to help shape pedagogical approaches for educators to draw upon as they move to transform their classroom practice and their field. Teachers require evidence-based theoretical frameworks that can be translated into practice and new directions for pedagogy.

For example, the *New York Times* article reporting the 2009 US Department of Education study of online education was itself unclear about the theory and pedagogy of online learning. The author of the article, Steve Lohr, began by noting that "until fairly recently, online education amounted to little more than electronic versions of old-line correspondence courses." Moreover, he writes, most schools and universities "use online learning systems primarily for posting assignments, reading lists, and class schedules, and hosting some Web discussion boards." This is a fair description. However, Lohr goes on to write that: "The real promise of online education, experts say, is providing learning experiences that are more tailored to individual students than is possible in classrooms. That enables more 'learning by doing', which many students find more engaging and useful" (Lohr, 2009). On the other hand, Lohr also cites Philip Reiger, the dean of Arizona State University's Online and Extended Campus program, who provides a very different perspective:

> The technology will be used to create learning communities among students in new ways. People are correct when they say online education will take things out of the classroom. But they are wrong, I think, when they assume it will make learning an independent, personal activity. Learning has to occur in a community.

Teachers are being confronted with many mixed and mixed-up messages and unclear demands, and this is where guidelines based on learning theory are urgent and essential.

Despite the growing support for online learning, another facet of the conundrum for educators is that online education has been poorly defined and theorized, with little explication of which pedagogies, approaches, tools and environments should be used, under what conditions, for the best results. In fact, a very important issue is what kinds of results should teachers be seeking? Moreover, do results link with process? Should teachers consider a more individualized approach to learning or one based on learning communities? Should new educational models draw on 20th-century behaviorist and cognitivist approaches, which focus on individualized, prescriptive instructional designs? Is the focus on constructivist learning activities, with the emphasis on "learning by doing"? What kinds of process and products/outcomes are relevant and necessary in 21st-century learning and how are these related to Knowledge-Age work and society? This conundrum, which is at base a lack of clear definition and strategy, may explain why the most common concern cited by the Sloan studies thus far has been related to faculty acceptance (Allen & Seaman, 2007). Teachers do not have the necessary tools, training or understanding of the next steps. They need guidelines framed by theory.

Definitions of Online Learning

The nature of online learning—the new kid on the block—is poorly understood and has been saddled with a variety of contradictory definitions that paint a conflicting set of processes and outcomes. The term has been applied to almost any educational activity that uses email or Web access, even the simple posting of lecture notes, student grades or PowerPoint slides online.

This section addresses the need to define online learning by identifying the different and contradictory learning models that have been encompassed within this term. Being able to identify the major learning models associated with learning online will assist educators in interpreting research or field results by understanding the pedagogy or process underlying the approach that led to those outcomes (for example, outcomes such as drop-out rates, user satisfaction, learning effectiveness or costs). Different online learning models lead to different results. Hence, understanding the underlying theoretical frameworks will help guide educators to better design their pedagogical approaches and to select the most appropriate technologies to implement effective online courses and activities.

At least three distinct models have been commonly subsumed under the title of "online learning": Online Collaborative Learning (OCL), Online Distance Education (ODE) and Online Courseware (OC) (Harasim, 2002). The three approaches *each* use the Internet and the Web for education, but in significantly different ways and with major differences in learning theory, learning pedagogies and learning technologies. OCL, for example, employs a significant teacher role and an emphasis on student discourse and collaboration; ODE uses a correspondence model of course delivery, self-study and individual communication with a tutor; OC is based on individualized learning with courseware without instructor or peer interaction.

These three approaches are described below.

ONLINE COLLABORATIVE LEARNING (OCL)

OCL refers to educational applications that emphasize collaborative discourse and knowledge building mediated by the Internet; learners work together online to identify and advance issues of understanding, and to apply their new understanding and analytical terms and tools to solving problems, constructing plans or developing explanations for phenomena. OCL emphasizes processes that lead to both conceptual understanding and knowledge products. OCL is based on peer discourse that is informed by the processes and resources of the knowledge community and facilitated by the instructor as a representative of that knowledge community. Most commonly, the discourse is text-based and asynchronous, taking place in a web-based discussion forum or computer conferencing system. OCL also uses multimedia technologies such as graphics or video to enhance the discourse. Educational applications may be offered synchronously instead of or in addition to asynchronous communication. The role of the instructor is key: the teacher structures the discussions into small or large groups around knowledge problems. The teacher is not merely a facilitator of the group discourse but acts as a mediator between the students and the larger knowledge community that he or she represents, and helps to induct the learners into the debates and research processes of that knowledge community. OCL theory and pedagogy are discussed in more detail in a subsequent section, illustrated with examples.

ONLINE DISTANCE EDUCATION (ODE)

ODE is primarily based on traditional 19th- and 20th-century correspondence education models, but replaces postal-mail delivery with the cheaper, faster and more efficient email delivery of course materials and tutor feedback.

Romiszowski and Ravitz (1997, pp. 755–756), in discussing online learning, make a valuable distinction between the "conversational" paradigm (which we can identify as OCL) and the "instructional" paradigm (termed here as ODE):

> It may help to compare and contrast two alternative paradigms, or maybe philosophies, which can be seen in the real-world practice of education—we shall refer to them as the "instructional" and the "conversational" paradigms.... The "instructional" paradigm is the one that has driven much (though by no means all) of the research and development of the past 30 years that has been performed under the label of educational (or instructional) technology. The "conversational" paradigm may be seen as much of the work done on small group study, group dynamics, experiential learning and so on. In relation to distance teaching specifically, one may notice ... that the self-instructional "study module" or typical correspondence course may serve as a good example of the instructional paradigm.

As Romiszowski and Ravitz note, the use of online communication by distance education providers has been based on the "instructional technology" model, rather than what they call the collaborative "conversational" model. The ODE approach reflects the cognitivist learning theory and pedagogies based on self-study and individualized learning modules discussed in Chapter 4.

Nonetheless, many institutions that employ ODE are beginning to incorporate OCL into their course design, thereby moving toward what may be described as a blended pedagogical model (OCL + ODE). This shift from ODE to increasingly OCL pedagogy is, more importantly, moving online learning into the conversationalist paradigm. A significant component of the course becomes the group discourse, while the instructional aspect is an informational self-study component.

ONLINE COURSEWARE (OC)

OC (also known as Online Computer-Based Training) refers to the use of courseware (pre-packaged content) that a learner accesses online. The learner uses an individualized self-paced pedagogy to interact with the courseware content, which is presented in a modular format. Upon completion of each module, the student takes a post-test (typically a multiple-choice test that can be computer graded) to "assess" his or her understanding of the content and to provide remedial action if the student fails the post-test. OC began as the use of Intelligent Tutoring System software that was posted on the Web. Online courseware is now designed specifically for web-based applications. Online course authoring software to build and customize OC content is being developed in the nonformal training sector.

OC, like ODE, is an example of instructional technology based on cognitive learning theory (discussed in Chapter 4). OC is based on a prescriptive model of instructional design emphasizing individualized learning pedagogies. There is no discourse among peers, or with a tutor or instructor. OC is most commonly employed in the training sector, where it represents a major investment by large corporations, governments and the military.

However, some OC providers are beginning to supplement this training approach with OCL and peer interaction in order to reduce high drop-out rates, to better motivate and engage learners and to emphasize understanding over retention of facts. Researchers and trainers in the field of courseware are expressing the need to shift "away from stand-alone instructional devices and toward using tools to aid in the more collaborative learning process" (Shute & Psotka, 1996, p. 595).

Table 6.1 outlines the basic characteristics of each type or category of online learning that has been discussed in the previous sections. It highlights the distinctive as well as common characteristics.

Having briefly introduced and distinguished the three major categories within the umbrella term "online education," the remainder of the chapter discusses OCL theory, pedagogy and technologies.

Online Collaborative Learning Theory

Online collaborative learning (OCL) theory addresses the needs and opportunities of the Knowledge Age. Ours is a knowledge-creating age and our theories and practice of learning are challenged to move beyond didactic and even active learning approaches to enable learners to become knowledge builders. Knowledge building is a term now widely used. Scardamalia and Bereiter (2006, p. 113) note that: "we were, as far as we can ascertain, the first to use the term in education, and certainly the first to have used it as something more than a synonym for active learning." The authors distinguish knowledge building as distinct in important ways from such terms as "active learning," "self-regulated learning" and "learning by doing."

TABLE 6.1 Three Types of Online Learning

Online Collaborative Learning	Online Distance Learning	Online Courseware
• Online discourse	• Online delivery	• Online presentation
• Group learning	• Individualized learning	• Individualized learning
• Instructor-led	• Tutor support	• Computer assessment
• Asynchronous	• Asynchronous	• Asynchronous
• Place-independent	• Place-independent	• Place-independent
• Text-based	• Text-based	• Multimedia
• Internet-mediated discourse	• Internet-mediated delivery	• Internet-mediated presentation

OCL theory provides a model of learning in which students are encouraged and supported to work together to create knowledge: to invent, to explore ways to innovate and, by so doing, to seek the conceptual knowledge needed to solve problems rather than recite what they think is the right answer. While OCL theory does encourage the learner to be active and engaged, this is not considered to be sufficient for learning or knowledge construction. Terms or techniques such as "active learning" or "learning by doing" imply that students' interest-driven activities are generative of knowledge and competence. Self-regulation, moreover, is an individualized learning strategy to teach a learner better control over his/her behavior; it typically emphasizes self-observation, self-monitoring and self-evaluation. But these approaches do not necessarily lead students to conceptual change or to construct knowledge. In the active learning model, the role of the teacher is not considered, and is sometimes diminished to being a participant. In the OCL theory, the teacher plays a key role not as a fellow-learner, but as the link to the knowledge community, or state of the art in that discipline. Learning is defined as conceptual change and is key to building knowledge.

Learning activity needs to be informed and guided by the norms of the discipline and a discourse process that emphasizes conceptual learning and builds knowledge. There is a need for students to have a relationship to the knowledge community, mediated by the teacher or mentor who represents that community. In OCL, the teacher has a very important role to play. Moreover, learning and knowledge building should be viewed as meaningful to society and not driven only by personal interest or done to fulfill a class assignment.

Discourse, Collaboration and Knowledge Building

A key aspect of knowledge creation is discourse. Discourse refers to written or spoken discussion and conversation. Discourse is also posited as the very catalyst for our civilizational development, the basis of thought, knowledge and civilization. Speech is the first paradigm shift (see Figure 2.2), and speech as the basis of thought also draws upon Vygotsky's views that reflective thought is internalized conversation (inner speech). Vygotsky's 1962 book, *Thought and Language*, makes the argument that thought is inner conversation with ourselves, a collaboration turned inward: "The relation between thought and word is a living process; thought is born through words. A word devoid of thought is a dead thing, and a thought unembodied in words remains a shadow" (p. 153).

Vygotsky was an early and major force in advancing the importance of collaboration for knowledge construction; he revised learning theory by moving the unit of analysis from the individual per se, to the individual in relationship to the environment and in interaction with others. He defined learning as a social process, based on language, conversation and the "zone of proximal development" (ZPD), whereby we learn through contact and discourse with an adult or peer more competent in the field. Bruffee (1999) writes along the same line: "We think because we can talk with one another" (p. 134). Knowledge is generated by speech and conversation with one another, a construct of the community's form of discourse, negotiated and maintained by local consensus and subject to endless conversation (Bruffee, 1999; Kuhn, 1970). "Education initiates us into conversation, and by virtue of that conversation initiates us into thought" (Bruffee, 1999, p. 133).

Collaboration and discourse are key to building knowledge, an endless human conversation of changing and improving ideas. Academic disciplines as well as the world of work reflect the growing recognition of collaboration in human development. Anthropologists have come to view intentional collaboration as being at the very core of human identity and the essence of civilizational advancement (Hrdy, 2009). Invention and knowledge are perceived not as products of individual genius, but of knowledge communities and collaboration. Michael Farrell (2001) defines the term "collaborative circles" as follows:

Figure 6.1 Examples of Online Discourse.

A primary group consisting of peers who share similar occupational goals and who, through long periods of dialogue and collaboration negotiate a common vision that guides their work. The vision consists of a shared set of assumptions about their discipline, including what constitutes good work, how to work, what subjects are worth working on, and how to think about them. For a group of artists, the shared vision might be a new style. For a group of scientists, it might be a new theoretical paradigm. (p. 11)

Kenneth Bruffee (1999) similarly emphasizes the importance of collaboration for knowledge construction. He cites the studies of Bruno Latour and Steve Woolgar, who concluded that

scientists construct scientific knowledge through conversation, and that the most important kind of conversation scientists engage in is indirect, that is, displaced into writing. Scientists, they tell us, are "compulsive and almost manic writers." Conversation among scientists illustrates, furthermore, how we construct knowledge in every field and walk of life. (Bruffee, 1999, p. 53)

OCL theory and pedagogy seek to initiate the learners into the processes of conversation (discourse) used by knowledge communities to create knowledge and improve ideas. As Bruffee has observed, discourse is the means of transitioning from one community of knowledgeable peers to the next as we become reacculturated through engagement with each new community.

From the very beginning of our lives we construct knowledge in conversation with other people. When we learn something new, we leave a community that justifies certain beliefs in certain ways with certain linguistic and paralinguistic systems, to join instead another community that justifies other beliefs in other ways with other systems. We leave one community of knowledgeable peers and join another. (Bruffee, 1999, p. 135)

In fact, popular statements such as "Science is talk" or "Science is argument" may be simplistic but true. It is also true within art and social and cultural sciences, and for all forms of knowledge and education as well. Knowledge is built by and through informed discourse, debate, agreement and disagreement about new information.

Collaborative learning refers to ways of teaching and learning based on talk, on discourse whereby students co-labor to produce a result whether to solve a problem, to discuss or improve an idea, explore a hypothesis or conduct a project (Harasim, 2004). However, unlike "cooperative learning" in which each group member contributes an independent piece to the whole in the form of a division of labor, with "collaborative learning" the group members discuss and work together throughout the process. The *process* itself is collaborative, not just the product. The process is one of conceptual change, in which learners in a shared context (a course, a seminar, or a discussion) engage in a process of progressing from divergent to convergent perspectives and understanding. Intellectual divergence such as individual brainstorming, disagreeing, debating, eventually leads, with facilitation, to considering new ideas and exploring the merits of the different perspectives generated by the others in the group. Through the role of the teacher or moderator and access to new sources of information, the group arrives at a position of intellectual convergence, a group position (albeit not homogenous) that reflects a deeper understanding of the content and also of the process of knowledge and possibly even contributes to practice or advancing the state of the art.

The primary role of discourse in knowledge communities is to not merely persuade but to generate progress toward the solution of shared problems. Scardamalia and Bereiter (2006, p. 100) propose the following criteria for knowledge-building discourse in a classroom:

- a commitment to *progress*, something that does not characterize dinner party conversation or discussions devoted to sharing information and venting opinions;
- a commitment to *seek common understanding* rather than merely agreement, which is not characteristic of political and policy discourse, for instance;
- a commitment to *expand the base of accepted facts*, whereas, in court trials and debates, attacking the factual claims of opponents is common.

Online Collaborative Learning Processes

The OCL process includes discourse, collaborative learning and knowledge building. Innovation and creativity are essential to building knowledge, and are key aspects of divergent thinking. Divergent thinking refers to a process that generates many questions, ideas, responses or solutions. It is associated with brainstorming and creative thought, that is, generating questions and drawing on ideas from different perspectives and many sources (including personal observations and experiences). While divergent thinking involves generating many ideas, the process associated with identifying the best ideas and discarding the weak ones is called convergent thinking. Convergent thinking refers to narrowing down the options based on existing information and analysis, and selecting the best. Linus Pauling, the great scientist who won two Nobel prizes in his lifetime, was credited with the following response when asked at a public lecture how one creates scientific theories: Pauling replied that one must endeavor to come up with *many* ideas—then discard the useless ones.

Determining the best solution involves considering many ideas and learning most appropriate to apply to the situation. The OCL theory has been characterized by Harasim (1990a, 2002) as comprising three processes/phases, describing a path from divergent to convergent thinking. Although identified and developed in the online context, it resonates with Bruffee's (1999) theoretical position that intellectual convergence through collaborative discourse is key. Jeremy Roschelle (1992) similarly posits that collaboration can lead to convergence of meaning. He studies how two or more people can construct shared meanings for conversations, concepts and experiences:

One compelling reason for exploring a convergence account as a complement to Piagetian and Vygotskian accounts follows from a fundamental commitment to collaborative inquiry, and the relation of collaborative inquiry to scientific conceptual change. Democratic participation, intellectual progress and gradual convergence are base attributes of social inquiry practices that enable scientists to undergo conceptual change. In contrast, Vygostkian theory lends itself to accounts of the reproduction of existing scientific knowledge, whereas Piaget suggests development through static, maturational levels. A convergence account alone suggests the attractive possibility that students develop their concepts in the course of learning to participate in the practices of inquiry that scientists themselves use to develop scientific concepts. (Roschelle, 1992, p. 272)

Harasim (2002) proposes the OCL theory of discourse in online educational applications and identifies the following three intellectual phases as key:

1. Idea Generating. The first phase, Idea Generating, refers to divergent thinking within a group; brainstorming, verbalization, generating information, and thus sharing of ideas and positions on a particular topic or problem. Participants engage in democratic participation and thereby contribute toward building a large and diverse set of ideas and perspectives.
2. Idea Organizing. The second phase, Idea Organizing, is the beginning of conceptual change, demonstrating intellectual progress and the beginning of convergence as participants confront new or different ideas, clarify and cluster these new ideas according to their relationship and similarities to one another, selecting the strongest and weeding out weaker positions (referencing, agreement, disagreement or questioning). This phase demonstrates intellectual progress through recognizing multiple perspectives and identifying how these relate or not to one another and to the topic.
3. Intellectual Convergence. The third phase, Intellectual Convergence, is typically reflected in shared understanding (including agreeing to disagree), a mutual contribution to and construction of shared knowledge and understanding. Idea structuring, through gradual convergence, reaches a level of intellectual synthesis, understanding and consensus, whereby participants in the discussion agree to disagree, and/or co-produce a conclusion—perhaps an artifact such as a solution to a problem, a design, an assignment, a theory, a publication, a work of art, or a similar output co-authored by the group or subgroup.

Figure 6.2 illustrates the three stages of collaborative discourse from Idea Generating (IG) to Intellectual Convergence (IC). At the IG stage, individual students contribute their ideas and opinions to the group. Through the process of brainstorming, the students express their own ideas and begin to confront other ideas as generated by others in the group. This leads to the second stage of the discourse—Idea Organizing (IO). At this stage, the students reflect on the various ideas presented and begin to interact with one another, to agree or disagree, clarify, question, critique, elaborate or reject some ideas and identify relationships and organizing linkages among other ideas. As a result, discrete ideas start to come together; several small ideas become a few large ones, individual understandings grow into group-shared understanding. And many ideas are discarded. At this point, the discourse advances to the third level—IC. By stage 3, the group actively engages in the co-construction of knowledge based on shared understanding. The group members synthesize their ideas and knowledge into explicit points of view or positions on the topic. The outcomes of this stage are consolidated, shared understandings and

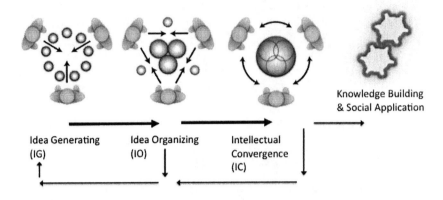

Knowledge Building
& Social Application

Idea Generating
(IG)

Idea Organizing
(IO)

Intellectual
Convergence
(IC)

Figure 6.2 Three Intellectual Phases of Online Collaborative Learning.

group convergence as evidenced by conclusive statements and/or co-production (such as theories, positions, strategies, tools, manifestos and scientific theories/hypotheses). These may lead to social applications, represented as gears. Or lead to further debate, discussion and refining of the concepts as suggested by the feedback arrows. The process is not circular, but one of continual growth or advance based on a feedback spiral. The phase of IO may move directly to IC, or it may trigger further brainstorming (IG). The role of the teacher/moderator is highlighted and discussed in the next section, on OCL pedagogy.

Online Collaborative Learning Pedagogy

Online learning has been adopted at all levels of education, from public schools and universities to training and continuing and corporate education. Many educators have tried totally online or blended classroom teaching. Online education is becoming ubiquitous, increasingly integrated into traditional classroom and distance education programs.

The major challenge and paradox, as discussed earlier in this chapter, is the need for a theory of learning and concomitant pedagogies that speak to the realities of the Knowledge Age. Teaching approaches and techniques for online education do exist, as evidenced by the growth of the field. Literature on how to design and moderate online seminars and projects is emerging and these books provide many valuable examples and techniques (see for example, books by Palloff & Pratt, 2001, 2005, 2007; Salmon, 2000; Collison et al., 2000).

OCL theory can enrich or contribute to the above pedagogical activities by providing a theoretical framework to help design and inform activities such as online seminars and group work with processes of conceptual change and intellectual convergence. OCL theory can also help in assessing conceptual change. OCL pedagogy emphasizes conceptual change and learning through advancing from the Idea Generating stage, to Idea Organizing, to the Intellectual Convergence stage. The pedagogical activities are linked with conceptual processes that encourage change and improvement over time.

In OCL theory and pedagogy, the teacher plays a key and essential role, a role that is neither as "guide on the side" nor "sage on the stage." Rather, the role of the educator is to engage the learners in the language and activities associated with building the discipline, inducting the learners into the language and processes of the knowledge community. Teachers are representatives of their knowledge communities, and as such introduce the learners to the appropriate language as well as its application within the particular discipline.

Everybody in such a knowledge community "speaks the same language," the language that constitutes the community. Among academic and public professionals alike, a major element in this constituting language is what to outsiders seems like jargon, the disciplinary locutions and terms of art that add up to the normal discourse of the community. Speaking that language fluently defines membership in the community. Not speaking it fluently marks a nonmember. Mathematicians speak fluent mathematics. Nonmathematicians do not. Sociologists speak fluent sociologese. Nonsociologists do not.... Thomas Kuhn has argued and Bruno Latour and others have confirmed that this principle extends as well to scientific thought and scientific communities. (Bruffee, 1999, pp. 153–154)

Teachers, professors and educators are members of their knowledge community and have the special role of representing that community and of inducting new members.

In accepting this responsibility, professors set out to help students acquire fluency in the language of those communities, so that they become, if not necessarily new professionals, then people who are "literarily-minded," "mathematically minded," "sociologically minded," and so on. That is, the students learn more than disciplinary jargon. Their education is reacculturation involving intense, flexible linguistic engagement with members of communities they already belong to and communities to which they do not yet belong. (Bruffee, 1999, p. 154)

To help illustrate this intellectual process, we examine a generic online group discussion or seminar approach, which begins with small group discussions on a topic, then progresses.

Figure 6.3 depicts the pedagogy of group discussion and the progress from divergence to intellectual convergence that approximates the knowledge community. The role of the teacher is as facilitator with the students and as representative of the knowledge community, reacculturating the students into the discourse of the knowledge community of that discipline.

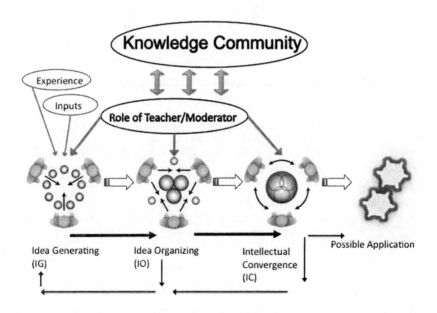

Figure 6.3 Example OCL Processes in a Class.

We can view this process exemplified by a group discussion (or seminar, debate, etc.).

1. Idea Generating. Learners engage in a group discussion of a specific topic, question or knowledge problem in the discipline that they are studying. Each participant logs on to the discussion to present his or her initial views on the subject. This is the process of idea generating and brainstorming, whereby participants articulate their views and generate a range of divergent perspectives on the topic. The teacher or moderator establishes the processes of discussion and the knowledge problem to be discussed. This phase is a highly democratic and engaging process: everyone presents one or several ideas.

2. Idea Organizing. Students interact with one another, confront new ideas and engage in relevant course readings suggested by the teacher/moderator and other sources of information proposed by group members. The input has grown and has enriched each learner's awareness and appreciation of how the topic can be viewed. Learners begin to organize, analyze and filter the range of ideas by agreeing or disagreeing with some of the ideas presented, elaborating, expanding or rejecting others. Inputs from the teacher/moderator such as course readings and facilitating the discussion reflect the influence of the knowledge community as the framework of reference. The teacher introduces new analytical terms which are applied by the students to deepen the discussion and understanding of the topic. Some idea generating may occur but primarily this phase of the process is characterized by references to ideas and applying analytical concepts to cluster or organize common ideas into fewer and more refined categories.

3. Intellectual Convergence. Through informed discussion and analysis informed by the readings and supported by the teacher/moderator, learners reach a level of intellectual convergence and come to a position on the topic or a resolution to the knowledge problem. Intellectual convergence includes (and is most typically characterized by) agreement to disagree or in some cases reaching a consensus. Intellectual convergence may be reflected in a co-produced final product such as a report, a final paper, a group presentation or an intellectual statement such as a summary or landscape of the discussion. When a product is the goal (a paper, a presentation, a project or assignment), the intellectual processes aim toward a consensus on the shape of the final product. In more scholarly applications, the goal may be development of a design, a policy, an artistic or scientific statement. Or the process of convergence may yield a few key but distinct positions.

> The process of moderated group discussion in an educational forum is to provide students with access to the most relevant and timely information sources, to learn the analytical terms and concepts of the discipline and how to apply these appropriately, and to arrive at a position informed by the process. Students have engaged in learning and constructing knowledge by using the processes used by the knowledge community in that discipline, and thus approximate the processes employed by that knowledge community. The role of the teacher has been to mediate between the students and the knowledge community, representing the knowledge community by assisting access to state-of-the-art information on the topic and facilitating the collaboration and knowledge-building processes. In a course, the process will likely end here, a final paper or project applying the conclusions. Or possibly the process may repeat, in a loop or a spiral, to deepen the intellectual processes. Another option is that the process leads to real-world applications, such as a course involving preservice or inservice training.

4. Final Position. The process encourages conceptual change. It may trigger further consideration and analysis by recycling (at an ever deeper or more advanced level) intellectual

processes of Idea Generating and Idea Organizing or in other cases, such as applied sciences and professions, the final conclusions may be decisions or strategies to influence real-world applications.

This example takes into consideration the process of reacculturation that learners experience as they confront new problems or new perspectives on an existing problem, learn new analytical terms and apply new analytical processes to problem solving. Learners typically enter the course with an existing view on a topic or problem. Through group discussion and interaction with the teacher and information resources, they come to a new and deeper understanding of the knowledge problem and how to address it in the manner of the knowledge community to which they wish to gain entry, upon graduation.

The role of the teacher is essential to facilitating the process and providing the learners with the resources and kinds of activities that will help them to build knowledge collaboratively, using the Internet. Key as well is the role of the knowledge community, which represents the state of the art in that discipline. The teacher or professor, as a representative of that knowledge community,

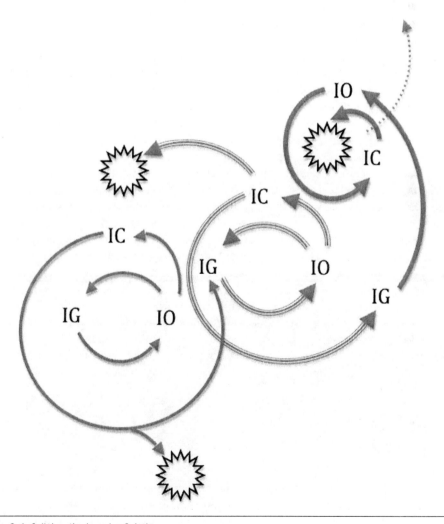

Figure 6.4 Collaborative Learning Spirals.

mediates between the learners and the knowledge community and inducts the learners into the processes for building knowledge in that discipline. Collaborative learning discourse and processes contribute to the growth of understanding and knowledge in a cyclical or spiral manner (not linear), progressing and improving through experience, discussion and new information over time.

Online Collaborative Learning Technology

The nature of online technologies is another key to understanding and engaging in effective online learning. Online technologies can play various and very distinct roles. Some online technologies facilitate learning tasks while others facilitate learning processes. The former are referred to as online tools, the latter as online environments.

The next two sections discuss in greater detail online learning technology's essential roles:

1. Technology as learning tool(s);
2. Technology as learning environment.

Online Learning Tools

The concept of online learning tools refers to web tools that can facilitate or enable particular tasks in a learning activity. These may be tools generic to the Web or education-specific tools. Educators and learners use both. Generic web tools include search engines such as Google, web browsers for accessing the Web, email tools, productivity tools such as online calendars, document-creation tools and graphic presentation tools. Generic tools associated with Web 2.0 (also referred to as the Social or Collaborative Web) include blogs, wikis, podcast-authoring tools, web-authoring tools, social networking tools and tools to enable social networking by user-generated content.

Education-specific tools include websites or portals with resources specifically aimed at teachers, students or particular disciplines: for example, sites that offer lesson plans; assessment information, tools or inventories; learner support or tutoring; content for specific disciplines and age levels; and/or links to related sites. Other online tools that are popular with educators are online gradebooks, online quizzes, web portals that contain course materials and (audio and/or video) podcasts.

Nonetheless, such tools do not provide online "spaces" conducive to facilitating collaborative learning. They offer potential enhancements to collaborative discourse and group conversations, but they are not shared spaces or environments, able—in and of themselves—to support collaborative learning and knowledge building discourse. Blogs, wikis and social networks are excellent for their purposes as diaries, collaborative-authoring tools or social spaces, but they were not designed for nor are they appropriate as learning environments which can support group discussion that deepens and progresses over time.

Web tools are important pieces in the learning process, but attempts to date to concatenate the tools to form an environment for learning, such as linking a gradebook with a quiz tool, are inadequate for effective learning. Central to collaborative learning and knowledge building is the need for a shared space for discourse and interaction. This shared space is the heart of an online learning environment that can support OCL.

Online Learning Environments

The term online learning environment refers to web-based software that is designed to host or house the learning activities. An online learning environment is the online equivalent of physical architecture such as a classroom, a campus, a student cafe, a seminar room, a student lab or office. Allen and Otto (1996) refer to the educational ecology of media as "lived environments," whereby users exercise their powers of perception, mobility and agency within the constraints imposed by the various technologies and learning theories and pedagogies (p. 199). Online learning environments are not mere channels for transmitting information (such as broadcasting by television and radio, or lectures delivered by podcasting). They are environments where users can construct knowledge and negotiate meaning through conversation and collaboration, not just receive communication. They are experienced as lived spaces, to the extent that they facilitate both the perception of opportunities for acting as well as some means for acting (Allen & Otto, 1996, p. 199).

Online learning environments, just as their physical equivalents, are typically content-free. Unlike courseware applications, the content in OCL is discourse generated primarily by the learners. OCL applications typically use generic group-discussion software such as forums, bulletin boards or computer conferencing systems. Group-discussion software can be organized by the instructor into various forums and subforums, virtual spaces that can be designated by the instructor to represent different topics, different group activities, with different group sizes, scheduled for specified times during the online semester. Students navigate around the online course and select (click on) the appropriate forum to read and write comments or to work on individual or group assignments.

Online learning environments have the potential to support highly effective learning and knowledge-creation processes. Creating customized learning environments based on pedagogical models and frameworks remains a major challenge, although early steps have been taken in this direction. Tools embedded within the environment could provide relevant information, suggestions or scaffolds for particular learning processes. The need for tools and environments customized for online learning was first expressed in the late 1980s, for group-discussion forums that went beyond generic design to those intentionally designed to support collaborative learning and knowledge-building discourse. This did not mean generic online forums linked to quiz tools, nor sites preloaded with curricular content. The need was for online educational discourse environments customized and informed by pedagogical principles and learning theory.

> Generic network tools—such as e-mail, computer conferencing and newsgroups—impose significant user overhead because they were not specifically designed to support educational activities. Instructors have had to expend great effort to reformulate their traditional classroom activities. Doing so with models or tools to shape the learning environment involved substantial administrative, organizational, and pedagogical challenges and cost. Many experiments failed and discouraged early enthusiasts. (Harasim, 1999, p. 44)

In the 1990s efforts to develop an online learning environment to support and encourage the use of collaborative learning online led to the creation of the Virtual-U web-based learning system.

> The goal of our system, now known as the Virtual-U, was to provide a flexible framework to support advanced pedagogies based on active learning, collaboration, multiple perspectives, and knowledge building. This framework employs various instructional formats, including seminars, tutorials, group projects, and labs. (Harasim, 1999, p. 45)

The Virtual-U software employed a spatial metaphor in its interface to represent different "spaces" or forums for hosting individual and group educational activities. Virtual-U was distinguished by a pedagogical vision and framework that guided the software design. That framework was explicit: to support collaborative learning and knowledge construction. This was done by designing a seamless online environment with embedded teacher and learner tools that could generate discourse spaces that could be configured and customized in a variety of ways, for individuals or groups using various communication features (asynchronous group conferencing and synchronous chats). The asynchronous computer conferencing system, named VGroups, was designed to enable users to gain multiple perspectives on the discourse: users could organize the online message transcripts according to subject, thread, author, date or reader-set keyword. VGroups provided instructors and moderators with tools to customize the discourse space by group size and user privileges (i.e., create, delete, read-only) to define discourse categories. The Virtual-U environment was based on geographical metaphors to help students and instructors navigate the virtual space: different spaces for each seminar, each discussion or work group, labs, cafe, personal workspace, course library, chat space, course-design tools, administrative tools, personal calendar and course gradebook. Messages could be text or multimedia and include web links. Virtual-U also prototyped educational scaffolds and templates to support instructors and learning in the use of such pedagogical techniques as debates, case-based learning and tools to measure different dimensions of learning processes. VUCat, the Virtual-U Course Analysis Tool, enabled monitoring of user participation (logins, number of messages read, messages written, replies) and generated graphical displays of summary data. Such data could be accessed by the teacher/moderator or by participants (depending on how user privileges were set up by the moderator). Templates for transcript analysis by categorizing the messages according to the three phases of OCL discourse were also developed for researchers, instructors and students. Students reported that such OCL templates were valuable for moderating online seminars and in orienting their own participation in online discussions: VU-Cat helped moderators view the volume and nature of messages, analyze the phase of discourse and thus help them to facilitate and advance the learning. Virtual-U exemplifies one approach to customizing an online environment to support collaboration and knowledge-building discourse.

Other important innovations in online learning and knowledge building were also developed and implemented in the 1990s. Knowledge Forum (KF) was designed as a knowledge-building environment, defined as: "Any environment (virtual or otherwise) that enhances collaborative efforts to create and continually improve ideas" (Scardamalia, 2003, p. 269). This definition can refer to educational as well as work or other organizational environments and includes essential characteristics or requirements for a knowledge-building environment, such as: support for collaborative creation and revision of conceptual artifacts; shared, user-configured design spaces with supports for citing and referencing one another's work; systems of feedback to enhance self- and group monitoring or ongoing processes. Bereiter and Scardamalia (2006) note that "a knowledge building software environment does not merely promote Knowledge Age soft skills but embodies the essential characteristics of creative knowledge work" (p. 709). Moreover, as noted earlier, Scardamalia and Bereiter (2006) distinguish knowledge building from didacticism and constructivist learning: "traditional educational practice—with its emphasis on knowledge transmission—as well as the newer constructivist methods both appear to be limited in scope if not entirely missing the point" (p. 98). KF is an asynchronous web-based technology that provides a shared discourse environment. It emphasizes collaborative knowledge-building strategies, textual and graphical representation of ideas, and reorganization of knowledge artifacts.

KF intends to be used as an online learning system or an in-class technology. For each course there is a database. The main feature is called a note. Users have access to the following options:

- search for existing notes;
- write a new note;
- co-author, when more users share the authorship for the same note;

- reference and quote an existing note;
- annotate an existing note without creating a new one;
- reply (build on) to a specific note;
- create "rise-above" notes, which subsume sets of related notes.

The main technique that KF employs is scaffolding (Scardamalia, 2004). Learners use a specific set of scaffolds (a set of six note types) that support cognitive operations intended to help learners improve their understanding. The basic scaffolds are notes that are labeled, categorized, organized and linked as one of the following options or note types:

- "my theory"
- "I need to understand"
- "new information"
- "this theory cannot explain"
- "a better theory"
- "putting our knowledge together."

A learner or participant writes a note and labels it according to one of these six options to categorize the content, before sending it to the group database. The categories can also be customized. According to Bereiter and Scardamalia (2003): "a comprehensive knowledge building environment would provide a means of initiating students into a knowledge-creating culture—to make them feel a part of humankind's long-term effort to understand their world and gain some control over their destiny" (p. 18). Key to the choice of learning environment and tools is the view or theory of learning that is supported by the technology. Virtual-U, KF and similar online environments were developed to facilitate collaborative knowledge building. Courseware authoring tools, on the other hand, are based on knowledge-transmission models, and are centered on the course designer who prescribes the content to be delivered and determines the sequence, hierarchy and quantity of the presentation. The learner does not engage in co-constructing the knowledge, but is charged with accessing and repeating the content correctly.

Other web tools based on knowledge-transmission models are broadcasting tools such as lectures delivered online using audio podcasts, long text messages or PowerPoint slides with audio and/or with video clips. Live communication tools such as video feeds are another tool that encourages one-to-many instructor broadcasting rather than many-to-many collaboration and communication.

Online tools such as presentation tools, document tools, productivity tools, web browsers and search engines can be used in concert with shared discourse spaces, to enhance and expand discourse and knowledge building. Such tools can be used by students to generate content and to enhance their ability to engage in learning and constructing knowledge together. But a shared discourse space remains key to OCL.

What is key to these environments is the existence of a shared space—not just an assemblage of tools—and how the shared space is designed and structured. A famous quotation attributed to Marshall McLuhan is relevant here: "First we shape our tools, and then our tools shape us." This is true for online as well as physical environments, and it is essential that the technologies be designed with the intent to facilitate shared space and knowledge community processes.

As a final note to this section, it is critical to clearly understand the purpose for which a particular software tool was designed and to use the software systems and tools appropriately. A technology is designed for a particular purpose, and in such a way as to facilitate that purpose. Designing and customizing new educational environments and tools is a high priority.

There are few environments that have been especially customized for educational discourse available today. The rise of the open-source software movement holds promise for collaborative, global construction of new and customizable OCL environments, but the potential has yet to be realized.

In this next section, we explore the attributes of OCL environments, from the perspective of potential benefits and limitations of online forums in supporting collaboration and knowledge-building *discourse*. What is key, in addition to the access of the learner to educational offerings, is the nature and quality of the intellectual and social discourse that can be supported online. The next section discusses the attributes OCL environments for facilitating knowledge-building discourse.

Attributes of Online Collaborative Learning Environments

The environments in which we live, learn, work and socialize are all characterized by attributes that enable certain kinds of activities and communications, and limit or negate others. Face-to-face environments have particular attributes and affordances while online environments have others. OCL environments, specifically discussion forums, are characterized by discourse with the following five attributes:

1. Place-independent discourse;
2. Time-independent (as well as synchronous) discourse;
3. Many-to-many discourse (as well as one-to-many and one-to-one communication);
4. Text-based (with multimedia) discourse;
5. Internet-mediated discourse.

OCL environments benefit discourse in certain unique ways, but limits it in others. OCL environments introduce new opportunities for learning. Below is a brief discussion of some of the ways in which the attributes can affect OCL discourse.

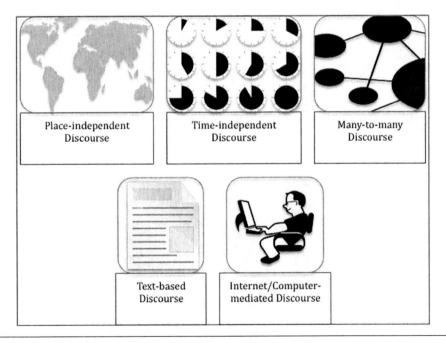

Figure 6.5 Types of Online Discourse (Screenshot of University of Phoenix).

1. PLACE-INDEPENDENT DISCOURSE

Among the most obvious and powerful attributes of the Internet is place-independent discourse. The ability to communicate and collaborate beyond the classroom walls has introduced profound shifts in teaching and learning.

Perhaps the primary implication of place-independent discourse is access, a critical goal of school, college, workplace and corporate education. Online education has a global reach and this offers learning a tremendous advantage. Place independence enables educational access for learners in remote areas, in parts of the world without access to particular disciplines of study, particular expertise or appropriate levels of study. It enables educational access to learners who may have to travel for work, and thus can participate in online education while on the road or who have family or other responsibilities or have physical disabilities that preclude travel to a place-based campus.

Place-independent discourse also has significant implications for the quality of learning and knowledge building. It enables greatly expanded student participation, and hence the quality and nature of the ideas generated and debated are potentially enriched. Discourse in OCL environments benefits from access to new cultures, perspectives and input: multiple perspectives are encouraged given the inclusion of participants from diverse locations and backgrounds. Place-independent discourse also enables the inclusion of guest experts or participants from outside the class, to enhance the discussions.

Place-independent discourse also introduces new challenges. In the case of global or cross-cultural discussions, there is a need for participants to become sensitized to cultural differences and nuances (some cultures may be more loquacious, while others value more formal interactions). Students participating in online classes may also face difficulties in creating suitable learning spaces at home or in their office (a parent in an online course may be challenged for computer access or by distractions if the computer is on the kitchen table).

2. TIME-INDEPENDENT DISCOURSE

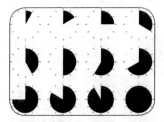

A second attribute of online learning is time independence or asynchronicity. OCL is typically asynchronous, although synchronous (real-time) course delivery and group interaction is available through videoconferencing and audioconferencing technologies such as Skype.

Asynchronous access means that the online class is available 24 hours a day, seven days a week: 24/7. Time-independent discourse introduces a number of benefits for learning and knowledge building. Students do in fact engage in online learning activities 24/7, to read and write messages at all hours of the day and night. Participation in the online conversations is ongoing. And the expanded access enables online discussions to be highly active and interactive. There is no limit to airtime and students can always make input. Feedback on ideas posted online can be relatively immediate and discussion and debate can refine and advance an idea over time. Or students can take more time if needed to draft a thoughtful response and access resources to inform and enhance their input. Students can also take advantage of spell checkers or grammar guides, to write and edit a comment. Asynchronous discourse also offers participants time to reflect on an idea or message, and to take as long as necessary to formulate a response. Learners can participate at their best learning-readiness times, especially important if they have family or other obligations that are time sensitive. They can participate at a time most convenient to them and appropriate to the course activity. Asynchronous communication also facilitates discourse across time zones.

On the other hand, students in online discourse activities such as seminars may experience communication anxiety while awaiting a response to their comment, or frustration if the discussions begin to lag. Long periods of time between messages can distract from or diminish the significance of input and undermine the communication flow.

3. GROUP (MANY–MANY) DISCOURSE

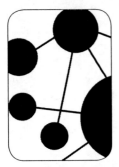

The ability to engage in group, or many-to-many, discourse is the basis for collaboration and knowledge building. As has been discussed throughout this chapter, group input enables multiple perspectives to enrich consideration of an idea or topic. Online forums or conferencing systems were developed to enable group conversations, and hence allow all participants to input their own ideas and thereby create a diversity of ideas, reactions and feedback on the discussion topic. Forums have proven to be excellent environments for communicating divergent input, such as verbalization and brainstorming. Online forums support creativity by enabling participants to draw on ideas from many perspectives and diverse sources; the ability to respond to and interact with a range of ideas allows us to refine and improve understanding and knowledge.

Current online forum systems, however, are not well designed to facilitate convergent thinking and this requires the instructor or moderator to organize and structure the group discussions into intellectual processes that lead to intellectual convergence and conclusions. Online discourse requires moderating and facilitating frameworks and techniques to organize the diverse and potentially voluminous input and to encourage intellectual progress. Online forum software also enables one-to-many communication such as broadcasts or lectures, and one-to-one communication as needed or appropriate.

4. TEXT-BASED DISCOURSE

OCL discourse is primarily text-based, although multimedia tools such as audio, video, animation and even avatars may be incorporated into online course activities and discourse. While some educators may question the use of text as the primary medium of communication in online learning (in preference to audio, video or animation), text is the groundbreaking mode of academic, scientific and intellectual discourse. The most important type of conversation in knowledge building is text or writing. As Bruffee (1999) notes, scientists are "'compulsive and almost manic writers.' … Conversation among scientists illustrates, further, how we construct knowledge in every field and walks of life" (p. 53). Vygotsky (1962) posited the importance of writing to the process of knowing. The articulation of thoughts into written speech involves analytical deliberation: "The change from maximally compact inner speech to maximally detailed written speech requires what may be called deliberate semantics—deliberate structuring of the web of meaning" (pp. 99–100). Discourse and writing are powerful articulations and representations of our thoughts. It is how we express and communicate our thoughts, to others and ourselves. McGinley and Tierney (1989) emphasize the importance of writing in the construction of meaning and how we come to know, and cite this insightful statement by J. Gage (1986):

> Writing is thinking made tangible, thinking that can be examined because it is on the page and not in the head invisibly floating around. Writing is thinking that can be stopped and tinkered with. It is a way of holding thought still enough to examine its structure, its flaws. The road to clearer understanding of one's thoughts is travelled on paper. It is through an attempt to find words for ourselves in which to express related ideas that we often discover what we think. (Cited in McGinley & Tierney, 1989, p. 24)

Writing is thinking made visible, whereby it is subject to consideration and comment. Whether on the screen or on paper, writing is a way of discovering what we think and also a means to improve our ideas and discourse. Online discourse, moreover, is archived by the forum or computer conferencing software. This creates an accurate and verbatim transcript that learners and educators can access for replying to comments, reviewing the discussion, making multiple passes through the transcript and for retrospective analysis or assessment.

Online text is a compelling attribute for peer discussion and debate. Given the transmission speeds required for sending and receiving text, online text is accessible around the globe. Moreover, the Net Gen prefer texting to talking by cellphone. This trend is growing among all sectors of the population, even in the United States: Americans sent 110 billion text messages in 2008, double the number sent in 2007. The nation's 270 million cellphone subscribers each sent an average of 407 text messages in 2008. "We are seeing a clear trend of huge increases in text messaging," writes Amanda Lenhart, senior research specialist at the Pew Internet and American Life Project.

"If teens are a leader for America, then we are moving to a text-based communication system. For them, there is less interest in talking." Lenhart's research found that the average American teen sent over 2000 text messages per month, and that two-thirds of all teens use text messaging. ("Texting over Talking," *Globe and Mail*, December 21, 2009)

The popularity and expertise with text-based communication may bode well for online educational discussion forums. Until recently, text was widely (and unwisely) derided as too narrow in bandwidth to support student interest in learning online. The rise of texting by the Net Gen may turn attention to how, and not whether, to use this powerful discourse medium for best educational practice.

At the same time, online learning activities are incorporating more multimedia, such as the introduction of sophisticated simulations and immersive environments (see Chapter 7 for examples).

5. INTERNET-MEDIATED DISCOURSE

This final attribute is perhaps the most potent, given the range and scope of information, the vast repository of tools and resources, and the astounding number of people participating on the Web that are all accessible to online educational discussion forums. And the capacity of the Web, already unparalleled, is growing. The rise of the Internet and the scope of future plans and projections are beyond anything human society has experienced to date, and education will certainly be influenced.

Today, we have easy access at our fingertips to a global knowledge network whereby we can learn from all kinds of people and resources. Internet-mediated discourse already provides access to an astounding myriad of resources that can be linked/hypertexted into our messages, blogs or discussions to provide new perspectives, information or evidence. The Web is an incredible repository of information and expertise that is easily accessed and yet offers immense rewards. We may intentionally seek specific data or resources, or serendipitously discover new insights and ideas or expand/refine existing ones.

Text, graphics and videos are easily incorporated into our discourse to enrich or illuminate our position. And the rate of technological change and increased computing power is astounding.

Within a few decades computers have gone from storing 1 byte (equal to one character), to a kilobyte (1,000 bytes), to a megabyte (1,000 kilobytes), then gigabyte (1,000 megabytes). Today, gigabyte is a common term in referring to the storage space on our computers and storage in a terabyte (1,000 gigabytes) is becoming mainstream. Major advances in storage capacity are evolving rapidly.

New web tools are emerging at a tremendous rate to create qualitatively new dimensions of discourse, collaboration and knowledge construction. Cloud computing refers to new ways of storage, that dramatically expand computing power. Cloud applications such as enormous repositories of information could be linked with problem-solving or analytical tools to enrich online collaboration and knowledge building.

The vision of the Semantic Web was conceived by Tim Berners-Lee, the inventor of the World Wide Web, as the next step in web evolution. Berners-Lee has called the Semantic Web as "a web of data that can be processed directly and indirectly by machines" (1999, p. 177). By this, Berners-Lee means that whereas the current Web can only search and retrieve information that a user requests, the Semantic Web would be able to identify and display the most relevant information in a given circumstance. Data as well as documents would be on the Web and accessed by the Semantic Web technologies to process, transform, assemble and possibly even act on the data as needed. Data itself will become part of the Web and be able to be processed independently of application, platform or domain. This is in contrast to the World Wide Web as we know it today, which contains boundless information in the form of documents. We can use computers to search for these documents, but they still have to be read and interpreted by humans before any useful information can be extrapolated. The Semantic Web will be able to do the reading and interpretation for us, to yield even more profound analyses.

Data analysis and visualization tools are becoming major applications and potentially very valuable for educational research and assessment. Today, online quantitative data-analysis tools are common and more advanced ones are in the pipeline. However, qualitative data analysis remains underdeveloped, with few online tools to provide even simple and illuminative transcript analysis (or qualitative data) analysis. Analytical tools like Latent Semantic Analysis, text mining and data mining demonstrate some potential but remain complex and unwieldy for educational practice. However, major advances are under way.

Visualization software shows immediate promise. Visualization is a technique to graphically represent data. A simple example is the use of classic business charting software to visualize data using line charts, histograms or pie charts. Even such simple visuals can contribute to better understanding and have value in analyzing usage data or transcript discourse data in online education. Visualization software that is simple to use and which can reflect change over time (akin to line charts) is of particular value for studying educational discourse—to educators, learners and researchers. Histograms and pie charts help visualize content or categories. Many new visualization tools are appearing free, as open-source software, or as commercial products, representing an opportunity for educators, researchers and educational technologists to use or create such tools and techniques to study OCL processes in online discussions.

A final thought on the potential of Internet-mediated discussion is that in addition to unprecedented access to people and resources, the rise of the open knowledge and open content movement has enabled access to a wealth of academic and scholarly content that has been created but not traditionally made public, for free. *Open Knowledge* is a term used to denote a set of principles and methodologies related to the production and distribution of knowledge goods in an *open* manner. As set out in the Open Knowledge Definition, knowledge is open if "one is free to use, reuse, and redistribute it without legal, social or technological restriction." Open knowledge and open content have led to the creation of, or access to, large repositories of data, information and content such as educational course manuals, curricula and lesson plans. Major open-content repositories and directories include:

- OpenCourseWare Consortium: portal linking to free and openly licensed course materials from hundreds of universities worldwide;
- MIT OpenCourseWare: free and openly licensed course materials from more than 1,800 MIT courses;
- Connexions: global open-content repository started by Rice University;

- OER Commons: OpenEducationResource Commons is a network of open teaching and learning materials, with ratings and reviews;
- Google Directory: open Content;
- OpenLearn: free and open educational resources from the Open University;
- Comprehensive Knowledge Archive Network (CKAN): directory/registry of open data/content packages and projects;
- UNESCO Open Training Platform: network for international development issues;
- Open ICEcat catalog: worldwide open catalog for product information.

The next three chapters will focus on OCL in practice. Discourse on the Web, organized in online courses and within knowledge communities and other associations introduces unprecedented opportunities for a paradigmatic shift in how we teach and learn, as will be discussed in Chapters 7, 8 and 9.

Summary

Chapter 6 introduced online collaborative learning as a theory and as a framework for pedagogical and technological design. The chapter discussed the context of the 21st-century Knowledge Age and why a new theory of online learning is necessary.

The history of online learning was introduced to provide a timeline and a view of the development of online collaborative learning over the past four decades.

An exploration of the definitions of OCL theory and pedagogy was provided to enable readers to distinguish among the various models that may be implicit in the concept of "online education," and the need to clarify the theoretical foundations embedded in the use of the related terms.

Effective online learning tools and environments were also discussed, with some illustrations from the field to demonstrate new directions in OCL technologies.

The attributes of OCL environments were identified and discussed to provide a context for understanding online discourse and its potential for collaborative learning and knowledge building.

Chapter 7 provides examples of OCL pedagogies in practice: the use of online simulations for group case studies, student-led online seminars, co-production of real-world products by online teams and immersive role-playing learning environments.

7

OCL Pedagogies in Practice

We are the inheritors, neither of an inquiry about ourselves and the world, nor of an accumulating body of information, but of a conversation, begun in the primeval forests and extended and made more articulate in the course of centuries. It is a conversation which goes on both in public and within each of ourselves.... And it is this conversation which, in the end, gives place and character to every human activity and utterance.

—Michael Oakeshott, 1962

case studies   collaborative learning   convergence   dqs   educational games   four students   group discussion   high school
students   idea generating   idea organizing   immersive learning environments   intellectual convergence   interaction   learning
environment   moderators   one-week online seminar discussants   one-week online seminars   online case studies   online collaborative
learning   online communities   online course activity   online courses   online discussion forums   online discussions   online educational
games   online game whyville   online games   online learning contexts   online multiplayer games   online pedagogies   online role
plays   online simulations   online social café   online students   online universities   other online university
programs   participant   participants   pedagogies   pedagogy   perspectives   scenarios   seminars   student-led online
seminars   successful online seminars   teamwork   textbook case   transcript analysis   video games   virtual organizations

Chapter 7 illuminates online collaborative learning (OCL) pedagogies in practice and:

- Introduces four fictional students who are participating in online courses;
- Presents four OCL scenarios to provide a sample of how online courses can be designed and how the students engage:
  a. Scenario One: Online case studies (virtual simulations)
  b. Scenario Two: Student-led online seminars
  c. Scenario Three: Online global training program for third-world union educators
  d. Scenario Four: Online educational games and immersive learning environments.

Introduction

Chapter 7 offers readers a means to understand online learning, some of its different forms and how differing approaches and processes can be used to support effective learning and educational change. Four scenarios are drawn from online and blended learning models; applications that are appropriate for both formal (K-12 and university) and nonformal (professional development, training) educational contexts around the world.

The use of scenarios allows us to visualize what happens in "virtual classrooms" and online learning contexts. These scenarios offer snapshots of how an online course activity may be designed by an instructor and be experienced by the learner in terms of social and intellectual interaction online. Specific examples from semi-fictionalized online learning applications help readers to envision typical "real" curricula and student interactions. Four OCL pedagogic scenarios from real online schools and courses are presented, although some of the details have been changed for privacy.

1. online simulations and case studies of virtual organizations;
2. student-led online seminars;
3. co-production of real-world products and programs;
4. online educational games and immersive learning environments.

To get started, we introduce four fictional students who are studying in an undergraduate degree program, online. The fictionalized students' accounts are composites of real student experiences.

Living the Online Student Life

Jennifer

Jennifer is a busy professional who nonetheless wants to complete the undergraduate degree that she started some years ago but left when she entered the job market, then married and had a family. Given her responsibilities, a place-based university with courses rigidly scheduled at specific times and locations is not realistic. "For the last ten years, I have been attempting to find the time to go back to school. I attempted the traditional classroom settings, but due to work schedules and demands I never was able to stick to it."

Barry

Barry works in sales and travels extensively, but is serious in seeking a university degree for job promotion and personal satisfaction. He regrets never attending post-secondary education. His challenge is how to pursue a university degree when his job takes him weekly around the world to destinations such as Bangkok, London and Paris, to name a few, as well as numerous cities in the United States throughout the year.

Curt

Curt is in his 12th year serving in the United States Army and, given the demands associated with the role of a soldier, has found it difficult to work toward a degree: "I have attempted many times to complete an undergraduate degree to no avail. I have had to withdraw from a number of college courses due to last minute training requirements and deployments."

LeAnne

LeAnne was born, schooled and now and works in the high-tech sector in Hong Kong. She is fluent in English and her goal is to move to the United States in a few years to work in the same industry and advance her career. An American degree is important to her and she believes it is essential to realizing her professional plans.

OCL Pedagogical Scenarios: Four Students and Online Study

These four students seek a university program to meet their needs. They found that they have many options to choose from: every year, almost six million students in the United States alone take online courses. Some of the online universities are based on distance education (ODE) or courseware (OC) approaches, so instruction is not provided by a professor. Our four students are seeking courses that have a professor or an instructor and involve peer interaction and collaborative learning. "Having peers to talk to, to share the work, the fun and the challenges makes the learning more enjoyable and more effective for me," writes Jennifer. LeAnne agrees, and adds that learning teamwork skills is important for her professionally as well.

The four found many accredited universities that offer online degrees using the OCL model. There are differences, however, in how each university structures its programs. Some online universities offer undergraduate and graduate degree programs based on 6 weeks per course, with approximately 12 participants in each course. Students are limited to one course at a time. Upon completion of that 6-week course, students move to the next course in their program. Other online university programs offer courses that are 12 or 15 weeks in duration, like traditional university semesters. Still other online degree programs offer a cohort system, whereby courses may start at any time, once a certain number of students have registered. Regardless of how the online courses are scheduled, all of these approaches are based on an OCL model and limit the number of students to between 10 and 25 students per course.

For those of us who are unfamiliar with online study, we are curious to know more about the experiences of these four students and how an online classroom functions. Our fictional four students select to study in the same program at the same university: their online classroom is available 24 hours a day and 7 days a week. They have access to their course any time of the day or night, from anywhere in the world.

The workload is demanding but well structured and the students feel that they are learning valuable knowledge and work habits. Barry comments that:

> The knowledge I am gaining through the program's curriculum has changed my personal and work habits. The structure almost "forces" you to get regimented to stay on track with your assignments. As a result, I have become more organized at work, which gives me more "free" time to tackle company projects. In my personal life, it's so organized, I sometimes find myself with too much free time (I am not complaining).

All of the courses use a curriculum based on individual and group assignments, and group discussion with topics that change (typically each week), leading the students into deeper and more analytical consideration of the subject matter. Once Jennifer, for example, registers for a course, she receives the textbook and all additional course materials, or resources, either by courier or posted online. Using the Web, Jennifer logs on to the university's password-protected learning environment where each course is accessible. She will gain entry only to the course for which she is registered. While online she "meets" with the instructor and her classmates, exchanging greetings and learning about her fellow students through "self-introductions." The discussions are primarily text-based and asynchronous. The virtual classroom comprises a variety of group conferences or forums (think of "virtual rooms"); the forums or "rooms" change each week according to the topic, task and group size. Some forums are based on a full group discussion of a topic; others involve small-group discussions or projects. One forum may be "write only" where students submit their assignments to the professor, but cannot read one another's submissions. In other cases, students can access and even comment upon the work of their peers. Initially, to help facilitate the dynamics among the students who participate independently on their own time and in their own off-campus setting, the instructor begins with a full group discussion forum based on assigned readings each week. Rather than a question-and-answer format, students are encouraged to reflect on the issues raised by the instructor, consider the readings and send in a thoughtful response online. Students are encouraged to submit multiple comments and ideas, and then to reflect on and respond to one another's comments—agreeing, disagreeing, expanding and advancing the ideas presented. The tone should be considered but not unnecessarily formal. As in any discussion or debate, informed opinions based on the readings or other resources are expected. This sets the tone for the course. Eventually, students will progress to other collaborative learning activities such as the virtual simulations described in Scenario One or to lead their own seminars, as described in Scenario Two. Social interaction is encouraged and an online social café is available for students to chat and socialize.

The tone of the seminars is not meant to be rigid but thoughtful and to emphasize evidence over emotion in the group discussions. Still, students are friendly toward one another, use first names and often start their message with a joke or social comment (for example: "Boy, is it ever snowing out here!! I am cozy in my kitchen logging on from home! It has made me reflect on the reading about access…"). Each week the topic changes as students progress in their learning, advancing from the familiar to the less familiar, and relating the concrete with the conceptual, and the specific with the analytical. Students are introduced to analytical terms relevant to the course topic/field and through their discussions and course readings and resources, they gain fluency in the language of analysis and its application in the field.

Typically students work in learning groups or project teams to complete an assignment. Assignments may be brief or complex, individual or group-oriented. The role of the instructor is to serve as the representative of the knowledge community in that discipline: to provide the learning materials, provide the orientation through presentations on a topic (either by text or audio/video podcast), introduce key analytical terms and concepts through course readings and other resources and organize the learning processes to encourage student learning and problem solving. Group seminars encourage students to learn to apply new terms and concepts and to engage in knowledge-building processes. The instructor plays an important role in organizing the seminars, especially in the case where students will serve as seminar leaders or moderators. Student-led seminars require important instructor input to assist students to learn how to be a moderator, as well as how to be a discussant in the seminars. These are new roles for traditional classroom or distance education instructors and students. Moderators will need to learn about online group dynamics, the subject matter and how to facilitate collaborative learning and intellectual progress. Moderating requires more than group dynamics; it requires that moderators engage the discussants in knowledge building on the topic. In educational seminars or group discussion, the moderators become the most knowledgeable about their particular topic, because they have done significant background study in order to prepare to lead the seminar and facilitate the discussion to advance the discourse from Idea Generating to Idea Organizing to Intellectual Convergence (the OCL framework is discussed in Chapter 6). Moderators must understand how to guide and facilitate the group discussion to ensure that there is learning, that the discussants are advancing in their understanding of the topic and that they are engaging with the knowledge problems and contributing to meaningful interaction and improving ideas on the topic. Students are learning to solve problems and construct knowledge together, knowledge that reflects state-of-the-art thinking in their discipline (the knowledge community) and that has real-world relevance. They learn the analytical terms of the field and they learn how to apply these terms and concepts to real-world problems, to generate knowledge artifacts such as new designs, prototypes, processes or solutions. Learning is part of the process of problem solving: students must identify what they need to learn to resolve the problem.

Scenario One: Online Case Studies (Simulations)

A case study is an analysis of a system by observing specific situations or processes in order to solve problems. Case studies are used in many higher-education academic and training disciplines to simulate real-life scenarios. Students are assigned cases and typically work in small groups to gain understanding of their case, diagnose and develop solutions to resolve the problems posed. Traditionally, educational case studies have been presented in hardcopy, either in textbook or casebook format.

The use of online case studies is an innovative OCL pedagogy that promotes interaction and use of real problem-solving tools and processes. Online case studies offer important new features and learning opportunities beyond traditional textbook approaches, such as expanded opportunities for interactivity, variety and hence increased realism. In traditional textbook case studies, students are provided with a large amount of background information. The problem with the traditional textbook cases is that students have no way to find additional information, and no one to ask questions of in trying to clarify the problem. "There are none of the simulated interviews, none of the memos, none of the electronic correspondence that we have in the virtual organizations. So if you have questions on a case, the students have to make assumptions" (Wasley, 2008). Another benefit of online case studies is that students can use real software tools to problem solve and become more proficient in applying these tools and behaving as they would in a real-world context.

Given the access to vast arrays of data, online case studies can be designed to be imperfect and thereby encourage significant problem-solving efforts by students. Whereas textbook case studies are by necessity neatly packaged so that students can use the data that is available to problem solve, online case studies may be far more complex and provide what is referred to as ill-defined problems, which require students to solve problems by trying out various tools to access and manipulate different data. An ill-defined problem is often considered to be a real-world scenario in that there is no simplistic correct answer. Textbook case studies, in contrast, typically employ "well-defined problems" to facilitate an easier solution, given the constraints of information that can be provided to students.

In the past, if instructors wanted students to engage in typical real-world cases, a major obstacle was the amount of student time required to access and organize the data. A further and very

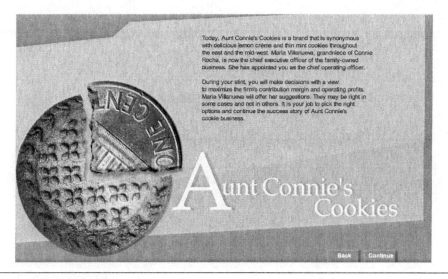

Figure 7.1 Aunt Connie's Cookies.

difficult problem was access to the necessary information, which required both time and permission to work with confidential and/or proprietary data.

An example of the use of a state-of-the art educational simulation is the virtual organizations software developed by the University of Phoenix for their onsite and online students. Hundreds of case studies of virtual schools and businesses have been integrated into the virtual American town of Kelsey. Unlike a static textbook case study,

> Phoenix students, instead, can tap into a virtual world where each fictional school or corporation comes with detailed, simulated scenarios that "real-world" employees are likely to encounter in the workplace. These virtual-world scenarios are not fully interactive like *Second Life*—they do not provide second-by-second feedback—but they do bring real-world problems to life. (Wasley, 2008)

The use of the online case studies also provides students in a course with a range of issues or knowledge problems, while the ability to access common data enables students to collaborate on assignments. All of the virtual organizations are located in fictional Kelsey, which has a population of 53,000 and features eight corporations, four schools, a hospital and municipal offices. Approximately 500 University of Phoenix courses (online and onsite) feature the virtual organizations in course assignments. Students may do cost–benefit analyses of outsourcing in the hospital or school cafeteria, or rewrite the menus based on new health or policy considerations. Students in Information Technology (IT) courses may analyze the user logs or IT service requests to diagnose software problems. Students in education may be asked to examine the student records to identify learning problems in particular areas and propose activities to address the problems.

"Students say the software gives them a view of how the parts of an organization work together. Most schoolteachers see test scores and other data only for the grade levels they teach," says Katy Wilkins, an assistant principal at a middle school that used Phoenix's virtual school program in two master's level education courses. "The Kelsey schools allow you to access the full picture," she says (quoted in Wasley, 2008).

In a course on instructional design, Wilkins noticed that the parent–teacher communication logs at Kelsey's elementary school mentioned that certain students had comprehension abilities above their grade levels, but that the school district had no program for gifted students. For her final project in the course, she proposed a professional development program to help Kelsey teachers steer gifted students toward more challenging activities.

Wilkins presented a similar proposal to her Arizona middle school, transferring the learning of the Kelsey simulation to her own school district. "With Kelsey schools right there in front of you, it makes you scratch your head and say, I wonder if we actually have something like that in our district," she says (quoted in Wasley, 2008).

Scenario Two: Student-led Online Seminars

Scenario Two depicts student-led online seminars. This pedagogy is appropriate for learners at all levels: secondary school, undergraduate or graduate school, professional development and training or continuing education. The pedagogy could also be used to inform moderating of online communities of practice (discussed in Chapter 9).

THE ONLINE SEMINARS

Our virtual four students are taking an online course with 12 other students. The course curriculum features four 1-week online seminars, each on a different topic and each moderated by a team of four students. Like all students in this course, our four will engage in two distinct roles, each with specific timelines, activities and assessment:

- moderators work in teams of four to lead a 1-week online seminar;
- discussants participate actively in three 1-week seminars.

MODERATING

Moderating represents 30% of the final grade. Jennifer, Barry, Curt and LeAnne form a team to moderate a 1-week online seminar together. Each seminar involves three distinct activities:

- seminar presentation: 10%
- seminar facilitation: 10%
- summary and transcript analysis of the discourse: 10%.

SEMINAR PRESENTATION

Our team has identified their seminar topic and is now preparing the Presentation to launch their seminar. The Presentation is a very important, in fact critical, component since the quality of the Presentation can determine the quality of the seminar discussion input and the quality of the learning experiences of the seminar discussants. The Presentation provides the background and key information about the topic and includes categories such as those shown in Figure 7.2.

Once the moderating team has welcomed discussants to the seminar and introduced the topic, they present three Discussion Questions (DQs). Our team realizes that effective Discussion Questions are the key to successful online seminars. Well designed DQs encourage multiple perspectives on the topic, and generate thoughtful discussions that advance intellectual organization and convergence. Excellent DQs are fuel for thought; DQs should be relevant and real, and not answerable simply by "yes" or "no." A DQ should not encourage repetitious responses (or a series of "me too!" messages). A seminar, moreover, is not a question-and-answer activity: seminars involve questions that advance understanding. Online seminars benefit from considered and thought-provoking DQs, which provide focus to the discussion, motivate learning new concepts and promote deeper reflection and understanding of a topic. Discussants build on one another's

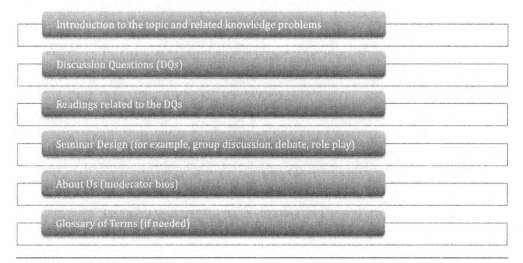

Figure 7.2 Online Seminar Presentation.

input; they may agree or disagree, but through this process they should arrive at a conclusion or a position on the topic.

Jennifer, Barry, Curt and LeAnne spend considerable time shaping their DQs in relation to what they would like to see discussants accomplish during the seminar. Drafting thought-provoking DQs is a challenge. The team must also seek readings that can help provide discussants with information and data related to the discussions. The team decides to focus DQ 1 on a key problem in the field to stimulate the generating of various ideas or perspectives on the topic. They search for relevant readings. They then teamwork on shaping DQ 2 to encourage the discussants to reflect on the various perspectives that have been generated and identify commonalities among the diverse ideas.

The team is unsure of how to design DQ 3. The final seminar question should lead the discussants to a level of convergence. Jennifer suggests that they bring the seminar to a conclusion by synthesizing all of the discussion into a few points. Curt disagrees, pointing out that it is for the discussants to come to a convergence themselves, not for the moderators to do it for them. The seminar has a fixed timeline, so time is of the essence. Barry suggests using a wiki. "The discussants could each post their position." LeAnne agrees that it would be cool to use a wiki but points out that a wiki does not necessarily encourage convergence. However, using a technique or tool to help discussants come to a final position is a good idea. Jennifer suggests: "What about developing a report card where discussants grade each of the three major options?" "Or we could have them rate or rank the three options." The team decides that DQ 3 should link to a voting tool whereby discussants vote on the three major options, and provide a brief rationale for their choice. The final decision (and seminar conclusion) would be the majority vote, with dissenting views. With their Presentation completed, the moderators are now ready to launch and facilitate their week-long seminar.

The goal of a good seminar is not unified agreement, but that the discussants learn the analytical language of a field and use the analytical concepts to identify and discuss various perspectives on a topic to arrive at an informed position. Discussants may not agree on one position, and they may agree to disagree. Or, in the case where a single final product is required, as in the case of the team developing three DQs, there is a need to converge on the final product. Whether the conclusion is convergence or consensus, the class has progressed beyond divergence to develop an analytical and informed position.

FACILITATION

It is Day 1 of our team's seminar. They post their Presentation at noon. The seminar is open 24 hours a day for the next 7 days. Already the team is excited to engage in the discussions, but also anxious. What if no one participates? What is taking everyone so long to respond? Are the DQs too difficult or too simplistic? However, it is still early in the seminar: only 1 or 2 hours have passed since the Presentation was posted. Soon the first response arrives: "Great Presentation, Team! The topic is intriguing and I can't wait to get into discussing it. I'll be back online as soon as I do the readings." Another comment is posted and a third and a fourth, and the discussion is launched.

Jennifer, Barry, Curt and LeAnne are encouraged by the participation and camaraderie. They begin to facilitate the comments, to keep the discussion flowing and focused and to help build knowledge about the topic. Facilitating also requires balancing the number, volume and timing of moderator comments. The moderating team must not overwhelm the conference with too many notes, but be active in stimulating discussion, responding to unanswered questions, encouraging others to participate in Idea Generating. They also provide additional questions to either deepen or advance the discussion as needed. Discussants may become too involved in brainstorming; the moderators need to help maintain informed discussion by asking discussants to cite evidence for their views, such as reference the readings and to then advance the discussion to initiate convergence, posing such facilitating questions as: what are the key ideas presented? Are there links among them? By acknowledging valuable ideas, and synthesizing or weaving the contributions thus far, moderators can also encourage Idea Organizing. Some students may have begun to reference one another's comments through referencing, and the moderators build upon those initiatives.

Idea Organizing can benefit from weaving, a process of synthesizing the discussions to date, highlighting the important areas covered, and suggesting new directions that the discussion might productively cover. Weaving the comments does not mean that moderators should acknowledge each individual's comment, but rather illuminate and highlight the important points made in relation to the DQs and to the topic overall. Encouraging progress from Idea Generating to Idea Organization and on to Intellectual Convergence facilitates the learning process.

Also, the team moderators remind themselves that they are there to facilitate, not to judge or dictate "right" and "wrong." While moderating, they resist the desire to become too involved with the actual debate, keeping in mind that the task is to help each participant to formulate their understanding of the topic with the assistance of the DQs and by facilitating the interaction of the group.

SUMMARY AND TRANSCRIPT ANALYSIS OF THE DISCOURSE

The final portion of the student-led seminar asks moderators to produce a summary of their 1-week seminars; assessing how well their seminar design functioned, level of user activity (volume and pattern of messaging by day, gender, role or other categories) and lessons learned. Moderators also conduct a transcript analysis by categorizing each discussant message as social or cognitive, and if the latter, then whether it is primarily Idea Generating, Idea Organizing or Intellectual Convergence. The data are organized by day of the week to plot number and kind of message each day. The results are input into simple visualization software such as Excel to generate graphic displays such as a line graph showing intellectual change over time.

Scenario Three: Online Global Professional Development Program

Thirty-three participants from 24 developing countries are studying together in an online education course that will last for 8 months. None of these participants have ever engaged in online computer conferencing or online discussion forums. Thirty participants perceive their email usage skills as high, three do not. Most use the Internet regularly and report feeling comfortable with computers. The number of male and female participants is almost equal. While many of the participants have computers at home, few have home Internet access. As this course is work-related, most of the online discussions and online project teamwork are conducted using the workplace computers—usually during the off hours, when the few Internet-based computers are not being used by others for work.

This scenario is a fictionalized rendition of a real story involving trade unions. Participants in this course access web-based software, which is based on computer forums (also called conferences) that serve as an asynchronous learning environment to support group discussions, team projects, debates and seminars. Participants enter the learning environment, which is open 24 hours a day, 7 days a week, at any time they want. The system is available worldwide through the Web.

Participants log on to the Web and enter a password-protected environment to access the group activities related to their course. The system organizes the topics into different forums. Users send their messages to the particular forum to which they belong, featuring the topic or

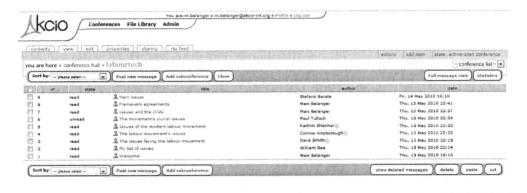

Figure 7.3 Asynchronous Learning Environment.

unit of that week. When participants log on, they read the messages that others have submitted to the forum and they then reply or post a new message. Messages are organized chronologically.

Accessing the forums opened by the course instructor, participants log on to text-based "mini-lectures" provided by the instructor and read postings by their peers that relate to the current topic of readings and resources. Participants discuss the topic and, based on the course readings, debate its relevance and consider its application for their first major task.

The course is a nonformal, professional development course for trainers in developing countries. The course curriculum is new to union trainers as is the delivery method. The course comprises four distinct categories of activity:

• seminars based on active reading and discussion of concepts, implications, processes and so on (active reading is when learners are asked to read material with particular, instructor-provided questions to which they must respond);
• seminars based on active reading, as well as discussion and questions and answers;
• technical workshops (learning how to use particular tools);
• teamwork seminars that involve the co-production of a series of documents.

Participants in this particular course live and work in different countries throughout the Caribbean, Africa and the Middle East. The 8-month course is conducted entirely online.

Much about this example is intriguing, including: the geographic span of the participants; the developing world locations; a supportive organization with meager resources and not generally viewed as "on the cutting edge" with respect to innovation or new technology; and the pedagogical design, which involved significant engagement and commitment throughout the 8 months to apply OCL and knowledge building to solve real-world problems. The OCL model continues and grows among union educators in the developing world.

As learners everywhere, their initial few weeks are characterized by questioning, challenging, brainstorming and divergent thinking: "When I first came across that concept I was skeptical. I wondered what it was about and it left questions in my mind." As other participants begin to share their questions, their experiences and perspectives, the discussion grows richer. One participant writes: "The volume of material folks are churning out is amazing … we surely have a lot to say and to learn.…" Another writes: "More folks are logging on and asking the right questions and making important and salient points." Participants begin to come together, to converge as a group and start referencing one another by name. "Marc's comments on open source were very valuable and I think that we should ensure that they are included in our first document that we are developing."

Over the first days and weeks, participants each contribute a variety of perspectives, and as they do, they begin to identify linkages among their ideas and perspectives offered by others. Some reflect common viewpoints, others are different. This first round of "idea-generating" sessions will not necessarily present final positions but reflects initial positions with widespread differences. Perhaps as a result, almost everyone feels comfortable in offering a perspective. A typical comment: "I have so far looked at contributions done by many members of the group and they have all presented good cases.... Below is my contribution to the debate." Others also contribute reflections on the issues and input new ideas, but often end with a note such as: "My ideas are not final."

As the discussion continues, it advances in terms of the quality of the debate or exchange. New resources are provided to justify a particular position. Increasingly ideas are linked, either in support of a position or debating another: agreement and disagreement become a stimulus to seek further information, and in some cases to refine one's own position, recant and/or recognize the value of others' input. Ideas are clarified, associations between ideas are identified, and they become clustered into categories.

As with all real problem-solving scenarios, there is a looming deadline for producing a group document. The participants increasingly focus on and move toward Intellectual Convergence, based on shared understanding. Their messages reflect an increase in substantive comments, closure and a framework for co-production of a document. There is also a shift from the use of the pronoun "I" (which categorized the early weeks of discussion) to the use of the pronoun "we" and "our," as the first sessions converge toward co-producing the document.

Intellectual Convergence, it is important to emphasize, does *not* signify a homogeneous conclusion. In fact, Intellectual Convergence is often characterized by conjunctions—but, and, or— reflecting a convergence that is rich with multiplicity. Often, there may be two or three final positions and participants agree to disagree. Intellectual Convergence refers not to acquiescence but rather to the fact that participants now understand the various perspectives proposed in the discussion and how these perspectives relate to one another. In the case of co-productions, convergence reflects a consensus or it may represent a range of conclusions.

A common remark might include, "I just want to add this because, like Anikka, I share the views of everyone so far." Closure is evident in this comment: "Frankly I am very impressed with the ability to pull all the varying comments and suggestions into the document and make sure that you captured everyone." Signing off, another participant writes "I think that we have all done brilliantly so far. Thanks for all your comments and input ... I do believe that we are a great team and group."

Scenario Four: Online Educational Games and Immersive Learning Environments

Virtual video games are immensely popular among youths and adults. Estimated numbers of players are in the hundreds of millions. One of the most popular online multiplayer games is *World of Warcraft*, a fantasy game with over 10 million current subscribers, of which 2.5 million are in North America. Educational applications of online video games also have tremendous appeal in the market, although many educators and parents are skeptical about the educational benefits. There is justification for skepticism, but emerging research, as well as new developments in online educational games, is providing evidence of positive potential for learning. While educational video games are not a magic bullet, teachers and researchers report powerful learning possibilities in games with well designed pedagogies.

Online educational multiplayer games such *Food Force,* produced by the United Nations to educate users on food aid distribution through the use of online role plays, gained one million players in the first six weeks, four million players in the first year, and is now available in 10 languages, according to the United Nations. The game contains six different missions for players, who are faced with a number of realistic challenges. In a race against time, they must feed thousands of people in the fictitious island of Sheylan: they pilot helicopters, while looking out for hungry people; negotiate with armed rebels blocking a food convoy; and use food aid to help rebuild communities. *Food Force* is designed especially for classroom use and offers teaching resources as part of the lesson plans. It can be downloaded without cost.

Online games are typically multiplayer in design, meaning that problems are set up to be solved collaboratively by teams. The online game *Whyville*, oriented to K-12 math and science education, has four million subscribers (90% are North American), with the dominant demographic being 8–14-year-old girls (Mayo, 2009). Teachers and educational researchers report positive outcomes. One teacher on the site reports that

> My sixth graders love it! *Whyville* supports the use of computers by kids the way that scientists use computers: for data collection, data visualization, simulation and modeling and scientific communication. The site also reflects what we know about learning communities and the kinds of interaction kids seek while learning and having fun.

Others who left comments on the site include Joan Korman, author of *Internet Resources for Women*, and professor of English, University of Maryland, who writes:

> *Whyville* is an imaginative web site that aims to help elementary, middle, and high school students understand and enjoy science. It differs dramatically from most science education sites in its use of avatars, games, computer simulation and modeling, a *Whyville* newspaper, and interactivity among *Whyville* participants. Though *Whyville* is not designed specifically for girls, girls make up more than 60% of its users, an exceptionally high percentage for a science-and-technology-focused site.

Another collaborative, virtual environment for use in school classrooms is *River City*, which uses lifeforms or avatars something like those in *Second Life*. *River City* is targeted at students in grades six through nine and portrays how three diseases simultaneously affect health.

The National Science Foundation-funded *River City* multiuser virtual environment is centered on skills of hypothesis formation and experimental design, as well as content related to national standards and epidemiology. Students learn to behave as scientists as they collaboratively identify problems through observation and inference, form and test hypotheses and deduce evidence-based conclusions about underlying causes. Collaborating in teams of three or four participants, they try to figure out why people are getting sick and what actions can remove sources of illness. They talk to various residents in this simulated setting, such as children and adults who have fallen ill, hospital employees, merchants and university scientists (Dede, 2009, p. 67).

More highly sophisticated game content exists. An example is the games developed by the Federation of American Scientists on such topics as immunology. In the *Immune Attack*, the player controls drones that activate the release of immunity enzymes. For more information on this game, see http: fas.or/immuneattack.

Researchers studying online games have found promising results for the importance of pedagogy. Good pedagogy leads to positive educational outcomes, while weak pedagogical design in the software yields poor results. Mayo's (2009) review of the research literature on gaming notes that "where learning benefits appear, they are attributed to effective pedagogical practices embedded in the game design" (p. 80). The collaborative learning pedagogy has increased student engagement and conceptual change. Multiplayer game-based activities require students to work

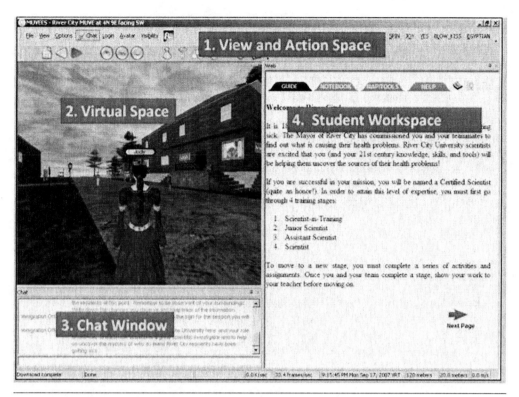

Figure 7.4 *River City* Multiuser Virtual Environment.

in teams to form a hypothesis, experiment with various options and come to an intellectual convergence on which actions to take and then the consequence of those actions.

Mayo (2009) raises an interesting point about the importance of pedagogy: she notes that students in a typical classroom ask 0.11 questions per hour, whereas educational games offer constant interaction—almost each keystroke yields a response. The active participatory nature of gaming is a vast departure from traditional passive lecture learning. Researchers describe a near universal antipathy to the undergraduate lecture format: 98% of students who leave science and engineering majors and 86% of those who stay report "poor teaching by faculty" (Seymour & Hewitt, 1997) to be a major concern. Mayo cites a meta study of 6,542 students in 62 introductory physics classes that found "switching to any interactive mode of instruction (for example, group projects, Socratic lectures and participatory demonstrations) easily improved learning outcomes in introductory physics by 108 percent" (2009, pp. 80–81). She also reports that other studies have found that video games can yield a 7–40% improvement in learning over lectures (Mayo, 2009).

Immersive learning environments are another feature of some video games, in which the user assumes an online persona and engages in a realistic digitally enhanced setting, a 3-D virtual world.

> Immersion is the subjective impression that one is participating in a comprehensive, realistic experience. Interactive media now enable various degrees of digital immersion. The more a virtual immersive experience is based on design strategies that combine actional, symbolic, and sensory factors, the greater the participant's suspension of disbelief that she or he is "inside" a digitally enhanced setting. (Dede, 2009, p. 66)

Dede reports that immersive interfaces aid in designing educational experiences that yield valuable results for learning: digital fluency, engagement, and learning and transfer from classroom to real-world settings. Learning is enhanced through the multiple perspectives enabled by the immersive interface, the situated learning and improved transfer from the classroom to the real-world context (2009, p. 67).

Online video games for learning are used by many disciplines in schools, universities and training settings. Immersive simulations are also used in corporate and military settings. One of the most successful and the earliest educational immersive simulation was developed for pilot training. Today, airplane flight and surgical simulators demonstrate highly successful transfer of learning from the educational setting to real-world application.

Research has demonstrated that visual skills developed by video games have implications for training in the case of laparoscopic surgery. Greenfield (2009, p. 70) notes that

> surgeons recognize that laparoscopy has changed the required skill profile of surgeons and their training needs. In laparoscopic surgery, a small incision is made, and a viewing tube with a small camera on the eyepiece is inserted through it. The surgeon examines internal organs on a video monitor connected to the tube and can also use the viewing tube to guide actual surgical procedures. Navigating through and operating in a three-dimensional space represented on a two-dimensional screen with minimal tactile feedback constitute basic parallels between laparoscopy and action video games. A study of the relation between video game skill and success in training for laparoscopic surgery yielded positive results: Action video game skill (as demonstrated in the laboratory) and past video game experience (assessed through self-report) predicted laparoscopic skills; in contrast, neither laparoscopic experience in the operating room nor years of training significantly predicted laparoscopic skill. The best game players (the top third) made 47% fewer errors and performed 39% faster in the laparoscopy tasks than the worst players (the bottom third). These results indicate the value of video game play as informal educational background for specific training in laparoscopic surgery, a finding that is applicable to other lines of work (such as piloting a plane) whose skill profiles overlap with those required by action video games.

Summary

Chapter 7 introduced a discussion and description of OCL pedagogies in practice. The chapter focused in detail on four pedagogic scenarios taken from real educational applications: online simulations and case studies of virtual organizations; student-led online seminars; co-production of real-world products and programs; and online educational games and immersive learning environments.

Four virtual students were introduced as examples to depict the experiences of learners in the first two scenarios. The level of detail provides in-depth illustration of how online pedagogies might function in real-world contexts.

OCL Cases of Institutional Innovation

And the one single factor that jumps out as you reflect on this history—is that this community has demonstrated agility and speed in implementation: speed in cobbling up the tools—software and hardware and networking and pedagogical practice to deliver online education, speed in implementing the courses and degrees, and speed in learning from experience, so that the second step was always surer than the first—and the third, surer still ... the quick implementation permitted experience to be gained which could be effectively applied when better tools, more bandwidth and faster computers arrived.

—Frank Mayadas, Sloan Consortium, 2009

centre online capabilities centre online courses distance education **distance education course** earmyu **group discussion** ids live online courses **new online faculty** ocl online briefing online campus website online collaboration online collaborative learning online conversations online course activities online course development online course enrollments online course offerings online degree programs **online discussions** online division **online educational activities online educational innovation online educational modalities** online enrolments online environments **online faculty preparation process** online instructors online learning environments online learning initiatives online learning systems online master online met online moderating online pedagogies online portal online student support services **online students** online technologies online tools **ou collaborative online environment** pedagogy phoenix online degree program seaman sln terminology **two-week five-hour online staff development program** upxo online degree versions

Chapter 8 presents the following topics:

- Context of OCL institutional adoption
- Institutional adoption
  - How many students are studying online?
  - Online delivery model
  - Blended learning mode
  - Totally online mode
- Institutional cases of totally online and blended learning
  - Case One: University of Phoenix Online
  - Case Two: State University of New York Learning Network
  - Case Three: UBC–ITESM Master of Educational Technology
  - Case Four: International Labour Organization
  - Case Five: Open University, UK
  - Case Six: eArmy U
  - Case Seven: Virtual High Schools
  - Case Eight: Online learning initiatives that did not reach targeted goals and other problems.

Context of OCL Institutional Adoption

Chapter 8 explores the use of online education delivery at the level of the institution or organization. The chapter draws upon examples from both formal and nonformal education to illustrate how institutions are involved in the design and implementation of the online delivery of certificate and degree programs.

Attitudes toward online education employed by schools, colleges and universities, or training institutions and continuing education providers have shifted dramatically over the past few decades. During the 1980s and early 1990s most online educational delivery of courses was the initiative and responsibility of individual teachers and professors, rather than an undertaking by institutions. The decision to create and implement online courses was left to the initiative and responsibility of teachers (Harasim et al., 1995). Teachers, instructors or professors who sought to offer courses online had no alternative but to do so using their own time and resources. They had to create the online pedagogies, access and structure the technological environments to support the learning pedagogies, and teach the courses. They represented the so-called "lone rangers" in the field (Bates, 2000, pp. 59–64).

Online educators were on their own; they were individually responsible for designing the course, developing the curriculum, organizing the resource and finding and obtaining access to online forums for the course activities. All this in addition to learning how to use the technology, creating online IDs and passwords for each student, establishing the conference or forum space for each course seminar or activity, organizing the group discussion or projects, training students in how to use the system, providing technical support and problem solving for the students, posting or emailing the training manuals and course materials to each student, implementing the course and grading the activities. There were no institutional policies, funding or resources allocated to assist the teaching of online courses. In fact, in the 1980s and 1990s (and even today) educators adopting online education might encounter collegial or institutional resistance from those who perceived online education to be a threat or insult to traditional "chalk-and-talk" teaching.

However, while it was the individual teachers and faculty who moved forward as the primary motivators of online educational innovation, it was the institutions, through their resource allocations and policies that were able to mainstream online education. The institutional adoption of online education was central to changing educational and social perception. As educational institutions and organizations incorporated online education into their integral mission, the resources and policies shifted to reflect these new priorities.

Most of the courses and programs offered online during the 1980s used a collaborative learning approach that became a framework for online education (Mason & Kaye, 1989; Harasim, 1990a; Hiltz, 1994; Harasim et al., 1995). The early examples of online education (as discussed in Chapter 6) anticipated Online Collaborative Learning (OCL).

In 1989, the Open University (OU) in the United Kingdom—an internationally renowned distance education university—offered a distance education course with a significant "online" component that featured group discussion. The OU was one of the earliest institutional adopters. Approximately 1,500 students were involved in this particular course (Mason, 1989). It attracted significant attention to online educational modalities and to online collaborative learning.

Also launched in the late 1980s, a far smaller endeavor but one that ultimately had a major impact on the field of online and higher education was the University of Phoenix's online degree program, known today as the University of Phoenix Online (UPXO). UPXO was launched in 1989 with around 40 students and was the first university to offer online degree programs.

Both of these online education "firsts"—the OU mass course and the UPXO online degree program—employed the technology of computer conferencing for group communication and collaborative learning. Students who participated in these programs dialed a proprietary, university modem phone line using modem speeds of between 300 to 1,200 bytes per second (bps).

Public access to the Internet in 1989 had a major impact on online education, and was instrumental in the tremendous expansion of online education applications, initiating a sea change in how online learning would be viewed by schools, universities and training organizations.

Many traditional educational institutions began to support the use of online educational activities and/or group discussions by providing an online environment, such as computer conferencing or forum software. Among the most innovative institutions were those that provided, in addition to the technology, a systematic approach to faculty training and support, student support and a vision of how the technology would link with the pedagogy to advance the learning mission.

Institutions that specialized in distance education and those that offered distance education in addition to their face-to-face (f2f) courses soon became aware of the potential of the Internet and integrated it into their distance delivery approach. It is important to recognize, however, that while most distance education providers adopted the use of the Internet, the majority has not yet transformed their pedagogical approach. They retain a correspondence model of education, substituting email for postal mail to send and receive educational materials or assignments more efficiently and inexpensively. The correspondence learning model simply went online, to become Online Distance Education (ODE).

The situation is the same among courseware providers. Largely as a consequence of public access to the Web in 1993 and graphical browsers, which improved access to and posting of multimedia content online, nonformal training organizations began to post their multimedia content on the net. Training companies, which utilized individualized learning, self-study pedagogies and multimedia courseware, were able to relatively easily upload and deliver their multimedia content via the Web. And internationally many universities and colleges began to develop individualized courseware for Web delivery. Here, too, as in distance education, the courseware pedagogy was not significantly changed from its original format, but remained based on individualized learning; that is, interaction between the students and the computer software, without access to an instructor or tutor. The Online Courseware (OC) approach was thus initiated.

Institutional Adoption

Institutional adoption of online learning, starting in the 1990s, has grown rapidly worldwide and become part of mainstream education. Yet, surprisingly, even today the underlying pedagogical model is seldom articulated or defined. Far too seldom do educators ask about the pedagogical approach used by a particular course or program. The three major models (OCL, ODE and OC) are largely parallel but isolated worlds, with little recognition or acknowledgment of one another. Some educational institutions do consciously emphasize one approach to online learning over the other; most, however, do not distinguish among the different models, and their online course offerings reflect some mix of all three models. Often the mixing is done by default, reflecting a lack of planning, faculty training, design or policy regarding online learning. In some cases, mixed-modes or blended learning are offered by design. Online and blended approaches are discussed further in this chapter.

During the 1990s, a rather fierce debate emerged regarding the quality of education delivered online. Typically (and unfortunately) the debate focused on the technology (the Internet or the Web) rather than on the pedagogy that was used. At the time, the question looming was whether online education was as effective as face-to-face learning. This debate was fueled by the media, and it influenced the public as well as skeptical university faculty. The debate was also characterized by the confusion surrounding the definitions of online learning. The debates, then and now, applied the term "online education" indiscriminately, without identifying which pedagogical model led to which educational results.

The misuse of online terminology and definitions was fuel for skeptical educators and fed their misunderstanding and mistrust about these new teaching opportunities. As discussed in Chapter 6, there is a critical need to clarify the terms and seek deeper understanding of the opportunities offered by online research and theory.

By the late 1990s, virtual universities began to emerge, many traditional universities began to offer online courses and attitudes toward online educational applications became increasingly positive—greater numbers of faculty at universities acknowledged the potential of online teaching. Indeed, one of the major breakthroughs to emerge was a growing acknowledgment that online learning, with attention to pedagogical design, could be not only as good as face-to-face classroom education but better. OCL offers the potential for a paradigmatic shift and advance in how we understand and practice learning. As noted in Chapter 6, one attribute of "online" learning is the text-based nature of the discourse that enables the instructor to see what the students are learning and how they are progressing (or not). Moreover, instructors can monitor how both the individual and the group are changing conceptually over time, and devise interventions or techniques to improve the learning. The ability to formatively "see the learning," both in terms of viewing the discourse and by applying analytical tools to study conceptual change, highlights the potential of OCL to emerge among the most powerful pedagogies. Moreover, studies and reports in recent years attest to the phenomenal growth of online education in formal and nonformal markets. Online education is outstripping the growth of onsite university enrollment.

How Many Students Are Studying Online?

The size of the market for online education is significant and growing rapidly, with almost six million students enrolled in online post-secondary education courses in the United States in 2010. Online enrollments have continued to grow at rates far in excess of the total higher-education student population, with the most recent data demonstrating no signs of slowing.

In the public education sector, the overall number of K-12 students engaged in online courses in 2007/2008 was estimated at 1,030,000. This represented a 47% increase since 2005/2006, and school districts anticipated their online enrollments will continue to grow (Picciano & Seaman, 2009).

In continuing and professional online education, online course enrollments accounted for about a fifth of continuing and professional education enrollments at the typical college or university (Ashburn, 2006). Ashburn cites the report based on a survey of 43 nonprofit institutions, which predicts that online continuing education enrollments will grow by about 20% each year for the next few years.

The figures cited above provide a valuable overview on the growth of online education in the formal and nonformal education sectors today, both in for-profit and nonprofit. However, there is little or no data on pedagogical approaches being used. There are some hints, particularly in the data on continuing and professional online education. The survey reported that

> about half of the institutions surveyed said they outsourced at least some aspects of their online continuing-education operations. About a quarter of the colleges had licensed noncredit courses from third-party providers, and some had completely outsourced their noncredit online operations. (Ashburn, 2006)

Licensing courses from third-party providers typically signifies the use of online distance education or courseware models of teaching.

Online Delivery Model (Totally Online or Blended Modes)

The concept of online delivery refers to the fact that the primary teaching and learning activities occur in an online learning environment or another application on the Web or the Internet. "Online learning" as a term does not signify a particular pedagogy: it could mean Online Collaborative Learning, Online Distance Education or Online Courseware. Hence, specification of the learning or teaching model is essential when discussing online education.

Another issue is that while online learning is conducted on the Web, it can and often does employ offline resources such as textbooks. It is often assumed that all aspects of an online course must be conducted online, but this is not necessarily true. Educators and students often combine working online with traditional textbooks and/or traditional tools (printing portions of online discussions or printing portions of online readings) to make notes in the margins, highlight ideas and annotate. Offline readers for online learning environments are also being developed (see Case Four in this chapter).

The term "blended learning" has attracted the attention of educators and institutions. The concept of mixed-mode courses was first used in the 1980s to define face-to-face education (or distance education) that had a significant online component mixed in with the traditional curriculum. (Harasim, 1990a). The application of mixed-mode or blended learning has definitely increased over the past two decades. Nonetheless, studies have found that blended courses in higher education are not more prevalent than those conducted fully online. According to Allen, Seaman and Garret (2006), similar proportions of schools offer blended courses as online courses, with slightly more citing more online offerings. There is also little evidence of growth in blended course offerings. According to the Sloan study, the number of blended courses decreased slightly between 2003 and 2005, while the number of online courses grew, and neither instructors nor students report that they view blended courses as holding more promise than fully online courses.

Institutional Cases of Totally Online and Blended Learning

Institutional case examples are presented to illustrate ways in which online learning is being offered in formal and nonformal education today. The cases intend to embody and exemplify some of the key aspects of institutional innovation.

Eight examples of totally online educational delivery are presented: Cases One to Five exemplify OCL practice, while Cases Four to Seven illustrate pedagogical and/or institutional blending.

1. University of Phoenix Online (UPXO)
2. State University of New York (SUNY) Learning Network (SLN)
3. University of British Columbia/Instituto Tecnologico y de Estudios Superiores de Monterrey Online Master's of Educational Technology (MET)
4. International Labour Organization
5. Open University (OU), United Kingdom
6. eArmyU
7. Virtual High School
8. Initiatives that did not succeed and other problems.

This section introduces institutions that grant degrees, diplomas and certificates that are delivered entirely online, using the Web or a designated Intranet, and the institutional policies and practices associated with online delivery. The shifting policies and practices at the institutional level reflect the process of innovation and paradigmatic change in education and, in particular, the growing use of OCL.

Case One: The University of Phoenix Online

The University of Phoenix Online (UPXO) is a leader in virtual universities, both historically and in terms of academic growth and public awareness. The UPXO was officially launched in 1989 with 40 students, and 20 years later the UPXO has had 32,000 graduates and an enrollment of 165,000.

The distinctive features of UPXO as a virtual university:

- History: the first virtual university
- Policy innovations:
  - employs OCL pedagogy and asynchronous learning environments
  - emphasizes small class size (10–12 students per class)
  - significant investment in teacher support
  - major emphasis on developing state-of-the-art educational resources
  - significant investment in student support services
  - standardized approach
  - significant investment in teacher training.

HISTORY

The University of Phoenix was founded in 1976 as an onsite institution whose mission was accessibility of higher education for working adults through face-to-face programs that emphasized group learning. In other words, the objective was to address the post-secondary education needs of adult learners. The collaborative learning approach was viewed as key for adult students, unlike the lecture-hall approach emphasized by traditional universities who target 18- to 25-year-old learners. The focus on accessibility was thus first addressed on pedagogical appropriateness (collaborative learning is viewed as a pillar of adult education).

OCL PEDAGOGY

In 1989, the University of Phoenix began offering courses and degree programs online, having created an online division (UPXO). The design of the online courses was based on the collaborative learning model, reflecting UPXO's commitment to online collaborative learning. One of the many advantages of UPXO was the use of a course instructor and the small class size. The ratio of students to instructor in the online class was approximately eight students per course/per instructor (today it is around 10 to 12 students per course).

UPXO employs a collaborative and participative educational pedagogy based largely on group discussion and project-based learning teams. Online students complete one course at a time (a course usually lasts about 6 weeks), just like students in onsite courses. The OCL pedagogy is delivered using an asynchronous text-based conferencing system, but may also include advanced simulation software. UPXO describes its pedagogy as follows:

- students complete coursework through electronic forums, including a main forum comprising debates and active participation in course subjects, as well as a chat room where students talk with classmates about any topic;
- in the course materials forum, students download the course syllabus, presentations or other resources;
- in individual forums, students submit completed assignments and access materials and notes provided specifically for them by their instructor;
- students log in and participate with their class when and where they choose, and participate approximately 3 or 4 days each week depending upon their degree program;

- students work closely with a small number of classmates in a learning team, whether they are working toward an associate's, bachelor's, master's or doctoral degree;
- communicate online with classmates, instructors and academic counselors;
- complete 100% of educational and administrative activities online (excluding doctoral residencies, nursing clinicals and internships and student teaching in education programs). (University of Phoenix, 2009)

Learning teams are the key pedagogy of all UPXO courses. These teams are established during the 1st or 2nd week of the course, with each team assigned to a specific online forum as their workroom.

STATE-OF-THE-ART LEARNING RESOURCES

Another aspect of UPXO's innovative policy is the significant financial investment into state-of-the-art learning resources, such as complex simulation software for its educational programs, both face-to-face and online. UPXO has developed detailed case studies of fictional institutions and companies within a virtual town called "Kelsey." Kelsey

> exists only online, in software designed by the University of Phoenix for its business, information-technology, education, and health-case courses. Kelsey and its elaborately constructed fictional companies are what the university calls its "virtual organizations"—online teaching tools designed to simulate the experience of working at a typical corporation, school, or government agency. (Wasley, 2008)

UPXO has invested significant financial resources in developing state-of-the-art learning.

STUDENT SUPPORT

UPXO emphasizes its investment in online student support services, with student assistance offered 24 hours a day. This includes student counselors working online. The online campus website provides students with access to email, student services and courses. All administrative activities are conducted online. Students are able to conduct a full range of academic functions online, such as registering for classes, paying tuition, ordering books, requesting transcripts, obtaining grades and conducting research for class.

STANDARDIZED APPROACHES

The University of Phoenix has developed standardized formats, curricula and teaching approaches for both its face-to-face and online courses. All courses are 6 weeks in length, and students take one course at a time. Both face-to-face and online versions of a course use the same textbooks and curriculum. Both versions of the course also use a collaborative learning pedagogy, although with some differences given the differing media attributes.

FACULTY TRAINING

A significant aspect of UPXO's effectiveness can be attributed to its investment in academic credentials and faculty training. UPXO emphasizes the importance of faculty credentials: faculty must hold a master's or doctoral degree from a regionally accredited US institution (or the international equivalent) related to the subject they teach and demonstrate significant work experience related to the subject area.

Training for online teaching is mandatory. The training activities include mandatory online training (4 weeks), followed by mentorship. Ongoing faculty development and communities of practice are also available. As participants have observed:

There are two main goals to the training course. The first goal is to prepare faculty candidates to use Outlook Express software skillfully and to communicate effectively. The second goal is related to the context and content of working with an institution of higher education online, including policies and practices, and learning how to create clear, respectful, and engaging communications in an online environment. The purpose of the four-week training course is to provide faculty candidates with the essential qualifications for the next step in the online faculty preparation process, the mentorship. A four week introductory course to the world of online education might be perceived as excessive to a novice administration wanting to provide online courses as quickly and as inexpensively as possible. However, the need for practicing the skills required to facilitate or to teach an online class, to manipulate the online environment, and to master the required skills of communication and interaction cannot be underestimated. (Muirhead & Betz, 2002)

The 4-week online training is a rigorous reality experience for prospective faculty. Active participation is essential for participants in the training course and is a key requirement for teaching in the UPXO courses. In other words, it is expected that faculty learn by doing as well as by reading numerous articles related to teaching online.

Candidates are required to thoughtfully read and respond to course readings, assignments, and discussions, as well as to visibly participate in cooperative learning groups or learning teams. Substantial contributions are required, consisting of several meaningful sentences and/or coherent paragraphs: one line email messages do not constitute valid participation in the Training course. Candidates who do not register full participation in the training course are usually not allowed to proceed to the mentorship. (Muirhead & Betz, 2002)

A second element in the training process involves the use of mentors who are veteran faculty members. Mentors assist new online faculty by helping them prepare their first classes and providing advice on how to create a syllabus, lectures, a personal biography and course notes. The mentor stays with the candidate throughout the first course and offers advice and feedback (based on student surveys) through frequent email to the candidate.

Case Two: State University of New York (SUNY) Learning Network (SLN)

The SUNY Learning Network (SLN) was introduced by the State University of New York as a virtual university parallel to the traditional campus(es) in 1995. The traditional place-based SUNY was officially established in 1948 when New York became the 48th state. Today SUNY has 64 onsite campuses, with more than 418,000 full-time and part-time students, and of those approximately 101,000 are distance education students enrolled in the SLN (Pickett, 2007). SLN offers students the option of taking a course over the Web rather than through the traditional face-to-face mode of lecture-hall or classroom instruction. Forty of the 64 campuses participate in SLN.

The SLN began in 1995/1996 with eight online courses and by 2004/2005, SLN offered 4,325 courses online. By 2007, SLN offered over 100 online degree programs and certificates (Pickett, 2007) with over 3,000 faculty teaching online. The investment in faculty training and support is a major element of SLN's success. In fact, SLN has won several major achievement awards for excellence in teaching and learning.

The SLN invests significantly in research and evaluation of their online courses. Surveys reveal that 90% of faculty and students express a high level of satisfaction with online courses. A fall

2004 survey that found 94% of the faculty reported being satisfied or very satisfied and that 98% would teach online again (Pickett, 2007).

Alexandra Pickett, the Associate Director of the SLN, identified five key elements of successful online faculty development:

1. Models: SLN's models for online faculty development, course design and training include: peer lead trainers; interdisciplinary cohorts of faculty to build communities of practice; access to experienced faculty; training that is online *plus* face-to-face *plus* individual support; templates and wizards; exemplar courses; and training for returning faculty to improve courses and collect best practice.
2. Support roles: These include individual instructional design support; technical HelpDesk support 24/7; resources and support in a variety of media; and access to the Academic Coordinator community.
3. Approaches: SLN emphasizes faculty-driven course design; faculty must develop the course themselves; and faculty can observe live online courses.
4. Evaluation: Evaluation is ongoing and occurs at both the course and institutional levels through faculty observation, research, collection and sharing of best practices, the SLN teaching surveys and longitudinal systematic data collection and analysis at the institutional level, with internationally recognized scholarly publication.
5. Quality: Course quality is addressed through such mechanisms as a wizard to scaffold pedagogic design with a quick-start course design; course templates/standards to help make the technology and instructional design process transparent; opportunities for faculty reflection, evaluation and revision; formal instructional design course reviews and training. (Pickett, 2007)

SLN uses group discussions and group activities in their online courses, and provides guidelines to online students in how to participate in online discussions.

Case Three: The UBC/ITESM Online Master of Educational Technology Program

The online master's program in Educational Technology offered jointly by the University of British Columbia (UBC), Canada (a major public research university) and ITESM (a highly regarded private university in Mexico) is a unique and valuable model that employs online technologies for both institutional and pedagogic benefit.

In 1989, Mexico's Instituto Tecnologico y de Estudios Superiores de Monterrey (ITESM) created a virtual university with the intent of taking advantage of satellite systems and video technology to offer graduate and professional programs. The pedagogic model was based on a television broadcast, distance education model using satellites for transmission of lectures and information. From 1995 onwards, the Internet was gradually substituted as a more effective delivery vehicle.

In 1996, ITESM and the Center for Continuing Studies at UBC joined forces to develop a totally online postgraduate certificate in technology-based distributed learning, focusing on teacher professional development and continuing education. In 2001, this program was redesigned and expanded to become a fully accredited Master's in Educational Technology (MET), although continuing education students can also enroll in one or more of the same courses for their professional development. The online program is entirely based on collaborative learning, using group discussions and group projects. The pedagogy also encourages students (who are educators) to reflect on their own educational practice and to work together to generate new insights into teaching and learning that they might apply in their own work.

Some of the program's distinctive institutional features are:

- the program is multinational (involving institutions in Canada and Mexico, and enrolling students from around the world);
- the program is bilingual (offered in both English and Spanish);
- the program is multi-institutional (involving UBC and ITESM);
- the program offers a joint degree from both institutions, as well as degrees from each institution, depending on the student's choice of courses;
- the program operates on a cost-recovery model that has enabled new, tenured professors to be hired within UBC's Faculty of Education.

The fact that this case example involved two very different institutions (each with its own policies, qualifications, history, norms, culture and staffing), in two countries, offering a credited, joint graduate program in two languages is a testimony to the efforts of the partners and their vision for a new way of teaching and learning. Dr. Tony Bates, then Director of Distance Education and Technology, Center for Continuing Studies at UBC and one of the visionaries behind this effort, noted that at UBC alone, 27 different policies had to be changed to accommodate the online MET (conversation with Dr. Bates, November 20, 2002).

The MET program uses the OCL pedagogy (conversation with Dr. Bates, April 20, 2009). The core of the courses are the group forums that enable online collaborative work, group discussions and other forms of learning such as "problem-based learning, cooperative and collaborative learning, and project-oriented learning" (Limón, 2006, p. 354).

When the Postgraduate Certificate program was being designed in 1995, there were no well-established, commercial, "off-the-shelf" learning environments, although software programs such as FirstClass incorporated online discussion forums. The first UBC/ITESM certificate programs were designed using a specially developed in-house html-based "content" framework combined with a free, off-the-shelf threaded discussion forum. Around the same time, WebCT was being developed at UBC, and in 1997, the Certificate program courses were moved to WebCT.

Because there was no precedent for these courses, both in terms of content and delivery, the course developers—staff in the Distance Education and Technology department at UBC—had considerable freedom in design, and they selected collaborative learning pedagogies. One of the program goals was to encourage communication and discussion between students from different countries and cultures. Many of the students were themselves teachers and course designers, so it was obvious to the program designers that the students themselves had much to contribute to the program. Another goal was to have students apply what they learned in the course to their own teaching context and the course designers felt it was important for students in this context to have opportunities for discussion and feedback not only with the instructors in the program but also with fellow students. Group assignments formed an important part of student assessment, so again online tools for discussion and collaboration were necessary.

Case Four: The International Labour Organization

The goal of the Training Centre of the International Labour Organization, a specialized agency of the United Nations, is to conduct educational programs aimed at people and organizations in developing countries. The center runs more than 450 educational programs and projects for approximately 11,000 people from over 180 countries every year. Its course/subject areas touch on all aspects of work including: employment policies, social protection, gender equality at the workplace, child labor, health and safety, labor migration and trade union education. The training courses are taught in face-to-face classrooms, whether at the Training Centre in Turin, Italy, or in other locations in the developing world.

In 2000, the center began using computer communications to augment its educational offerings. At first the online offerings were restricted to using the ODE pedagogy: students followed a syllabus individually with minimal involvement by a tutor. Course material was supplied online and the students were expected to complete a series of readings and tasks with assignments to be sent to the course organizer for evaluation. There was no interaction among the students participating in the course. Later, a computer conferencing (forum) facility was added to the center's online capabilities, but it was used only as a "café"—a common space in the conferencing system dedicated to informal discussion mainly unrelated to the course subject.

The center continues to use ODE for many of its online courses. But in 2002, the center began experimenting with the use of a discussion-based strategy for some of its online courses. In this scenario the students were expected to read assigned texts and perform individual tasks for evaluation, but also participate in group discussions. About five of the center's 20 online courses were designed to include a discussion component. These components, however, were quite loosely organized, promoting discussion among the participants but without clearly defined tasks or goals. The course organizers acted as discussion leaders guiding the online conversations toward the subjects being addressed in the course modules. According to Marc Belanger, director of the Training Centre, informal analysis of the participation patterns in these courses showed that most of the participants addressed their comments to the course organizer with minimal reference to the comments of the other students in the course. It became clear that the courses were instructor-centered and not taking advantage of the experiences and knowledge of the participants (personal communication, April 2009).

Consequently the center began experimenting with the OCL pedagogy to encourage course participants to take more control of the educational process. The trade union education unit at the center was given a lead role in developing the new strategy, because it had been designing new educational communication technologies and group-centered education is central to union education.

In 2004, the Training Centre decided to expand the use of OCL strategies in its online courses. Its first step was to systematically study one of the courses that were applying OCL principles. The course emphasized knowledge building through discourse, student maintenance of the learning process, instructor coaching of team leaders in a private side-forum, active reading assignments and the co-production of an artifact in the course such as a mini-manual or a document. According to Belanger, staff at the center found that in order to promote progress toward conceptual change, *new* information had to be brought into the discourse. Merely rehashing existing opinions based on the information the students brought into the course with them did not promote learning or new knowledge building or intellectual convergence (because the students, without new information to digest together, tended to hold on to their pre-course views and not move to common group positions).

The study showed that to promote effective OCL in its courses, the center would need to train its online instructors in the principles of the OCL theory, stress co-production in the courses and ensure new information was invested in the course discussions (Belanger, 2007). Existing technologies that would enable this strategy were reviewed, but it was clear that the center's unique mandate—to provide education and training for developing countries—would not be met by using any of the online technologies available at the time. Most of the center's clients are organizations based in countries without dependable electricity supplies and that have poor telephone facilities and expensive Internet services. None of the technologies available at the time were adequately designed to enable OCL given the difficulties of working in developing countries. Ordinarily the result of this mismatch of needs and available technologies would have meant that the organization would ratchet down its goals and work with whatever technologies were available at the time. However, because of the advent of the open-source free software movement, the center was able to develop a new communication technology that enabled OCL activity and addressed the constraints of online communication in developing countries. By studying the development and lessons of earlier online learning systems (primarily the Virtual U—an educational computer conferencing system developed in Canada in the late 1990s), building on previous open-source projects that the center had organized and working with the open-source community in Turin, the center was able to create a system that met its needs at an affordable cost.

Course participant surveys and analysis of previous online courses determined the need for an online educational environment that was designed to enable online groups to work more efficiently and effectively by including an audio component so that participants could listen to introductory comments by the instructors and comments provided by other participants (former participants who had been surveyed pointed out that their cultures were orally based and that listening to others speak would enhance the educational experience):

- be asynchronous, because course participants were usually dispersed over wide areas such as Africa or Asia, and therefore unable to go online at the same time;
- have the ability to work offline (not connected to the Internet) to save on costs and make it easier for those who had slow Internet connections;
- be able to search easily for new information to inform the discussions. (Belanger, 2007)

Studying the pedagogical framework that underlay the Virtual U technology, the developers of the new system identified lessons about how the technology could help online groups engage in discussions more efficiently (with a facility for displaying all the messages or a particular subset of messages) and all at once, instead of having to open messages one by one. The new software was designed based on the pedagogical framework advanced by Virtual U, but incorporated new features and tools. One new feature was a specialized search engine designed to help the discussion process by allowing participants to explore the Web and find information to bring to the discussions quickly and easily, without leaving the conferencing system. Another feature was an offline reader, which had been previously developed as an open-source project by the center, so participants could download forum comments, write offline and then post their comments when they reconnected to the Internet. With the help of the Polytechnic of Turin, the center also built an audio capability into the conferencing system that could be used efficiently by people in developing countries.

The result is a software called the Community Information and Participation System (CIPS). CIPS is an asynchronous computer conferencing system with audio capabilities and a built-in specialized search engine, which can be used for formal and informal learning. The Centre released the software and its documentation under the GNU Public License.

The first application of the center's newly developed CIPS was a system for trade union education called SoliComm. Development of a CIPS for social protection practitioners in Latin America was begun, and plans were made to apply the technology to other specialized groups served by the center, such as entrepreneurs, healthcare professionals and teachers. The publicly available CIPS called Akcio is released as open-source, free, software, which can be adopted by any organization and customized for its particular needs. In this way, the lessons learned by an organization in developing systems aimed at enhancing OCL can be shared by many other organizations and educational institutes.

Case Five: The Open University, United Kingdom (ODE + OCL)

It is interesting to note that as distance education providers began to adopt the Internet for course delivery, the pedagogy began to change from correspondence models of education to collaborative learning.

The Open University in the United Kingdom reflects the incorporation of OCL into a predominantly ODE model. The Open University was founded in 1969 as a single-mode, distance education institution offering a wide range of undergraduate and postgraduate degrees, as well as professional qualifications through correspondence learning pedagogies. Curriculum materials, educational resources and assignments are sent by postal mail or broadcast by radio or television. The Open University's programs are fully accredited in the United Kingdom and are highly regarded worldwide. The OU has served as a model to universities around the world interested in the open-university structure.

The United Kingdom's Open University serves around 220,000 students in the United Kingdom and mainland Eastern and Western Europe, with most programs featuring an online component (Salmon & Lawless, 2006, p. 387). The distance learning support system is still operating in what is referred to as the mass education of the "industrial model," but has changed to include a critical OCL component. Salmon and Lawless (2006) describe the new pedagogies as Phase One and Phase Two:

> Phase One consists of developing high-quality and paced-learning materials, originally through print and broadcast. Over the years, more new learning technologies such as CD-ROMs and Web sites have been included. The second phase is the delivery of group tutoring, feedback on individual assignments, and support by part-time tutors. Clearly, students' working together for knowledge sharing forms a critical part of the learning. Tutors have gradually learned to run their classes and groups in the online environments as well as face to face. (pp. 387–388)

In the OU Certificate of Management program, for example, the online groups are expected to be self-managing because online moderating of "large groups can be time consuming and participants benefit from becoming self-managing" (p. 395). There is, however, an opportunity for the tutor to facilitate the group-forming process, which includes:

- divide larger groups into smaller work teams. Give them ample time to complete an e-tivity and then report back to the larger group;
- where necessary, offer clarification about the task, the timescale and the form of presentation;
- leave the group to get on with the task, only intervening if they fail to post their contribution to the plenary on time;
- start a discussion on the results of the plenary contributions but do not dominate it. Summarize the discussion or ask an experienced participant to do this. (p. 395).

Additional training was introduced in 2004 for the OU Business School tutors related to the online course activities, with especial focus on solving real-world management problems collaboratively.

As a rehearsal for supporting their students, the tutors work through a 2-week, 5-hour online staff development program, instead of the usual face-to-face 1-day briefing. The course development team offers a Webcast, a dedicated website and also a set of e-tivities and discussion forums on the OU's collaborative online environment, FirstClass. Specially trained tutor-peers act as e-convenors for the forums and e-tivities, all of whom (willingly) went through the online brief-ing first (Salmon & Lawless, 2006, p. 396).

Case Six: eArmyU

The Army University Access Online (known as eArmyU) provides access to post-secondary edu-cation for enlisted American soldiers around the globe. eArmyU is an online learning initiative launched in 2000 and funded by the United States Army to provide degree and diploma pro-grams to eligible enlisted soldiers. eArmyU is not itself a university or a college; it is an online portal that leads to a consortium of more than 20 colleges and universities and multiple vendors that offer online delivery of courses, degree programs and student services. Launched in January 2001, eArmyU provides soldiers with the opportunity to earn a certificate or an associate bach-elor's, or master's degree in a wide variety of disciplines, including the arts, aeronautics, business, criminal justice, hospitality and information technology (IT). The soldiers earn degrees from a home college, while taking web-based courses from multiple colleges at any time and any-where. eArmyU offers approximately 146 programs from 29 different educational institutions. Since 2001, over 43,000 students—living or working in every state, as well 50 countries and four American Territories— have participated in eArmyU, resulting in more than 5,300 degrees being conferred.

In 2004, soldiers had over 146 academic programs to choose from and nearly 1,500 courses offered online by 29 participating institutions, with established agreements allowing credits to transfer among participating institutions. eArmyU offers "for-credit" college degrees and is looking to develop new online offerings that address the need for "new-skills" training or work-place training (see www.earmyu.com). While the institutions related to eArmyU use a pedagogy largely based on ODE and OC, the pedagogies used in military training are undergoing a major transformation.

The US Department of Defense (DOD) provides training and education for the 2.1 million members of its active and reserve armed forces that include 700,000 civilian employees and 85,000 dependent children. Each year 150 to 250 million dollars are invested by the DOD in research and development in education, training and relevant technologies.

As noted in Chapter 4, the military was the major investor in computer-assisted instruction (CAI), one of the earliest and most prominent educational software applications. Today, the focus is increasingly on simulations. "CAI concentrates on teaching, whereas simulation concentrates on learning through interaction with 'real world' experiences" (Fletcher, 2009, p. 73). Today's military operations increasingly involve incredibly complex tasks, which are cognitively highly demanding. "CAI is very good at producing journeymen from novices, but these tasks require higher levels of mastery, involving analysis, evaluation, and creativity" (p. 73). The military is thus now emphasizing simulations, involving collaborative learning, for training to address these complex learning needs in real-world settings. The origin of simulations, including collective simulations, came from training air crews. In fact, the first manned aircraft relied on simulation. Today collective simulations based on computer networks that link simulators and simulations together are used to enable crews, teams and units to train together.

Collaborative constructive simulation in the military "is best exemplified by computerized war games. Participants establish scenarios, parameters, and command decisions. They then use com-puters to play out missions and use the consequences of their decisions to support the develop-ment of tactics, techniques, and procedures" (Fletcher, 2009, p. 74). A review of the literature on collectives in business and industry cited by Fletcher reports a clear consensus "that work groups are the cornerstone of modern American industry" (p. 74).

Case Seven: The Virtual High School

One of the earliest examples of a Virtual High School was a project undertaken by the Concord Cortium to launch online courses or netcourses to train secondary math and science school teachers in how to develop and implement online high school subjects (Collison et al., 2000, p. 3). The netcourses were designed as an alternative to summer professional development institutes run by the National Science Foundation, and were also part of a graduate course. One aspect of the project, the International Netcourse Teacher Enhancement Coalition) was to introduce participants to the pedagogy of inquiry-based instruction and also show participants 11 exemplary curricula. Each teacher would select one unit for study, and then design and pilot a 2–4-week blended learning unit for his or her own classroom. A second aspect or related project was the Teacher Learning Conference (TLC).

> The TLC primarily serves teachers who are participating in the Virtual High School (VHS) collaborative of accredited high schools whose teachers lead a virtual course in exchange for seats for local students in the VHS. The collaborative now offers over two hundred teacher-designed netcourses for high school students.... In exchange for providing a teacher and a course taught by that teacher in the VHS catalog, each school in the VHS cooperative can enroll twenty students in any other netcourse being offered by other participating schools. (Collison et al., 2000, pp. 4–5)

The pedagogical model is online collaboration with the teacher serving as a facilitator or guide to online discussion groups and projects.

More recent survey data show that a significant number of US public school students are now engaging in online courses: "in 2007–2008 approximately 1,030,000 students were enrolled in fully online and blended courses. This represented an increase of 47% since 2005–6" (Picciano & Seaman, 2009, p. 5).

The study defined the totally online course as one where most or all of the content was delivered online and there were no face-to-face meetings. The blended course featured a substantial portion of the content delivered online with some online discussions and typically few face-to-face meetings (Picciano & Seaman, 2009, p. 5). The study also envisioned blended learning in K-12 schooling of the future, in which students might take some courses in face-to-face classrooms, while studying other courses entirely online, or where part of a course is held online and another portion onsite.

The Picciano and Seaman (2009) study is a survey of US School Administrators; it highlights issues of importance to administrators. The major issues perceived as important in relation to virtual or online high school programming were meeting the access needs of students, such as:

- meeting the needs of specific groups of students;
- offering courses not otherwise available at the school;
- offering advanced placement or college-level courses;
- permitting students who failed a course to take it again;
- reducing scheduling conflicts for students. (p. 11)

Issues of quality of learning or pedagogy were not addressed by the Picciano and Seaman (2009) study. Nor were respondents queried about pedagogical issues. Yet, the references to the significant use of third-party providers suggests that many, if not most, of the courses were developed as OC or ODE content provided to schools for delivery. Unlike the early VHS project, virtual high schools today used pedagogies based on individualized learning and students working at their own pace. It is stated that teachers can be contacted via email, phone or discussion board. For an extra fee many virtual high schools also offered an "enhanced support" option, which provides for more frequent contact from teachers and regular progress reports for parents. However, there is no discussion of teacher-led online classes or peer-group discussion.

Case Eight: Online Learning Initiatives That Did Not Meet Their Targeted Goals and Other General Problems

A significant source of data can be derived from initiatives that did not reach their targeted goals. In the field of online education, there is a wealth of undiscovered wisdom in such case examples. However, studies of failures are typically few and far between. In most disciplines, such studies are often not welcomed, either by the authors of the failures or by publishers.

It is hard to accept and acknowledge failure, even when we believe it does not matter and that we have learned from it. However, the collection and analyzing of data on online learning initiatives "that did not reach targeted goals" does continue to identify implications for the field. These include a study of the United Kingdom eUniversity, the Scottish Interactive University and the NHS University (Bacsich, 2005; Keegan et al., 2007; MacLeod, 2004). These studies focused on the "business" models—the primary motivation for these particular cases was profit rather than pedagogic effectiveness. The major problem identified was the poor and unrealistic nature of the business model.

The APLU[1]–Sloan National Commission on Online Learning was formed in May 2007 to engage the APLU Presidents and Chancellors in a discussion about the utility of online education as a means to achieve broader institutional priorities such as diversity, retention, internationalization and accountability. The two-volume report, *Online Learning as a Strategic Asset*, contains the results of 231 interviews with faculty, administrators and students and 10,700 responses from faculty across disciplines, teaching levels and tenure position. The survey was sent to approximately 50,000 faculty (Seaman, 2009).

The results of the survey indicate that more than one-third (34.4%) of faculty have taught at least one course online. And these faculty represent the spectrum of tenure and teaching experience. Among those who have had online teaching experience, the majority report that the learning outcomes are as good as or better than face-to-face instruction. However, important barriers were identified.

The major barrier was the effort required to teach online: about 64% of the respondents wrote that it takes "somewhat more" or "a lot more" effort to teach online over face-to-face instruction, and over 85% reported that it takes "somewhat more" or "a lot more" effort to develop an online course than a face-to-face course (Seaman, 2009). (It should be noted that the pedagogy and educational model employed were not identified.) Faculty thus perceived the effort of developing and teaching online courses as the greatest barrier to engaging in online learning.

The major problems were related to institutional support structures. Faculty ranked seven of the eight support dimensions as "below average." These included: support for online course development, course delivery and students; policies on intellectual property; recognition in tenure and promotion; and incentives for developing and delivering online courses.

The only dimension that faculty rated as "average" was technology infrastructure. There was no dimension in institutional support that was rated as "above average."

Issues of faculty support and engagement, structure and finance have long been identified as fundamental concerns for institutions adopting online education. The need for faculty training and support for online course development and delivery has been identified as urgent.

The responses indicate significant problems that must be resolved in order that online education be accepted universally by the academy. The results are insightful because they demonstrate that while faculty are increasingly adopting online education, there are also very important challenges that should be addressed by institutions to obtain the highest-quality education and educator efforts. Studies of institutional adoption are becoming available, such as the Seaman (2009) report and the Bates and Sangra (2010) book, *The Integration of Technology within Universities and Colleges*.

Summary

Chapter 8 introduced the examination of institutional adoption of online learning, particularly with respect to online (or blended) delivery of courses and programs. The chapter provided a wide variety of case examples from both formal and nonformal education to illustrate how institutions are involved in the design and implementation of the online delivery of certificate and degree programs. Six cases of totally online and blended course delivery were presented and discussed. In addition, there was discussion of virtual high schools. Very importantly, the chapter concluded with a discussion of online learning initiatives that did not succeed and some of the key problems that have been highlighted in relation to institutional adoption of online education.

OCL Scenarios
Online Communities of Practice

What counts as scientific knowledge, for instance, is the prerogative of scientific communities, which interact to define what facts matter and what theories are valid. There may be disagreements, there may be mavericks, but it is through the process of communal involvement, including all the controversies, that a body of knowledge is developed. It is by participating in these communities—even when going against the mainstream—that members produce knowledge.

—Wenger, McDermott and Snyder, 2002

collaborative learning communities of practice discourse gen seminars huge online community intellectual discourse knowledge building knowledge communities ocop online communities online community autonomous online community forum online educational game communities online monthly seminars online social communication online text-based communities online university courses participant participants perspectives postings practice-based learning community premier online reference destination professional practice project groups quantitative data reification research findings research projects scientific communities scientific community seminars social discourse social engagement social networks student-led online seminars task-based learning communities term community term online communities term online community textual communities traditional community transcript analysis transcripts usage statistics user-generated online content various communities virtual communities wenger wikipedia

Chapter 9 examines online communities of practice and presents the following topics:

- Context and definition of key terms such as:
  - Community
  - Communities of practice
  - Community of learning
  - Social networks
  - Online communities
- Definition of an online community of practice (OCoP)
- History of OCoPs
- Two OCoP exemplars
  - Global Educators' Network (GEN)
  - Wikipedia
- An analytical framework to study and design OCoPs.

Context of Communities of Practice (CoP)

Chapter 9 addresses a fascinating and key aspect of human learning, informal learning in online communities of practice. Informal learning refers to experiential learning, that is, learning outside of the classroom. There is no teacher or curriculum; nor is there a degree, diploma or certificate as a result. Informal learning is the way that we learn throughout our lives. We learn by doing, by observing and by experiencing life. As professionals, we hone and advance our knowledge through experience and informal learning with peers and experts in our field. While an exact figure cannot be calculated, a common assertion is informal learning constitutes around 80% of the learning in organizations (Cross, 2007, p. 17). With the advent of the Internet, online communities have become a new, important and highly popular destination for informal learning and knowledge building, as well as for social communication.

Chapter 9 builds on Chapters 6, 7 and 8 by examining the role and significance of online communities of practice. The chapter provides definitions and presents two real-world examples to depict how online communities of practice function and contribute to learning and knowledge building. Chapter 9 concludes by discussing features and indicators of online communities of practice and puts forward a Framework for Analysis to assist the design, implementation and assessment of OCoPs.

It is illuminating that the terms "communication" and "community" derive from common Latin roots, *communicare* and *communis,* which mean "to share." Sharing has enabled humans to survive and to thrive, and, as discussed in this book, has been the basis of civilizational advances. The ability to intentionally collaborate defines the fundamental nature of the human species (Hrdy, 2009). From the days of our earliest ancestors, the ability to communicate and to form community has been key to our survival. Communication is at the heart and soul of human development, individual and social. And in fundamental ways it is key to how we learn.

Moreover, the concept of the community is replacing the image of the solitary genius as the sole, primary or even preferred source of creativity, science and innovation (Farrell, 2001). In studying the major artistic, social and scientific transformations of the past two centuries, Farrell notes that "artists, writers, composers, scientists, social reformers and other creative people report that a collaborative circle played an indispensable part in their development" (2001, p. 1). He cites a passage from the American writer Henry James, who suggests that without a community of peers, creative work is far more difficult:

> The best things come … from the talents that are members of a group; every man works better when he has companions working in the same line, and yielding to the stimulus of suggestion, comparison, and emulation. Great things have of course been done by solitary workers, but they have usually been done with double the pains they would have cost if they had been produced in more genial circumstances. (James, 1909, p. 31, quoted in Farrell, 2001, p. 1)

Lave and Wenger (1991) coined the term "communities of practice" in the context of studying traditional apprenticeship. As Wenger later noted:

> Apprenticeship is often thought of as a relationship between a master and a student. Yet we observed that learning took place mostly during interactions with journeymen and more advanced apprentices. Community of practice is the term we used to refer to this social structure. Once we had the concept, however, we started to see these communities in many other settings, where there was no official institution of apprenticeship. (Wenger, McDermott & Snyder, 2002, p. 233)

The concept of communities of practice (CoP) has been adopted in education, training and management as well as related fields. The term refers to relatively tightly knit groups of professionals engaged in a common practice, who communicate, negotiate and share their best practice with one another directly. Sometimes these professionals work in the same organization. More typically CoPs exist outside of a particular workplace, but within a particular profession or area of skill. For example, high school biology teachers may participate in a CoP related to their specialization, even though they teach in different schools in different cities or countries. Heart surgeons may travel long distances to study one another's work and learn new techniques from peers or experts in the field.

CoPs may also be composed of hobbyists or interest groups. They may be antique car enthusiasts, foodies or self-help groups such as people who share news and information to learn more about their particular concern and deepen their knowledge on that topic. Most of us belong to various CoPs; we may be very active in some of these communities while we participate only occasionally in others.

> Communities of practice are groups of people who share a concern, a set of problems, or a passion about a topic, and who deepen their knowledge and expertise in this area by interacting on an ongoing basis.... These people don't necessarily work together every day, but they meet because they find value in their interactions. As they spend time together, they typically share information, insight and advice. They help each other solve problems. They discuss their situations, their aspirations, and their needs. They ponder common issues, explore ideas, and act as sounding boards. They may create tools, standards, generic designs, manuals, and other documents—or they may simply develop a tacit understanding that they share. However they accumulate knowledge, they become informally bound by the value that they find in learning together. This value is not merely instrumental for their work. It also accrues in the personal satisfaction of knowing colleagues who understand each other's perspectives and of belonging to an interesting group of people. Over time, they develop a unique perspective on their topic as well as a body of common knowledge, practice and approaches. They also develop personal relationships and established ways of interacting. They may even develop a common sense of identity. (Wenger et al., 2002, pp. 4–5)

CoPs not only accumulate knowledge, they also contribute to advancing knowledge. Solving new problems and documenting the solution in a manual, article, new way of working or new tool represents a knowledge artifact. Barab, MaKinster and Scheckler (2004) note that participation in a CoP

> results in some outcome, whether it is an idea, a tool, drawing, online post, or simply becoming more knowledgeably skillful with respect to the practice. This process of transforming experience and the outcomes of experience into a thing is known as *reification*. (p. 66; italics in the original).

The construction of a knowledge artifact is a very important phenomenon and output of practice, but there is a danger associated with reification that Wenger (1998) also addresses:

> Reification as a constituent of meaning is always incomplete, ongoing, potentially enriching, and potentially misleading. The notion of assigning the status of object to something that is really not an object conveys a sense of mistaken solidity, or project concreteness. It conveys a sense of useful illusion. The use of the term reification stands both as a tribute to the generative power of the process and as a gentle reminder of its delusory perils. (p. 62)

Knowledge is thus an outcome or a product, but it is also part of human practice. It is not just a "thing"; it is formed by communities and reification of practice. A tool or a book is most relevant to and understood by the communities associated with the practice represented by that artifact. Members of the community are most likely to understand a particular new tool or book. Attempts at knowledge management, to make knowledge into a static "thing" like a self-contained entity through the use of databases or other forms of IT, have proven elusive or challenging at least. Wenger et al. (2002) argue that knowledge should not be viewed as a static object and suggest several points related to the challenge of creating usable knowledge. They write:

Knowledge Lives in the Human Act of Knowing

…The knowledge of experts is an accumulation of experience—a kind of "residue" of their actions, thinking and conversations—that remain a dynamic part of their ongoing experience. This type of knowledge is much more a living process than a static body of information. Communities of practice do not reduce knowledge to an object. They make it an integral part of their activities and interactions, and they serve as a living repository for that knowledge.

Knowledge is Tacit as Well as Explicit

…Communities of practice are in the best position to codify knowledge, because they can combine its tacit and explicit aspects. They can produce useful documentation, tools, and procedures because they understand the needs of practitioners. Moreover, these products have increased in meaning because they are not just objects by themselves, but are part of the life of the community.

Knowledge is Social as Well as Individual

…Appreciating the collective nature of knowledge is especially important in an age when almost every field changes too much, too fast for individuals to master … this collective character of knowledge does not mean that individuals don't count. In fact, the best communities welcome strong personalities and encourage disagreements and debates. Controversy is part of what makes a community vital, effective, and productive.

Knowledge is Dynamic

…In short, what makes managing knowledge a challenge is that it is not an object that can be stored, owned, and moved around like a piece of equipment or a document. It resides in the skills, understanding, and relationships of its members as well as in the tools, documents, and processes that embody aspects of this knowledge. (Wenger et al., 2002, pp. 9–11)

CoPs are also represented in academic and professional fields, such as the pure and applied sciences, computer science, education and arts. Kuhn (1970) posited that scientists work in disciplinary communities and, through discourse (discussion, debate), generate the current state-of-the-art knowledge in that discipline. Bruffee (1999) used the term "knowledge communities" in a similar way. Disciplinary communities of scientists, artists and other professionals are the means of generating and advancing knowledge in their respective fields. Correspondence, books, tools or manuals that document processes, within the context of the field or discipline, not only reify but diffuse the knowledge among peers, inductees, apprentices and students.

Scientific advances depend on the speed and efficiency of communication. A scientific community interacts across time (even over generations) and geography. Historically, knowledge

Figure 9.1 Knowledge in Communities of Practice.

has advanced as communication technologies have improved. This was demonstrated with the role of the printing press, which, together with the rise of the early postal service and inventions in transportation, accelerated the development of modern science from the period of the 16th century (the time of Galileo) until today. Informal systems of communication such as meetings, letters and scholarly publications, which form the "nervous system" of science, were refined and improved. Scientific researchers communicated more often, more widely and thereby more intensively in their area of specialization. Scientific communities comprised specialists working in "invisible colleges" (meetings, publications, personal correspondence, reports). As the mechanisms to meet and share ideas improved, so too did scientific knowledge.

Brown and Duguid (2000) note the importance of text and documents in generating new schools of thought and practice. They portray the history of the Internet as extending a long tradition of communities forming around documents: textual communities. Schools of thought and practice, they argue, are based on shared texts. "The shared texts as much as anything else gave texture to the notion of a discipline, a profession, or an interest group, though most of the people in these 'worlds' knew little of one another directly" (Brown & Duguid, 2000, p. 190). The antecedents of CoPs actually go back much further than textual communities, back to the twilight of humanity. Wenger et al. (2002, p. 5) write:

> Communities of practice are not a new idea. They were our first knowledge-based social structures, back when we lived in caves and gathered around the fire to discuss strategies for cornering prey, the shape of arrowheads, or which roots were edible. In ancient Rome, "corporations" of metalworkers, potters, masons, and other craftsmen had both a social aspect (members worshipped common deities and celebrated holidays together) and a business function (training apprentices and spreading innovations). In the Middle Ages, guilds fulfilled similar roles for artisans throughout Europe. Guilds lost their influence during the Industrial Revolution, but communities of practice have continued to proliferate to this day in every aspect of human life.

Definitions of Key Terms

It is important to distinguish CoPs from similar but different concepts such as communities in general, communities of learning, task-oriented communities (work teams and project groups) and social networks. We will also briefly discuss the notion of *online* community.

Community: The concept of community is a difficult term to define because of the very wide and diffuse use of the term. While the term "community" may seem like a simple concept that refers to people who live in the same geographic area, there are in fact hundreds of distinct scholarly and popular definitions. For our purposes, we set out a simple but succinct definition of how the term is commonly used:

- a group of people living in a particular local area; "the team is drawn from all parts of the community";
- common ownership; "they shared a community of possessions";
- a group of nations having common interests; "they hoped to join the NATO community";
- agreement as to goals; "the preachers and the bootleggers found they had a community of interests";
- residential district: a district where people live; occupied primarily by private residences;
- (ecology) a group of interdependent organisms inhabiting the same region and interacting with each other.

(http://wordnetweb.princeton.edu/perl/webwn)

Communities of practice (CoP): The term "community of practice" has evolved from an emphasis on apprenticeship within an organization to that of members sharing a common profession or type of work beyond an institutional affiliation. In fact, the latter is the most common understanding of CoP: shared profession or work but not shared workplace. CoPs are informal, meaning that they are voluntary and not mandated or assigned by a workplace or organization. In the extract below, Wenger et al. (2002, p. 4) provide a broad description of CoPs, which includes communities of nonprofessional practice such as those related to hobbies as well as communities based on professional practice.

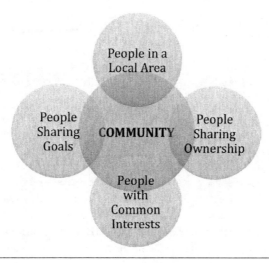

Figure 9.2 What is a Community?

Engineers who design a certain kind of electronic circuit called phase-lock loops find it useful to compare designs regularly and to discuss the intricacies of their esoteric specialty. Soccer moms and dads take advantage of game times to share tips and insights about the subtle art of parenting. Artists congregate in cafes and studios to debate the merits of a new style or technique. Gang members learn to survive on the street and deal with an unfriendly world. Frontline managers running manufacturing operations get a chance to commiserate, to learn about upcoming technologies, and to foresee shifts in the winds of power.

CoPs are those in which members share or develop several core commonalities. Members typically share: a common language or set of terms related to their profession, practice or interest; a substantive common focus; a common set of problems; common training or experience; a common way of working or doing things; a common set of tools or technologies; a common tacit understanding of the topic. And, CoPs also contribute to learning and to building knowledge, whether this goal is implicit or explicitly stated. Some CoPs reflect an intense passion or urgency to solving problems. Others are more oriented to social interaction. Nonetheless, there is generally a high level of cohesion and intentionality, if the group is to survive. CoPs with weak bonds, low levels of interaction or lack of relevant knowledge and experience typically do not attract new or sustained membership. Most CoPs reflect a mixture of problem-solving and socializing discourse. CoPs that specifically and intentionally commit to building the field of knowledge are most typically associated with scholarship, research, science, new technologies, new forms of artistic and cultural expression or social activism.

Community of learning: A community of learning is frequently associated with an educational program or course, guided or established by an instructor and linked to the curriculum of studies in some way and thus represents formal or nonformal learning. The instructor will induct students into learning communities as part of their course or program of studies. Most often a community of learning is related to accomplishing an assigned task or project, and is thus similar to a work group or project team. The topic, tasks and timeline are set by the instructor. Membership is mandated by the instructor, whether the instructor selects the team members or students self-select which group to join. A community of learning is neither voluntary nor ongoing.

> The learners' community is not perennial because its members are not engaged in a durable way in the activity at the base of its creation. It is born, grows, and dies at the rhythm of the stages of an educational program. In this aspect, it does not share the continuous activity that characterizes the community of practice in the work environment. (Henri & Pudelko, 2003, p. 481)

Communities of learning for educators are most typically associated with professional development courses, training activities or educational programs.

Work teams or project groups: Work teams or project groups are typically mandated by an organization to accomplish a specific task within a specified period. The members do not participate voluntarily but are recruited or assigned to meet a particular need within the framework of the organization or workplace. The task, the membership and the terms of work are set by the organization. A work team exists for a specific period and then dissolves. In the case of project-based teams related to research, the team may regroup or continue if further funding (external or institutional) is found.

Social networks: A social network refers to a set of social relationships, with the emphasis on the relationship and not on a particular topic or substantive focus. Social networks are voluntary and informal.

Online communities: The term online community is used throughout this book to mean the same as virtual communities and e-communities. These terms can generally be used interchangeably. An online community is any community that exists in a web-based environment, such as forums or social networks.

The Internet has been referred to as a vast online world, or set of online worlds and communities. Today, hundreds of millions of people participate in online communities and social networks—and these people view these worlds or virtual spaces as real, as authentic. Their experience is one of communicating and interacting with other real people, and while some may use pseudonyms or playful user IDs, most participate by using their real names or email IDs. It is thus important to recognize that online communities and online learning applications are real: they are not false or inauthentic forms of human interaction. Participant engagement varies depending on the task or nature of the community: an online hobby community may be less intense than an online community of professional practice—or it may be equally or even more intense and engaged. The level of participation may vary; the duration of the activity or the expectations or requirements of participation may vary. However, the perception of authenticity is that one is really participating, and the online experience can equal or exceed that of a real-time face-to-face event or community, even in online text-based communities.

A second aspect of online worlds, however, relates to some form of performance based on creativity, imagination, identity and embodiment of a character or role. For example, Sherry Turkle's book, *Life on the Screen* (1995), presents a view of the Internet as an exciting and creative space where virtual identities can be constructed and experimented with. Each online community and multiuser game has its own culture and rules of behavior: it may encourage the use of roleplay, variations on how the self can be portrayed and presented and/or anonymity or pseudonyms. Some online communities of interest as well as online games may allow or even encourage anonymity or pseudonyms. Many online SIGs and hobby groups are not particularly concerned with representation of self, as long as the user abides by the norms and etiquette of that "space." Similarly, many games and immersive worlds are premised on the construction and use of online personas. The early examples of immersive worlds, derived from online text-based multiuser games such as MUDs (multiuser dungeons and dragons and later renamed *mu*ltiuser *d*omains) and MUSEs (*mu*ltiuser *s*imulated *e*nvironments), expected and encouraged exploration or online personas and new behaviors and interactions.

While such use of online personas does not necessarily reflect inauthentic communication or misrepresentation, it is not the focus of this chapter and communities based on games, arcade roleplays or multiple representations of self are not considered here.

What Is an Online Community of Practice?

An online community of practice (OCoP) shares all of the features of a traditional community of practice (CoP), but it is conducted via the Web rather than onsite through face-to-face communication. The nature of the technology that mediates each type of CoP introduces different affordances. That is, the commonalities shared by members of a CoP are the same for an OCoP but the means for sharing and interacting have differences that can be significant. Face-to-face communication enhances some aspects of the communication but limits others; online communication similarly offers certain strengths and limitations. The Web, for example, enables far greater scope and scale of interaction and discourse than face-to-face meetings because of attributes such as place-independent, time-independent, many-to-many, text-based communication. On the other hand, the expanded access available online can also introduce potential disadvantages such as communication overload from a large number of participants or postings. The attributes of online collaboration were discussed in Chapter 6, and that discussion is applicable to online communities as well.

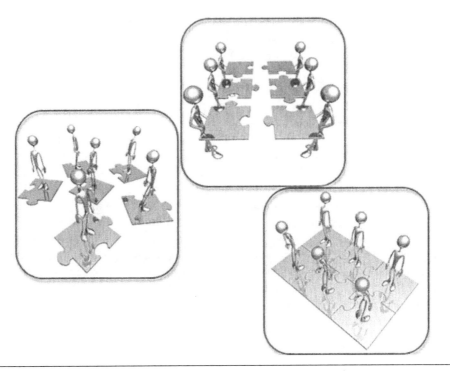

Figure 9.3 Three Conceptualizations of an OCoP.

CoPs, as noted by Wenger et al. (2002), have been part of human development since we lived in caves as hunters and gatherers. And they remain integral to our lives today. What is amazing, however, is the degree to which CoPs have populated the online world.

History of Online Communities of Practice

As discussed in Chapter 2, the invention of the Internet itself was the product of CoPs. The inventors were computer scientists who first worked together onsite and then, once the technology was invented and implemented, continued to work together online. And the Internet has gone on to support millions of online communities, users groups and social networks.

The Internet is characterized by an immense quantity, quality and range of online communication. Email has the highest number of users of all Internet applications, and online communities and social networks are close runners up. Online communities emerged during the 1970s, and their numbers snowballed from the 1980s. Scientists, academics, educators, professionals, all those who had access to computers and the network, soon began forming CoPs online.

Bitnet, the academic predecessor to the Internet, was an early world leader in network communications for the research and education communities, and helped lay the groundwork for the subsequent introduction of the Internet, especially outside the United States. The international Bitnet network (the "Because It's Time" network) began in the spring of 1981. Bitnet users shared information via electronic mail to individuals and shared-interest groups. Nearly 3,000 discussion groups on Bitnet covered topics of academic interest, from butterfly biology to theoretical physics, usually filtered and approved by a human moderator, and supported by the listserv software. Membership in an online community was anywhere from five participants to several thousand. The discussion groups based on mailing lists were the most popular elements of Bitnet.

Online communities based on computer conferencing systems or forums such as the west coast Whole Earth 'Lectronic Link (the WELL) emerged and became highly active in the 1980s, leading to online friendships and even marriages, as documented by Howard Rheingold's 1993 book: *Virtual Communities*. Online collaborative games such as MUDs and MUSEs emerged in the late 1980s and proliferated, providing members with programming tools to create new online worlds, societies and situations. Educators in the 1990s adopted multiuser environments for educational applications in their classrooms: for example, students might design and participate in an online world based on certain political or social principles (democracy, feudalism, dictatorship), assuming various roles within this online world. Or students might become pioneers in settling a new planet, scientists experimenting with research or environmentalists solving important problems. Such experiences then led to class discussion and analyses.

By the 1990s, millions of users participated in online academic, professional, educational, technical, political, social, special interest and/or hobby-related communities or discussion groups. User-generated online content became well established in educational applications such as online university courses, networked classrooms, online educational game communities and OCoPs (see Hiltz & Turoff, 1978; Harasim, 1993; Harasim et al., 1995; Riel, 1993; Palloff & Pratt, 1999, 2003).

Thus the rise of Web 2.0 and its designation as the "social" Web should neither detract from nor diminish our understanding and appreciation of the tremendous social role played by the early Arpanet and Internet in terms of communication, networking, online communities and collaborations and user-created content in the 1980s and 1990s.

The development of Web 2.0 group collaboration tools such as social networks, texting, Twitter, cultural production tools (YouTube, Flickr) and blogs since 2004 has built upon generations of online communities that first began in the 1970s. The computer conferencing system invented by Murray Turoff in 1972 was expressly aimed at facilitating group (many-to-many) communication, to expand and enhance electronic mail (email) invented in 1971 to facilitate one-to-one and one-to-many communication. And the earliest users of computer conferencing were professionals who employed this medium for professional discourse, problem solving, knowledge building and in general communication associated with their professional practice (Hiltz & Turoff, 1978). Email lists, bulletin boards, computer conferencing systems, discussion forums, synchronous chat lines and environments like MUDs and MUSEs were technologies that supported online communities since the mid-1970s, and many continue to be used today.

At the same time, Web 2.0 has definitely drawn public attention to online social communication and collaboration, and provided new collaboration tools and platforms that have been adopted by OCoPs.

OCoPs have also begun to generate significant interest by educational researchers. Lave and Wenger's (1991) concept of CoPs was initially related to studies of workplace learning and apprenticeship and then expanded to include both professional communities and communities of interest (hobbyists, for example). Riel and Polin (2004) focus on learning communities and identify three distinct but overlapping types: task-based, practice-based and knowledge-based online learning communities. They define task-based learning communities as "groups of people organized around a task who work intently together for a specific period of time to produce a product" (p. 20). A practice-based learning community refers to a larger group "with shared goals that offer their members richly contextualized and supported arenas for learning" (pp. 20–21). Knowledge-based learning communities "often share many of the features of a community of practice but focus on the deliberate and formal production of external knowledge about the practice" (p. 21). Henri and Pudelko (2003) discuss four types of virtual communities: communities of interest (people assembled to share ideas about a common topic); goal-oriented communities of interest (comparable to a task-force or project team vested with a specific mandate); a learners' community (guided by an instructor and linked to curricular objectives); and communities of practice (members share and pool complementary knowledge to enrich one another's professional practice).

Exemplars: How Do OCoPs Function?

A key question relates to how do CoPs become successful, and more fundamentally, what does "successful" mean in the context of OCoPs? What constitutes success in terms of participation, and particularly in terms of collaboration, learning and knowledge building? How are successful OCoPs launched, structured and sustained?

These are fascinating and profound questions. As Barab, Kling and Gray (2004, p. 3) noted:

> Too little of the education literature provides clear criteria for what does and does not constitute community; the term is too often employed as a slogan rather than as an analytical category. We also know little about the educational value of employing a community model for supporting learning.

Moreover, as these and other authors note, it is relatively easy to start an online community. At least in terms of technology, we have free access to listservs, computer conferencing systems and discussion boards, and more recently users have used blogs, wikis and social networks such as Facebook to start online communities. However, even by the early 1980s, there were discussions about "what to do if you host an online community and nobody shows up?" The Internet is littered with dead and abandoned online communities and special-interest groups (SIGs).

It is not just launching an OCoP, but building and sustaining it that is a significant challenge, especially if the task is knowledge construction. Thus important questions must be posed. As Barab et al. (2004, p. 4) state: "Building online communities in the service of learning is a major accomplishment about which we have much to learn." We must ask whether the OCoP is succeeding and what exactly it is accomplishing. We must also explore how we can define and determine success. And what designs, structures, processes and tools can best support success. These are critical questions and suggest areas for research and development.

Chapter 9 sets out two case examples of OCoPs and identifies some of the indicators of success that were reported, as well as the processes and tools involved, as a contribution to further research in this area. The two cases are:

1. the Global Educators Network (GEN)
2. Wikipedia.

For our purposes, the term online communities of practice (OCoPs) will be viewed as encompassing the voluntary association online of professionals, practitioners, scientists and/or interest groups who come together intentionally, actively and regularly for mutual gain and collective value. Typically the members of an OCoP share a common background based on work, practice or interest and, associated with that practice, common values, tacit understanding, common terms or language, exposure to common problems and common experience and/or training. Members will also share common purpose or intentionality for their OCoP, of which learning and building knowledge may be implicit or explicit.

The two OCoPs described below are drawn from real-world practice. They reflect examples of informal learning and thus exclude online formal education (which was the subject of Chapter 7) and online nonformal education (the subject of Chapter 8).

Both examples represent intentional collaboration, learning, sharing of information and the building of knowledge but each case does so in a different way and with differing emphases.

While many OCoPs exist related to educational professions, we draw upon examples that have been studied and have generated empirical data.

Global Educators' Network (GEN)

The Global Educators Network (or GEN) was an online community created "for online educators, by online educators." GEN was an international informal learning network aimed at encouraging information exchange, learning and knowledge building on the subject of online learning. Launched in 1999, GEN was based on asynchronous group communication using the Web-based Virtual-U software. GEN began as a way to link a small group of educators and researchers involved in research projects focused on online learning,[1] and then grew rapidly as educators from around the world learned of it and asked to join the discussions. As membership grew, a tool to enable self-registration to the online forum was developed and implemented. GEN soon evolved into an online community autonomous of the original research project but maintaining links that were considered mutually beneficial (these links are described below). Membership and participation in GEN were voluntary, and within 2 years membership grew to 2,400 members from 75 countries, reflecting users with various backgrounds and levels of expertise in online education. Members included K-12 teachers, trainers, university faculty, graduate students, software developers and educational and computer science researchers.

GEN became an OCoP with the goals of sharing best practice, encouraging collaborative learning related to online education and building and advancing knowledge in the field. The social design of GEN changed over time and in response to increased membership and active participation, from topical freeform discussions into an ongoing series of monthly seminars, moderated by the members. GEN members would volunteer to moderate a seminar on a topic of their choice; initially a seminar would be 2 weeks long, but they expanded to become 3 weeks in duration.

The seminars involved online peer collaboration linking conceptual learning with real-world problems and questions. GEN seminars often produced knowledge artifacts that synthesized the knowledge of the group on particular topics. Archives were one form of artifact, but summaries, wikis and resource lists were also produced by GEN members and circulated to other forums or disseminated to other practitioners through various means.

A GEN coordinator offered moderating tips and support through an online "metaconference" established for each seminar. Moderating suggestions also became "reified" into online documents available for members.

The design and goal of the GEN community evolved quickly as its size grew. The monthly seminar series became the backbone of the online community, since all members were automatically registered. A number of additional online activities also emerged: reading groups, an ecafé for socializing, special-interest groups and groups engaged in special projects.

The relationship between GEN and the research projects was relatively informal, in that the GEN community provided feedback on the social and pedagogical designs, content and membership. GEN did, nonetheless, benefit from the research project. At the practical level, funding was provided to hire a part-time coordinator to help manage GEN. Her role was to welcome new members, provide basic training in participation and moderating of the online discussions, troubleshoot and provide technical assistance. She also coordinated volunteers who were interested in moderating the online monthly seminars. With regard to the research activities, GEN members had ongoing opportunities to learn about the latest research findings and also to discuss and debate with researchers who were either directly involved in the research projects or were researching similar topics elsewhere.

The research project also benefited from GEN. GEN user feedback informed ongoing social and technical design of the online educational environment of the Virtual-U software, with respect to online collaborative learning, community and knowledge building. GEN was an opportunity to learn about and study online communities of educational practice, both by members and by researchers. In addition, GEN also assisted in the dissemination of research findings related to online learning and on occasion served as a sounding board for new research ideas.

CONTEXTUAL INDICATORS (QUANTITATIVE DATA) OF SUCCESS

The key indicator of success for any OCoP is basic: is it alive and is it well? The pulse of an OCoP is the level of member activity and participation, and this can be determined through quantitative data. Relatively basic and accessible usage data can provide insight into the life of the community, while qualitative indicators related to social and intellectual activities can illuminate its well-being.

Quantitative and qualitative data provided valuable insights into the level and nature of activity and participation. The Virtual-U software, which provided the GEN platform, was customized to automatically generate a variety of usage statistics to help users, moderators and researchers to monitor and view participation from various perspectives. For example, usage statistics indicate the number of seminars, the number of members, the change in membership numbers per month and level of activity overall as well as in specific categories. Usage data were also automatically generated by the system for each seminar, such as the number of messages in a seminar, number of messages *written* per participant, number of messages *read* per participant, number of messages posted per day, the number of new messages versus replies. Views of each seminar can be organized by date, by sender or by message threads. These data provide a valuable snapshot of which seminars had the most active participants, generated the most comments, the level of interaction and replies and the topics covered by threads. Analysis of message threads in each seminar provided an overview of the flow and development of a topic: showing which thread generated the most (and the fewest) comments and the scope of topics covered in a seminar.

SOCIAL AND INTELLECTUAL INDICATORS

The value of an OCoP such as GEN is the quality of its social and cognitive discourse. Discourse can be studied in online communities. The transcripts of the online text-based discussions are automatically recorded and archived by computer conference, blog or forum software and can be retrospectively studied (given participant consent). Three major types of discourse were analyzed:

1. social discourse
2. intellectual discourse
3. moderating discourse.

SOCIAL DISCOURSE ANALYSIS

The social nature and value of GEN for the members was studied by examining the transcripts of the seminars. Three subcategories of social discourse were examined:

a. community building
b. social engagement
c. user satisfaction.

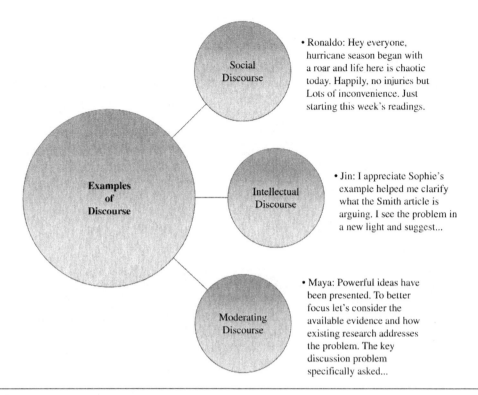

Ronaldo: Hey everyone, hurricane season began with a roar and life here is chaotic today. Happily, no injuries but Lots of inconvenience. Just starting this week's readings.

Jin: I appreciate Sophie's example helped me clarify what the Smith article is arguing. I see the problem in a new light and suggest...

Maya: Powerful ideas have been presented. To better focus let's consider the available evidence and how existing research addresses the problem. The key discussion problem specifically asked...

Figure 9.4 Examples of Discourse.

a. Community building:

Social comments, interactions and friendships form the glue for all communities and motivate active and regular member participation. Analysis of the transcripts determined that the volume of social exchange was approximately 25% of the total discourse in the GEN seminars. Social comments were typically part of a message, usually a prelude to a more substantive contribution. Messages that were entirely social, without any reference to the topic, were rare in the seminars.

Social and humorous discourse was a mechanism for participants to connect with one another, even if they had never met previously. Social comments appeared to spice up the discussion and reduce anxiety or pressure related to an exchange, inviting responses and contributing to a sense of commonalty.

Trust emerged as an important issue for community building and knowledge building. GEN participants noted the importance of trust in the intellectual exchange. Selected comments are presented below, with minor edits. The names have been omitted or changed to protect privacy. Comments are separated by asterisks (***).

I was fascinated to watch how this group managed to (a) make me feel welcome in a field I know little about and (b) convey sufficient atmosphere of trust that I could 'fess up to ignorance of things ... and seek help.

***

During a sharing phase, you test the waters ... and experience how others in the group present themselves. This builds trust and relief leading to confidence (or not) about offering your own linkages (thinking). Eventually, linkages lead (or not) to building (and agreeing to disagree or agree) and/or holding multiple perspectives as a way of appreciating and better understanding the complexity of things—once depth of understanding is collectively sought.

***

I sense that the measure of every step on this path is related to a collective culture of trust. Growth plays itself out in the later stages via the way that conflict among participants is received and engaged, leading to more or less trust and resulting in continued or less engagement.

Social comments should not be confused with comments that are viewed as without significance to the topic. In the quotation below, the role of the moderator is identified as key to encouraging substantive postings.

> I really like how Lucia honed what I was talking about. Empty praise postings (or any kind of empty reaction posts) don't contribute to the cognitive work being done and can be distracting/time-consuming.

Typically social comments are most prevalent at the beginning of a seminar, as a form of ice-breaking and self-introduction. And at the end of the seminar as participants offer concluding remarks, make reference to colleagues in the discussion, comment on the quality of the seminar and/or moderating, and say goodbye to that seminar.

b. Social engagement:
Social engagement refers to the nature and degree which members demonstrate commitment to the community. Both quantitative and qualitative data are illuminating. Active participation in the form of writing comments and responding to others in the seminar is a key indicator of user engagement. For example, during a 12-month period, 4,000 messages were generated in GEN seminars. During this period GEN hosted 30 seminars, averaging 100 messages each. Fifteen metaconferences to orient volunteer moderators averaged 38 messages per conference. In addition a number of SIGs were created but were not studied. Participation levels in GEN were found to be stable year-round. GEN seminars demonstrated a high level of active participation: per week, active participants posted three messages (including replies) and logged in five times.

Another factor that sustained the GEN community was the presence of a committed core of users. Four types of users were identified in the GEN community, according to their level of participation:

- a committed core who participated actively in most of the GEN seminars;
- regular participants who were active in many (about 50%) of the seminars;
- active lurkers who read many of the postings, but who infrequently wrote messages, depending presumably on the subject matter or their availability. GEN had many active lurkers, who regularly read the messages and remained current with the communication flows;
- new participants who had yet to demonstrate a particular pattern of behavior.

GEN seminars reflected high levels of user activity. Active participants would read all the messages in a seminar and post replies, comments, disagreements or questions. Level of user engagement is also reflected in the quality of the messages in a seminar, discussed in the section below, on Intellectual Discourse.

Other indicators of engagement included the voluntary participation in important community building and knowledge-building activities. Examples include: greeting new participants and introducing them to the group dynamics and the technology of GEN; helping to solve problems; providing new sources of information; creating knowledge artifacts such as seminar summaries, tip sheets, FAQs and manuals. For example, one participant introduced the concept and technology of the "wiki wiki" to GEN in the late 1990s, and educated GEN users in its use by using wikis to summarize several GEN seminars. Others provided summaries and syntheses of the seminar using concept mapping tools.

As one participant wrote:

> GEN operates on a basis of shared goals and experiences. Facilitators volunteer their time because they are committed to the advancement of both online education and the GEN community itself.

Another noted:

> The GEN community has evolved according to the needs of its members ... New events are scheduled by topic, so there is always something new and fresh to build expectations. The proposed seminar topics emerge through former discussions, or member suggestions and many participants take on new roles as leaders and facilitators.

c. User satisfaction:

An important indicator of the success of any community is the experience of the participants. A significant source of data on the social value of GEN's online seminars was user-satisfaction reports. Data on GEN user satisfaction were gathered through online interviews, group surveys, seminars on this topic, analysis of the transcripts for user comments and, more informally, through unsolicited email. During its 5-year history, GEN sought feedback from users as part of its process of continuous improvement of GEN's technical and social design. A sample of the comments on user satisfaction include:

> GEN provides an environment for exploration and sharing of ideas, where learning is a collective and participatory process. GEN is unlike traditional teacher professional development, which focuses on individual learning. Rather, collaboration and group learning are emphasized.
>
> ***
>
> GEN offers new opportunities for dialogue across disciplines, geographical borders, professions, levels of expertise, and education sectors.
>
> ***
>
> GEN provides a connection to everyday realities, current thinking and practices of education professionals. Participants typically draw upon their own experiences to link with, extend, or debate the seminar focus and presentations.
>
> ***
>
> There is no need to participate according to a strict structure. Reading along is acceptable and members are encouraged to join a discussion at any time that they have time, feel compelled, or feel comfortable. As such, there is an opportunity to become acculturated and ease in gradually if that suits the individual.

INTELLECTUAL DISCOURSE

Transcript analysis of the seminars was used to study the intellectual content and progress based on the OCL framework presented in Chapter 6. Approximately 75% of the content of the GEN seminars was related to intellectual discourse (the remainder was discourse related to social and procedural issues). Intellectual discourse was categorized according to three types and phases: Idea Generating (brainstorming), Idea Organizing (replying, referencing one another and clustering ideas) and Intellectual Convergence (reflecting final positions). Each online seminar was 2–3 weeks in length. Transcript analysis of the messages in the seminars determined that discourse related to Idea Generating and Idea Organizing (representing Phases 1 and 2) were most common. Intellectual Convergence (Phase 3) occurred when the moderator (or a participant) encouraged final-position statements or when there was a time-sensitive task to complete (such as co-authoring a report, coming to a decision or a position or preparing a presentation for an event).

Qualitative transcript analysis was conducted by coding each message in a seminar according to percentage of the message content that was social or intellectual, and if intellectual, to what degree did a message reflect: (a) Idea Generating, (b) Idea Organizing, or (c) Intellectual Convergence. The level of granularity or specificity of coding was flexible: a message could be coded, for example, as 20% social and 80% intellectual (primarily IG). Or coded at a finer level of analysis, as needed. A finer level of analysis may be desirable for moderators to monitor and facilitate progress. Instructors may wish to assess the seminar or the participant's contribution. Researchers may seek to identify change and progress over time, or to link moderator/instructor roles with discussant discourse. The analytical rubric can be customized according to the task and desired granularity.

Description of the OCL framework and examples drawn from GEN are provided below.

Phase 1: Idea Generating

The nature and quality of the messages is a key indicator. Phase 1 messages typically introduce new ideas and perspectives, and hence are categorized as exemplifying divergent thinking, whereby participants present individual points of view and thereby generate a multiplicity of perspectives. The kinds of discourse typical in this phase include:

- Introductions/initiations/contextualizations: A seminar begins with an introduction to the seminar topic by the moderator and sets the tone and norms for the discussion. Participants respond with self-introductions: "my name is … and I work at…" This typically provides a context for presenting their initial response to the discussion topic.
- Introducing ideas and understandings: This refers to new ideas, beginnings of threads, new topics.
- Opinion: Subjective, personal points of view on a topic.
- Examples: Personal examples drawn from work experience are used to illustrate a position, a particular point, or an opinion.

Phase 2: Idea Organizing

Phase 2 activities are characterized by messages in which participants begin to link ideas, identifying where ideas may be clustered as related, thereby moving from individual comments to collaboration. Phase 2 discussions reflect progress through such quantitative indicators as:

- increased number of reply messages;
- increased number of references to previous messages;
- increased number of references to other participants by name.

Qualitative changes in the nature of the discourse include:

- Agreement/disagreement statements: These statements reference a previous message and may present an alternative point of view or request clarification, for example: "Michelle, your comment really got me thinking about this issue because I don't see it the same way. Can you say more about your concerns?"
- Enhanced individual understanding: This again is a response to previous messages, exemplified by such comments as "now I understand." Such a comment may indicate incorporating a new perspective into one's thinking, elaborating an existing idea with an example, or lead to further questioning.
- Shared understandings: Enhanced individual understanding connects with the collective understanding of terms and/or frameworks.
- Weaving key ideas: Weaving together discrete ideas, and rising above or building on them is an important marker of collaboration:

We find things are really cooking if an author pulls a piece from here and a piece from there, citing more than one previous contributor and weaving multiple ideas together. Often, the most powerful of these kinds of posts offers an analogy that takes off in the community as particularly explaining of explored phenomenon [*sic*].

Phase 3: Intellectual Convergence

Phase 3 messages reflect an increased level of density, for example:

- an increased number of substantive contributions, such as messages that compare, rate, structure, rank or synthesize the ideas discussed;
- increased use of adverbial conjunctions such as: and, or, but;
- increased number of conclusion or position statements.

Phase 3 generally consists of convergence and summaries, or landscapes.
Convergence Typically, convergence is most evident when participants are engaged in co-production, whether it be producing a report, a presentation, a point of view, a work of art or a scientific theory. Few GEN seminars focused on production, but there were cases where the seminar involved organizing a panel presentation. An example of such discourse:

Thanks Mary for keeping us focused. I like the ideas that the seminar has proposed and think that you have done a good job in selecting the top five issues. Debating these five, citing examples from our own experiences with online learning, is a great format.

Summaries/landscape What follows is an excerpt of an online exchange on the topic of creating summaries, landscapes, and sidelines in online seminars and discussions:

Subject: Convergence and summaries
Anyway, we've been talking about effective strategies for summarizing—who should summarize, when, and should there be a term other than "summary". One suggestion is to have a "sideline" type of ongoing summary. (I feel like I'm not explaining this very well!—need pictures!) Have you used similar tools/strategies in your work?

Subject: landscapes instead of summaries

Hi Terry,
We've found the term "landscapes" more useful for this kind of work because the term is not so value-laden or argument-based as a "summary" which is a lens particular to the author (traditionally the group leader, instructor or chief administrator in a business meeting "summarizes" what's been established to this point—from their view).

In describing a landscape, there is more of a sense of the whole in a descriptive sort of way which lessens the pressure for others (readers, in our case) to release other pieces they might have thought worthy until a "summary" was made. Specifically, an author can describe a piece of the landscape, thus leaving it open to bring up and further unpack/explore/re-visit other pieces because they haven't been "discounted" (it's a tone thing more than anything else) in the same way as a summary tends to shed whatever is left out.

It also doesn't require any new "design" features (like a sideline suggests to me, are you thinking of a sort of extra left-hand column?), just training in listening-oriented collaboration.

Subject: re: landscapes instead of summaries

Dear Sara: Landscape. I like it! It sent sparks across my synapses. It provides opportunities to explore the landscape, returning to the same place at different times with new ideas and perspectives.

And you read my mind well, Sara! I was thinking about a sideline tool—something to facilitate the process of pulling out (more like linking to) bits and pieces. But that may be complicating a process that can be achieved nicely within the discussion space itself. Just traversing the landscape of this discussion I continue to pick up new gems I hadn't noticed before, or understand earlier.

MODERATOR DISCOURSE

GEN seminars were launched with a brief presentation by the moderator that posed a topic (problem or discussion question), followed by group discussion that involved debate, multiple perspectives, learning new ideas and coming to some level of convergence, even if it was preliminary. Various approaches to moderating GEN seminar were employed. However, moderator discourse was typically organized around three segments:

1. Introduction—presentation of topic (or problem posing): Each seminar began with a presentation by the moderator: it typically started with welcomes and an introduction to the topic and key question/problem for discussion. Whereas the student-led online seminars described in Chapter 7 posed three discussion questions drawn from the literature, the GEN seminars focused principally on practice-based issues and problems, such as questions related to new pedagogies, technologies or research findings that could advance the field. An overview of the problem helped to anchor the discussion. Seminars generated examples of practice from participants, readings or websites offering specific information, case studies, exemplars, tools, or particular research findings that addressed the problem and contributed to knowledge in the field.
2. Monitoring/facilitating the discussion: This refers to moderator activities to motivate active participation and to keep the discussion focused and progressing. Regular (daily) moderator presence enables the moderator to check and maintain the flow of the

discussion. Moderators can encourage input by requesting comments from participants or directing queries. Phase 1 activities encourage democratic participation and a range of perspectives. Moderators may also encourage feedback whereby participants seek clarification: "What do you mean by that?" "Can you pls. explain that term?" "What are some examples of that approach?" The moderator or the participants may request evidence to create a tone of informed opinion and discourse. "Why do you state a, b and c?" "What is the evidence for that claim?" "Do you know of any research on that position?" These kinds of evidence questions lead to Phase 2, Idea Organizing. Participants begin to reference one another's ideas, and to find linkages. "How does Joe's comment relate to Ira's point?" "Let me elaborate a bit on Ellen's example. I had a similar problem." Some ideas are challenged and dropped, others strengthened. Linking or referencing comments organize the perspectives into common themes or clusters. As much as possible, create the expectation that everyone is learning together to avoid a Q&A (question and answer) session with the moderator. (This is key—feeling the need to respond to each participant plus answer *all* the questions takes too much time and is not effective moderating.)

3. Conclusion: Drawing conclusions and arriving at a position on the topic is an important part of the seminar, reflecting and articulating the knowledge generated through the discourse interaction. This is Phase 3, Intellectual Convergence. Some seminar moderators asked discussants to identify the two most important ideas that each gained, or to vote on a list of five outcomes, or to rank the outputs. Wikis and concept maps were generated. Other seminars co-produced position papers or documents. GEN members noted: "Ideally we like to generate some sort of resource for the public archives as a seminar outcome—for example seminar highlights, annotated resource list, or summary of issues."

Transcript analysis of an online seminar can be valuable for studying the intellectual content and progress of the discussion. It is also valuable to help understand, design and implement online seminars: the framework offers a guide for moderators to facilitate and advance the discussion.

Threading analysis is also useful for the moderator to view and intervene in shaping the conversation flow, to decide which areas of the topic needed (or not) further discussion and, together with qualitative transcript analysis, what type of discussion is required. The moderator could thus assess how the discussion was flowing, both in terms of covering the topic, as well as advancing from divergent Idea Generating to Intellectual Convergence and decide on appropriate interventions.

TECHNOLOGICAL INDICATORS

The quality and ease-of-use of an online community forum is essential to facilitating member participation. A web-based forum should be easy to install, maintain, administer and use. Opensource online forums are emerging and have the advantage that many developers can contribute to build more advanced features. At the same time, there is a challenge to creating open-source educational environments, since the design is not only computational but pedagogical: it requires expertise in how people communicate, collaborate and build knowledge if features to support these key functions are to be developed. This is still a problem in that people with programming talents typically do not have expertise in learning theory and practice, and vice versa: few educators have the technical expertise to build state-of-the-art learning environments. The lack of a theoretical framework to guide the software development can lead to many tools that were developed ad hoc and do not form a coherent whole.

At the same time new technological developments are emerging to assist collaborative learning and knowledge-building processes, such as tools for scaffolds, annotations and multimedia communication (synchronous and asynchronous), and tools to enable online surveys, voting, ranking, rating and usage analyses. A whole new area of qualitative research analysis is emerging with promising research and development in data visualization, semantic analysis and transcript analysis. These can be the basis for discourse analysis and discourse scaffolding features in online education and OCoP applications. The GEN platform, Virtual-U, was an early example of development in this direction. New initiatives are needed to build software tools and cohesive environments that are based on theoretical frameworks like OCL.

GEN CONCLUSIONS AND INITIATIONS: LESSONS LEARNED

GEN lasted for approximately 5 years and came to an end when the research projects concluded. Nonetheless, the OCoP continued in different online venues and forms. For example, the Virtual-U software was adopted by the UN's International Labour Organization and informed the conceptual framework for the AKCIO open-source software developed by the International Labour Organization. The lessons from GEN have influenced not only technical but also educational design for formal (university) and nonformal (training) courses and projects. The transcript-analysis approaches have been refined and used in many online course applications.

Wikipedia

Wikipedia, the largest encyclopedia in history, is a work-in-progress constructed by a huge online CoP and operates as a free, collaborative and open process whereby anyone with Internet access can contribute and/or make changes to the entries. Since its creation in January 2001, Wikipedia has become a premier online reference destination, with approximately 400 million unique visitors per month in 2011. According to the website, in 2011 there were more than 91,000 active contributors working on 16 million articles in over 270 languages. By October, 2011 there were over 3.5 million articles in English and there were over 13 million registered users, including 1,755 administrators. "Every day, hundreds of thousands of visitors from around the world collectively make tens of thousands of edits and create thousands of new articles to augment the knowledge held by the Wikipedia encyclopedia. (See also: Wikipedia:Statistics)" (http://en.wikipedia.org/wiki/Wikipedia:About).

Because of its quality and uniqueness, the process of collaboratively building such a knowledge artifact is important. Wikipedia states that

> People of all ages and cultural and social backgrounds can write Wikipedia articles. Most of the articles can be edited by anyone with access to the Internet, simply by clicking the *edit this page* link. Anyone is welcome to add information, cross-references, or citations, as long as they do so within Wikipedia's editing policies and to an appropriate standard. Substandard or disputed information is subject to removal. Users need not worry about accidentally damaging Wikipedia when adding or improving information, as other editors are always around to advise or correct obvious errors, and Wikipedia's software is carefully designed to allow easy reversal of editorial mistakes. (http://en.wikipedia.org/wiki/Wikipedia:About, retrieved July 27, 2009)

Openness and inclusivity is thus the first feature of the Wikipedia process. The openness, inclusivity, size and scope of Wikipedia require editorial administration, oversight and management. This is a second key feature of the Wikipedia process: editorial administration processes developed to ensure quality, validity, reliability and civility to an appropriate standard. Editorial administration is provided through several mechanisms. Approximately 75,000 editors (volunteers who range from expert scholars to casual readers) regularly edit the articles. Methods such as peer review, article assessment and a featured article process intend to provide a rigorous review of articles in order to meet the highest standards and showcase Wikipedia's capability to produce high-quality work. Editors also provide stylistic consistency by applying the Wikipedia *Manual of Style*. The construction of the manual is another artifact of Wikipedia's collaborative knowledge building.

The administrators working on the English Wikipedia are an important mechanism to maintaining high standards of quality and civil discourse.

> Editors are able to watch pages and techies can write editing programs to keep track of or rectify bad edits. Over 1,500 administrators with special powers ensure that behavior conforms to Wikipedia guidelines and policies. Where there are disagreements on how to present facts, editors work together to arrive at an article that fairly represents current expert opinion on the subject. The administrators can temporarily or permanently ban editors of Wikipedia who fail to work with others in a civil manner.

A central quality of Wikipedia is that, whereby the quality of an article or contribution improves over time, the process is based on a conversation. Over time and with much discussion and editing, the Wikipedia article (and the encyclopedia itself) matures and progresses.

> As a wiki, articles are never complete. They are continually edited and improved over time. In general, this results in an upward trend of quality and a growing consensus over a fair and balanced representation of information.
>
> Users should be aware that not all articles are of encyclopedic quality from the start: they may contain false or debatable information. Indeed, many articles start their lives as partisan; and, after a long process of discussion, debate, and argument, they gradually take on a neutral point of view reached through consensus. Others may, for a while, become caught up in a heavily unbalanced viewpoint which can take some time—months perhaps—to achieve better balanced coverage of their subject. In part, this is because editors often contribute content in which they have a particular interest and do not attempt to make each article that they edit comprehensive. However, eventually, additional editors expand and contribute to articles and strive to achieve balance and comprehensive coverage. In addition, Wikipedia operates a number of internal resolution processes that can assist when editors disagree on content and approach. Usually, the editors eventually reach a consensus on ways to improve the article. (Wikipedia)

By 2011, there were over 450,000,000 edits to the English Wikipedia.

The high level of traffic to Wikipedia generally results in responses, disagreements or reports of errors (although this is not foolproof). Nonetheless, as a work-in-progress and with the input of a diverse, global readership, Wikipedia has the advantages of a short editorial cycle. Unlike a paper encyclopedia, which stays the same until the next edition, editors can update Wikipedia at any time to help ensure that articles stay abreast of the most recent events and scholarship. Wikipedia also has the advantage of multiple perspectives and input, unlike a traditional hardcopy encyclopedia that is the product of a select small group of authors and editors who may represent particular slants or perspectives. There are, nonetheless, strengths and weaknesses to the wiki process.

> Wikipedia is written by open and transparent consensus—an approach that has its pros and cons. Censorship or imposing "official" points of view is extremely difficult to achieve and usually fails after a time. Eventually for most articles, all notable views become fairly described and a neutral point of view reached. In reality, the process of reaching consensus may be long and drawn-out, with articles fluid or changeable for a long time while they find their "neutral approach" that all sides can agree on. Reaching neutrality is occasionally made harder by extreme-viewpoint contributors. Wikipedia operates a full editorial dispute resolution process, one that allows time for discussion and resolution in depth, but one that also permits disagreements to last for months before poor-quality or biased edits are removed. (Wikepedia).

Many other mechanisms for addressing issues of quality exist. For example, technologies to support the open, collaborative and asynchronous nature of the discourse have been constructed and refined. The technologies are open source.

> The MediaWiki software that runs Wikipedia retains a history of all edits and changes, thus information added to Wikipedia never "vanishes". Discussion pages are an important resource on contentious topics. Therefore, serious researchers can often find a wide range of vigorously or thoughtfully advocated viewpoints not present in the consensus article. Like any source, information should be checked. A 2005 editorial by a BBC technology writer comments that these debates are probably symptomatic of new cultural learnings that are happening across all sources of information (including search engines and the media), namely "a better sense of how to evaluate information sources"[4]. (Wikipedia)

Contributions remain the property of their creators, while the Creative Commons Attribution-Sharealike 3.0 Unported License (CC-BY-SA) and the GNU Free Documentation License (GFDL) licenses ensure the content is freely distributable and reproducible.

Toward an Analytical Framework for OCoPs

Understanding how online communities function and can contribute to learning and to building knowledge is a critical area requiring further discussion and research. The availability of system-generated usage statistics and archived transcripts of the discourse offer powerful quantitative and qualitative data for empirical analyses of OCoPs. Such analyses could proceed along many different paths, for such purposes as monitoring, assessment or research. Some suggestions for descriptive analytics are provided below.

Contextual Indicators

Contextual indicators refer to data that help us to understand the setting and the pulse of an OCoP. Both qualitative and quantitative data are valuable for this purpose—whether for perusing OCoPs to determine which ones suit our interest or for more in-depth investigation. Our first connection to any OCoP will be its name, in other words, qualitative data. When we first encounter an OCoP, we are most likely to survey the topics being discussed in order to gain a sense of the nature of the community and its scope. The topics and message subject headers offer an overview of the considerations of the OCoP. Additional data may be obtained through documentation related to the site as well as examining the transcripts for information such as: (a) when the online community was created; (b) its intent or purpose; (c) how it is organized to meet that purpose; (d) the nature of membership; (e) affiliations with other organizations, such as a professional association or a journal.

We then are likely to scan the size and currency of the community, for example by looking at the number of topics being discussed, the size of membership, the level of messaging and the message dates: this information is provided by numbers or quantitative data. For example, what is the level of activity: is the community alive? How do we know? What signs of life are evident? Are messages being posted? How recently? How actively? Are members posting hourly, daily or infrequently? How many topics or forums exist and are active (or inactive)?

Using a sample of the most recent postings, we can determine whether these were sent by many different participants or the same few. Is there an active core group of members?

We can determine level of activity through system-generated usage statistics that are typically available online and/or by "eyeball analysis," simply scrolling through the transcripts to see and count the number of messages, size of messages, date messages were posted and the sender.

What is the size of this community: what is the number of members? how many members are currently active? How long has the community been in existence? Does membership seem to be growing, maintaining, or declining?

Change over time is perhaps the critical benchmark of an OCoP, illuminating community building and knowledge building through both quantitative and qualitative data. These are discussed in the next section on social and intellectual indicators. A subsequent section, technological indicators, explores some of the online tools that can currently be used to analyze quantitative and qualitative data, as well as the promising new advances in areas such as visualization and semantic analysis.

Social and Intellectual Indicators of Success

Study of an OCoP at the contextual level is useful for a general overview or scan of the community. However, to understand the value of an OCoP, it is essential to study community building and knowledge building at a deeper level. Social and cognitive indicators are data that can demonstrate how well the online community is developing/advancing socially and intellectually. Powerful opportunities for discourse analysis are possible online, given the system-generated (and archived) transcripts and usage data. Here we discuss three types of discourse:

- social discourse
- intellectual discourse
- moderating discourse.

SOCIAL DISCOURSE

A key indicator of the success of an online community is active and sustained engagement by the members. The formation of an online community in which members identify themselves as belonging to the group, participate (read and write messages) actively and regularly, and contribute to the sustenance, stability and growth of the community signals an important level of success. Social engagement also reflects intellectual value in an OCoP, since members are motivated to contribute.

Community development and success can be determined by both quantitative and qualitative data. One source of data has already been mentioned in the discussion of contextual indicators: usage statistics can tell us whether the community is alive and well. Levels and volumes of messaging and replies over units of time (hour, day) provide such evidence. Quantitative indicators or measures include system-generated usage statistics such as number of conferences created in a given period of time (a week, month or year); number of messages written per conference in total and per participant; number of messages read per participant; volume of messaging; pattern of messaging (by time of day, by date, by thread or topic) to view ebbs and flows.

Another source of data is user reports. Quantitative data can be compiled through user surveys or polls to determine subjective reports of satisfaction level. Qualitative analysis of the discourse transcripts can identify user comments expressing satisfaction or not. Moreover, the level of social commentary does contribute to and reflect the existence of a community. Social discourse creates social glue: to encourage members to develop friendships and thereby motivate them to participate regularly.

Social discourse occurs in most formal and informal educational settings and can contribute a tone that invites participation. The volume of social comment ranges around 25% of the total exchange, enough to be welcoming but not disrupt the discussions.

Qualitative indicators refers to the nature and quality of the discourse. As noted in Chapter 6, the archivable text-based nature of the discourse enables retrospective analysis. The transcript provides a verbatim copy of the discourse that can then be subject to discourse analysis. Quantitative data and qualitative data are available from the transcripts. Quantitative data are often most easily obtained and analyzed as system-generated usage statistics, which are available on most forum software.

Qualitative data are easily available as the transcripts of the discourse, although few analytical tools and analytical frameworks exist as yet to study online discourse.

INTELLECTUAL DISCOURSE: COLLABORATIVE LEARNING AND KNOWLEDGE BUILDING

Social relationships form an important component in the "glue" of a community. Nonetheless, for online communities of practice, the purpose and the draw is the nature and the quality of the intellectual discourse. The quality of the discourse is what distinguishes an OCoP, and what draws, motivates and sustains active engagement and membership.

Both quantity and quality of messages in an online community offer important indicators of knowledge building and each should be studied and be used to deepen understanding of the nature of engagement and degree of success. Success here is understood as the continuity of activity, nature of activity, and user satisfaction. The quantity of messaging should not be taken as a sole indication of success, but nor should it be ignored. Levels of participation (such as number of messages per day, per person, per topic, size of a message and other quantitative measures) are an obvious and important indicator of the pulse of an online community. It is important in assessing the distribution of communication and the level of democratic participation and verbalization in a group.

Qualitative transcript analysis based on the OCL framework offers indicators or a rubric to understand, monitor, facilitate and assess online collaborative learning and knowledge building discourse. The GEN case example demonstrated the application of this framework in studying the social, cognitive and moderating discourse of that OCoP. Messages in a seminar or discussion can be analyzed as comprising one of three categories or phases of conceptual change: Idea generating, Idea Organizing, Intellectual Convergence. Discourse analysis may identify the predominant type in each message, or assess the level that each type is present in a message.

MODERATING/FACILITATING DISCOURSE

Moderating or facilitating an online discussion benefits from a theoretical framework to guide the process, advance the discourse, and to encourage progress toward intellectual convergence. Many manuals and books on facilitating techniques have been published or posted online, but without a theoretical base whereby to determine what constitutes progress and how to facilitate intellectual convergence. The OCL framework is a contribution to this important area.

Moderating benefits as well from content knowledge, as well as technical skills and experience with group dynamics and problem solving. Conceptual knowledge of the discipline or topic as well as pedagogical knowledge related to collaborative learning and knowledge building are very valuable, and it is expected that knowledge of the latter will grow and improve with experience.

Procedural Indicators

Processes and policies to enable and ensure high quality and fluid progress are essential for any community engaged in knowledge building. The Wikipedia example demonstrated the importance accorded to procedure, in order to develop a process and product of the highest standards. Procedures are continuously being assessed and new processes being developed by Wikipedia. To enable open, inclusive and yet high standards, Wikipedia has implemented a very powerful administrative framework with such components as:

- 75,000 volunteer editors to provide rigorous review of each article submitted;
- a *Manual* for stylistic consistency;
- 1,700 administrators to ensure guidelines and policies are followed;
- open-source tools and software to maintain a historical archive of everything, to facilitate editing and feedback, and other processes;
- a policy of continuous improvement of policy and technology;
- articles that are consensus-based for the general public, and discussion pages for more in-depth exploration of a topic;
- editorial dispute resolution process.

Technological Indicators

The quality and ease of use of an online learning environment is fundamental to its effective use. It should be easy to access, navigate and interpret. The quality of the technology from the user's point of view should be interesting, satisfying and motivating. However, it should also have embedded support for effective collaborative learning and knowledge-building processes. Some of these supports may be scaffolds that fade away as the user gains proficiency. Others may be tools or templates that are always available. Tools that have shown promise within online learning environments for OCoPs and for online courses include: customizable scaffolds for various types of discourse; system-generated usage data; annotation tools; multimedia tools; and usage analysis tools, transcript analysis tools, visualization software and online evaluation tools to support voting, surveys, ranking and rating. Technological designs and environment are of tremendous interest and importance for advancing online education to support collaborative learning and knowledge building.

OCoP Framework for Analysis

Contextual Indicators (quantitative data)

- Level of participation (per person/per day/per topic)
  - active messaging (# of msgs posted pp/pd)
  - active reading (# of msgs read pp/pd)
- Volume of messaging (stabilizing, growing, declining)
- Stability (levels of participation changed over time)
- Existence of active core group
- Longevity (how long has it been around?)
- Change over time in each of the above indicators.

Social and Intellectual Indicators (qualitative data)

- Social discourse
  - community building
  - user engagement
  - user satisfaction
- Intellectual discourse
  - idea generating
  - idea organizing
  - intellectual convergence
- Moderator discourse
  - introductions/context setting/design/agenda
  - monitoring and advancing
  - conclusions/meta analysis.

Procedural Indicators (qualitative data)

- Administrative discourse, establishing
  - goals and objectives (definition of the OCoP)
  - policy guidelines
  - statement of netiquette
  - what is expected of members, role of members
- Coordinating functions
- Policy/procedures implementation.

Technological Indicators

- Ease of use, access
- Availability of features to support collaborative learning and knowledge building, such as:
  - scaffolds for various discourse types
  - visualization tools (qualitative and quantitative)
  - transcript analysis tools
  - usage analysis tools
  - content-generating tools
  - organization and annotation tools
- Quality of system features
- Technical help/assistance.

Summary

Chapter 9 focused on OCL in the context of informal learning, exemplified by online communities of practice (OCoPs). OCoPs function like a knowledge community by building knowledge related to practice. This process is described in some detail in the initial part of the chapter, which focuses on the context of OCoPs. The chapter discusses CoPs and proceeds to provide definitions of key and related terms such as community, community of practice, community of interest, community of learning, work group, social network and online community.

This provided a context for examining specific OCoPs related to the field of educational practice. Chapter 9 did not include examples of online communities that were related to formal or nonformal educational settings since these had been covered in Chapters 7 and 8. Two OCoP examples were presented and described in some detail: the Global Educators' Network (GEN) and Wikipedia. A final section of the chapter considered key indicators of success for an OCoP, such as contextual indicators, social and intellectual indicators, procedural indicators and technological indicators. These indicators, it was suggested, could contribute toward a framework for OCoP analyses.

10
In Retrospect and In Prospect

In Retrospect

In October 1969, the first online message was sent. The message was sent from the University of California, Los Angeles, to the Stanford Research Institute, some hundreds of miles away. The content of the message, a test, was intended to be "LOGIN," but after the first two letters were transmitted the system crashed. Hence the first online message ever sent was "LO."[1] It was sent by an undergraduate student, Charley Kline.

The Internet revolution represents a tiny sliver of time in the history of humanity, and yet the impact has been profound. The growth of the Internet and the Web has been world changing. But the beginnings were small and seemingly inconsequential. The vast majority of scientists, academics and educators initially had no interest in computer communication, and the rest of society and business had even less. By 1981, only 213 computers were on the network. However, by 1995, 16 million people were online. Email was beginning to change the world. As discussed in Chapters 2 and 6, educators and professors were among the early adopters. They had begun to use Arpanet (the precursor to the Internet) in the mid-1970s. The 1980s were a time of educational exploration of this new medium, although the going was tough: the logistics were terrible as network connectivity with schools and homes was sparse. (Schools in the 1980s and even 1990s did not have modem connections and the only phone in the school was usually in the principal's office, who had no interest in classroom use of his phone even if it was a hookup to the sole computer in the school, which was also typically in his office.) Despite the logistical challenges, however, online education took hold even as the field of online technology was taking its baby steps.

The World Wide Web was made public in 1993. In January 1994, there were only an estimated 623 websites online, in total. Then: Amazon was launched online in 1995, Google was launched in 1998, Wikipedia in 2001, Facebook in 2003. In 2001, there were 513 million people online; in 2010, there were two billion.

The Internet has become a condition of daily life in today's world. It is an integral part of our work, social and personal communication. Yet, this is not true for the world of education. The Internet remains largely extraneous to the "real" work of teaching and learning in the class, where it is treated as an add-on. Surprisingly, despite the early sparks of interest and innovation by educators, the Internet revolution has not significantly impacted how we teach.

This chasm has left education seriously isolated from the lives of its students, teachers and the rest of the world. Nonetheless change is imminent. Today everyone in school, college, university and the workplace in most parts of the world has an email account (at least one) and a cell phone, and likely a blog, a website and membership in a social network. Fundamentally, the infrastructure is in place and the users are fluent in its use. It is time for an educational paradigmat shift to transform learning from didactic instruction to the collaborative knowledge-building discourse that reflects and coheres with the 21st-century Knowledge Age.

When early users were first introduced to email and the Internet, the common response was: "What now?" (What do I do with this technology? And why do I need it?) This is similar to the introduction of the telephone in the early 20th century; users were initially suspicious and resistant, and the term "phoney" reflected this negative view of telephone communication. The education system is beginning to overcome its suspicion of online communication and collaboration, but has yet to figure out: What now?

The field of formal education or schooling has historically been uncomfortable with technology, although as this book has argued, learning and technology are integral to human development. Nonetheless, technologies associated with behaviorist, cognitivist and even constructivist learning theories did not have a significant impact on or adoption by the education system. In fact, the inventors of early educational technologies had little contact with teachers and learners, and vice versa. However, as computing and online technologies have mainstreamed, online education has gained ground. Nonetheless, the field remains at an early stage of development, requiring a theory to guide and advance the practice and to ignite the discourse of our knowledge communities toward bolder visions and strategies.

Learning Theories and Online Technologies addresses this need. It examines how learning and technology integrate to advance human development. In particular, *Learning Theory and Online Technologies* has focused on learning theories in the 20th century and introduced Online Collaborative Learning (OCL) as a theory of learning for the 21st century.

As discussed in Chapters 1 and 2, learning has historically shaped and been shaped by technology. Forty thousand years ago, the invention of speech enabled our prehistoric cave-dwelling ancestors to better communicate and learn from one another. Agrarian societies, emerging approximately 10,000 years ago, accumulated production and developed human settlements, and thereby came to require the ability to account for stored goods for purposes of ownership, trade and taxation. Writing was invented to enable the recording of information and its reproduction, transmission and archiving. Literacy, the ability to read and write, required people with the skills to keep records and accounts. Formal instructor-led education was invented to ensure that appropriate literacy skills were taught, learned and assessed.

Until the late 19th century, however, the vast majority of society learned through nonformal education (such as mentorship) and informal (experiential, observational, trial-and-error) approaches to learning. Formal education and schooling, based on literacy, was restricted to a small elite.

The extension of formal education and literacy to the mass population came about only around the 19th century, thousands of years after literacy was invented. The machine age both enabled and required a literate society. The relatively recent invention of the printing press had made reading materials far more available. The rise of the manufacturing era needed literate workers who could read and follow simple instructions to run the machines; this led to mass schooling and the efficient didactic model of learning. The term "didactic" means "intended to teach or to instruct." The term originated in the mid 17th century from the Greek *didaktikos* and *didaskein* ("teach"). The didactic approach focuses on instruction and is teacher-centered.

The rise of manufacturing coincided with the historical period of the scientific revolution. With the rise of modern science, came the development of human sciences such as psychology and by extension, a focus on learning and education. Theories were developed that could be tested by positivist (empirical) methods and which could inform human and natural sciences.

Chapter 1 introduced theory as a point of view or premise whereby we observe and make "sense" of the observations. Learning theory provides educational researchers and practitioners with a framework for viewing the field and for connecting how we understand learning not only with our practice, but with research and with knowledge within our own and in other disciplines.

A theory of learning is based on empirical evidence. A theory asks questions of "why" or "how" and seeks to answer these questions through evidence-based study and by drawing on empirical data and verifiable facts. Until the emergence of positivism in the 19th century, natural philosophy (science) in the Western world was largely based on metaphysical belief or the religious beliefs on the divine origin of thought. Positivism challenged and changed the emphasis from metaphysics to modern science based on empirical evidence. This led to theories of human science, like learning theory, as well as theories of natural sciences. Learning theories do continue to have a relationship with philosophy (such as epistemology and ideology) but are grounded in observable and demonstrable conditions, to physical evidence rather than metaphysical or spiritual explanations.

With the rise of positivism, the emphasis on empirical data and evidence gained authority over belief-generated ideas, contributing to scientific method. Scientific method, prevalent throughout the natural sciences, required "proof" rather than conjecture or "belief." Learning theories were first developed in the 20th century, and the term theory was initially fundamentally linked to positivist science. This has changed in recent decades, as new models of learning are based less on clinical experimentation and are more field-oriented. Chapters 3–5 discuss 20th-century theories of learning, to help us understand the broader field and to reflect on our own ideas and practice.

The earliest theories of learning, behaviorism and cognitivism (discussed in Chapters 3 and 4), were strongly informed by the positivist ethos. Experimental controlled studies in the lab were echoed in instructional theories that were didactic and highly controlled in practice, with the instructor assuming a prescriptive role. The focus was to create explicit conditions for learning that would yield the intended results, in an empirically observable manner. The role of the instructor (or instructional designer) is emphasized over the role of the learner. Instructional design prescribed specific steps to achieve particular results, whether these steps be articulated by the instructor/trainer or embedded in a software to run instructional technologies such as a teaching machine, computer-assisted instruction or intelligent tutoring systems. Effective learning was understood as accurate reproduction and repetition of existing knowledge.

Constructivist learning theory, discussed in Chapter 5, emerged to some degree as a counter position to the objectivist epistemology and instructor-centered approaches that characterize behaviorist and cognitivist learning theory. Constructivism, particularly social constructivism, posited a view of knowledge as constructed through peer discussion and interaction with the environment. Didactic instruction associated with behaviorist and cognitivist theories was critiqued and rejected by constructivist pedagogies in favor of student-centered learning. Constructivist learning pedagogies emphasized active learning and learning-by-doing and characterized education in the 1980s and 1990s.

Chapter 6 presented Online Collaborative Learning (OCL) theory, which focuses on collaborative knowledge-construction discourse mediated by online technologies as a new paradigm for learning to address the challenges and needs of the 21st-century Knowledge Age. The focus of OCL theory is on collaborative discourse and knowledge-building processes associated with knowledge communities. OCL provides a theoretical framework based on three phases of collaborative discourse that progress from divergent thinking to intellectual convergence. These phases characterize conceptual change and knowledge building. They also inform OCL pedagogical and technological design and assessment.

Chapters 7, 8 and 9 provide practical cases to demonstrate how OCL works in the real world, with scenarios and case examples drawn from all sectors of formal, nonformal and informal educational applications. Online education is being successfully adopted and implemented by institutions and organizations worldwide, and the lessons inform OCL theory building and educational practice.

Learning Theory and Online Technologies provides an overview of learning theories in the 20th century and introduces OCL as a 21st-century theory of learning to guide educational practitioners and researchers in realizing the full potential of online technologies for the Knowledge Age. The book provides a retrospective analysis of learning theory but given its vantage point on the cusp of a paradigmatic shift, it has also looked ahead at imminent prospects.

In Prospect

The term *prospect* is rich in meaning: it can be a vision, a promise, a likelihood or an undertaking. As a verb, it denotes exploration. OCL represents and can realize all of these possibilities. Online education, for example, is being designed in myriad ways to revolutionize and improve how we understand and practice learning and knowledge creation. We are on the verge of a breakthrough, beginning to see new educational horizons unlike any known to date. Without becoming futuristic here are some potential scenarios that are already or almost available.

1. Online Communities of Practice: as professional development, lifelong learning and curricula OCoP become a major force in education

One of the major events of the next few decades will almost certainly be an unprecedented investment in professional development and lifelong learning for educators. The dearth of options to date will be addressed in response to the pent-up demand and need. One of the major and most interesting options will arguably be the heightened role of OCoPs for educators. These are already emerging and in fact were among the earliest applications of the Internet in the 1970s and 1980s. OCoPs will grow and improve to become a major force in Knowledge-Age education.

Peer interaction and engagement with experts, scholars and scientists in related fields open unprecedented opportunities for educators to learn, to progress and improve, through participation in the relevant knowledge communities. OCoPs will improve the abilities of educators and expand their opportunities to shape the future. OCoPs can help teachers to improve their disciplinary knowledge skills. For example, participation by science teachers (at all levels) in online communities of knowledge enables school teachers to engage in scientific discourse and research and thereby learn the concepts, appreciate the scope and nature of the issues and understand the methodologies whereby these issues are addressed empirically. OCoPs could similarly benefit teachers and scholars in other fields. OCoPs do already reflect a variety of knowledge practices, from the more pragmatic to the highly conceptual and educators in the discipline can both contribute to and learn from participation.

School curricula might similarly be transformed by engaging students as well in online knowledge community discussions, at various levels of theory and practice. Many opportunities can be envisioned as students and teachers engage in OCoPs, with peers, scholars, scientists and practitioners in the discipline. Online discourse communities might be one way to transform classroom, curriculum and pedagogy to advance beyond "teaching to the test."

2. Open Source, Open Knowledge have a tremendous impact on how we think about design, process and product, and who can engage in these activities

The rise of the open-source movement in software and subsequently in educational resources and curriculum has introduced a radical departure from commercial off-the-shelf, prepackaged content to free, user-created designs, content and products. Open Knowledge is a term used to denote a set of principles and methodologies related to the production and distribution of knowledge goods in an *open* manner. Knowledge is interpreted broadly to include data (for example, scientific, historical), content (such as music, books, video) and general information. As set out in the Open Knowledge Definition, knowledge is open if "one is free to use, reuse, and redistribute it without legal, social or technological restriction" (see www.opendefinition.org).

Open knowledge and open content have led to the creation of large non-commercial repositories of data, information and content such as educational course manuals, lesson plans, etc. The availability of open-content repositories and directories such as the OpenCourseWare Consortium (a portal linking to free and openly licensed course materials from universities worldwide), the MIT OpenCourseWare site with materials from 2,000 MIT courses or repositories of curricula that cover almost all disciplines and levels from schooling to training, is truly remarkable. The challenge is how to use and benefit from these curricula. The options range from outright adoption of these course curricula to modifying or adapting the content or to using the material as a benchmark or even inspiration for new pedagogies or ways of teaching particular concepts.

Without theoretical or pedagogical frameworks however, there is a high risk of teachers importing or reproducing the content and employing didactic teaching approaches at the expense of encouraging learners to construct knowledge and create their own content. The intent of open content may be excellent, but the implementation requires careful consideration.

3. State-of-the-Art Technological Advances: Semantic webs, visualization and other analytic tools will transform and enhance learning, teaching and the study of learning

The Semantic Web vision was conceived by Tim Berners-Lee, the inventor of the World Wide Web. Calling it the next step in Web evolution, Berners-Lee describes the Semantic Web as a web of data that can be processed directly and indirectly by computers.

The Web as we know it is an amazing repository of documents, with almost boundless amounts of information. However, while our web browsers can easily access this information, it must be read and analyzed by humans in order to extrapolate any useful conclusions or insights. The developers of the Semantic Web propose to have data as well as documents on the Web so that computers can process, transform, organize and even act upon the data in useful ways. In the Semantic Web data itself will become part of the Web and be able to be processed independently of application, platform or domain.

New developments and experimentation with new qualitative and quantitative analytical tools such as latent semantic analysis, text mining and data mining promise powerful and much-needed advances for the study and practice of learning. Visualization tools to graphically represent data can help us to understand social and cognitive processes in online education. Such tools are beginning to emerge. Visualization software that is simple to use and which can reflect change over time (such as line charts) is of particular value to educational transcript analysis and visualization—for educators, learners and researchers.

4. Increased Magnitude of Computing Power and Storage

New computing tools are emerging at a tremendous rate to create qualitatively new dimensions of discourse, collaboration and knowledge construction. Cloud computing, for example, is dramatically expanding computing power and capabilities. Cloud applications such as powerful repositories of information are being linked with problem-solving analytical tools to enrich online collaboration and knowledge building. Nanotechnology, the science of building machines at the subatomic level and scale, suggests profound implications for educational software and hardware, radically revolutionizing social, physical and intellectual architecture.

The scale of change in computer processing and storage will be increasingly astounding, as evidenced below.

Bit: A Bit is the smallest unit of data that a computer uses. It can be used to represent one of two states of information, such as Yes or No. This was the earliest computing power, akin to Turing's computer.

Byte: A Byte is equal to 8 Bits. 1 Byte could be equal to one character; 10 Bytes could be equal to a word.

Kilobyte: A Kilobyte is approximately 1,000 Bytes (actually 1,024). 1 Kilobyte would be equal to this paragraph, whereas 100 Kilobytes would equal an entire page. The Commodore 64 and Apple IIe computers of the early 1980s had 64 Kilobytes of memory.

Megabyte: A Megabyte is approximately 1,000 Kilobytes. 100 Megabytes will hold two volumes of an encyclopaedia.

Gigabyte: A Gigabyte is approximately 1,000 Megabytes. 100 Gigabytes could hold the entire library floor of academic journals.

Terabyte: A Terabyte is approximately one trillion Bytes, or 1,000 Gigabytes. A Terabyte could hold 1,000 copies of the *Encyclopaedia Britannica*. 10 Terabytes could hold the printed collection of the Library of Congress. Cellphones and personal computers are rapidly approaching this capacity.

Petabyte: A Petabyte is approximately 1,000 Terabytes or one million Gigabytes. 1 Petabyte could hold 500 billion pages of standard printed text.

Exabyte: An Exabyte is approximately 1,000 Petabytes or one billion Gigabytes.

Zettabyte: A Zettabyte is approximately 1,000 Exabytes.

Yottabyte: A Yottabyte is approximately 1,000 Zettabytes. It would take a few trillion years to download a yottabyte file from the Internet using high-power broadband.

We can see the story of human communication in reverse, in terms of today's technological storage capacity of human communication:

1 Yottabyte = the Web
5 Exabytes = speech: all the words ever spoken by mankind
5 Petabytes = printed text: most of the words ever printed by mankind.

The Internet Revolution introduced us to unprecedented access to other people. We now interact with friends, family, peers, colleagues, experts and relevant others on a local and global basis. We are a species distinguished by intentional collaboration and communication. Our survival and development is based on our ability to collaboratively learn and innovate. Online communication has exponentially expanded as well as transformed our opportunities to learn and create knowledge together. Schools, laboratories, libraries and knowledge communities of the 21st century will be networks. Online networks, by facilitating collaboration and discourse, have become crucibles for knowledge and innovation. Teachers and learners today have the fortunate opportunity to contribute to and participate in shaping this new online environment, and thereby, most importantly, fully engage in their mission of advancing the conversation of humankind.

Glossary

Army University Access Online (eArmyU): A program by the US Army to provide access to education via computer communications for its soldiers around the world. Key eArmyU members are IBM Business Consulting Services, the Council on Academic Management, learning technology and infrastructure support providers and a group of 30 educational institutes which provide more than 145 degree or certificate courses entirely over the Web.

Arpanet: The precursor network to the Internet. It was established in 1969 when the US Advanced Research Projects Agency (ARPA) created a wide-area network between computer systems in four universities. The network used a newly created technology, packet switching, which allowed the breaking up of electronic signals into small units of information called packets which could be routed over different pathways and reconstituted at their destination. In the 1970s the development of TCP/IP protocols enabled the expansion of the original project to become a network of networks, the Internet.

Asynchronous: Originally used to refer to data transmission without the use of a clock to coordinate (synchronize) the data transfer. The term has come to mean communication occurring at different times such as when users send email messages to each other that are stored until read by the recipient.

Asynchronous online learning: The use of computer communications to enable learners to participate in common educational activity without having to be in communication at the same time.

Asynchronous online forums: A group communication software on the Web/Internet where users can enter (post) messages and read messages which have been left by other users at other times.

Bitnet: A computer communications network founded in 1981, which allowed mainly university-based users to transmit messages and files. By 1991 it had some 500 organizations hosting more than 3,000 nodes (points of communication). With the advent of the Internet in the early 1990s Bitnet began to decline in usage and by 2000 had ceased to exist. It is still remembered for having created the first Multiuser Dungeon game in 1981.

Blended delivery: In the context of education, refers to the use of a combination of technologies and locations such as communications, classroom activities, teleconferencing and/or videoconferencing to create learning situations. Also referred to as blended mode.

Blended learning: Refers to the use of a combination of learning environments, particularly the mix of online learning with onsite classroom education.

Blog: A website used by an individual on a continuing basis to post comments, opinions, diaries and other personal communications mainly in text but increasingly incorporating videos, graphics and images; blogs are associated with online journalism and the word "blog" is a contraction of the phrase "web log."

Bits per second (bps): The rate at which one computer bit—a 0 or a 1—can be transmitted to or from a communications device such as a modem in one second. The rate is usually expressed in thousands (Kilobits or Kbits), millions (Megabits or Mbits) or billions (Gigabits or Gbps).

Case-based learning (CBL): A method of learning where students use real-world examples to build knowledge in a particular discipline.

Computer-assisted instruction (CAI): Computer software offering instructional modules or programs. The student proceeds through the prescribed material following the instructions provided by the software to do the readings and the assignments using an individualized self-paced pedagogy. There is no immediate feedback from human instructors. Users interact with the computer at their own speeds, on their own. Common CAI activities include: drill-and-practice arithmetic, language tutorials, educational games and basic computer simulations.

CERN: The French acronym for the European Organization for Nuclear Research, which is the world's largest particle physics laboratory. Based in Geneva on the French border, CERN has 20 European state members with over 2,000 employees and 7,000 affiliated researchers worldwide. It is the birthplace of the World Wide Web.

Chat groups: Online discussions in which participants enter comments and read messages from other participants in synchronous (real) time, as the messages are being entered.

Cloud computing: A method of computing which, rather than depending on personal computers or local network servers, relies on sharing computer resources to provide supercomputing power. To do this, large groups of servers, usually personal computers, are connected via high-speed transmission systems so they can share data-processing resources and tasks.

Computer-based training (CBT): See **Computer-assisted instruction**

Computer conferencing/forums: Computer software designed to support group communication, connected to a network system such as the Web/Internet whereby users can enter (post) messages and read messages which have been left by others. Conferencing or forum software organizes messages by topic—and within each topic the software can present the messages in different configurations, such as by date or author—provides editors for creating, formatting and spellchecking messages and includes options such as online libraries to store files.

Computer conferencing systems: Computer programs that provide computer conferences or forums in which users can read and leave messages. See **Computer conferencing/forums**.

Content management system (CMS): Computer programs which are used to manage, search and present various kinds of digital media and electronic text. In educational situations they are used to provide facilities such as forums, online quiz tools, student lists, online gradebooks and other administrative tools.

CSILE (Computer-supported Intentional Learning Environment): Is a computer-based learning environment and communal database, with both text and graphics capabilities. This networked multimedia environment allows students to generate "notes" containing an idea or piece of information relevant to the topic under study. Notes are available for other students to comment upon, leading to dialogues and an accumulation of knowledge. CSILE was developed by Marlene Scardamalia and Carl Bereiter at the Ontario Institute for Studies in Education.

Discussion forum software: See **Computer conferencing/forums**

Distance learning: Learning activities which occur when instructors and students are separated by geography and time. Distance learning employs a correspondence model in which learning materials are sent to the student who completes and submits the assigned work. The student also has access to a tutor for assistance. Enabling communication technologies include the postal system, telephones, television, videoconferencing, email and computer conferencing/forums.

Distributed problem-based learning: An educational process in which students and instructors, separated by geography and time, participate in collaboratively solving problems. The students work in small groups to study and resolve open-ended problems. The teachers become guides and facilitators of the process.

Download speed: The speed at which electronic data (such as a file, email or video) is transferred from the sending computer to the receiving computer. Speed is measured in kilobits (kps), megabits (mbps) and gigabits (gbps).

EARMYU or eArmyU: See **Army University Access Online**

Educational CMC/Elearning: Educational Computer Mediated Communications (CMC) is the use of computer communication technology to enable educational processes. The term was widely used in the 1980s and 1990s but has been supplanted by the terms elearning or online education.

Enhanced/adjunct mode: Use of online learning to enhance traditional face-to-face or distance education curriculum, but not as a substitute. Enhanced or adjunct mode is distinguished from mixed-mode/blended or totally online mode because enhanced involves minor use of online activities.

Facebook: A social networking website which allows users to join geographic or interest-based networks to interact with other users. People can add friends to their personal lists, create personal profiles and send messages.

Face-to-face (f2f): In an educational context face-to-face refers to students and instructors being in the same physical space (onsite) at the same time.

Flickr: A video-hosting and image-storing website which includes computer conferences/forums. Used by people to share photographs or as depositories attached to their blogs.

Formal education: Primary, secondary, post-secondary and tertiary institutions of learning accredited by a government agency.

Forums: See **Computer conferencing/forums**

Hypermedia: The linking of several types of media such as text, graphics, audio and video. Usually associated with the World Wide Web.

Hypertext: Text (usually) online, in a form readable by a web browser, in which the reader navigates from one section of text to another (on the same or another computer) by clicking on words or phrases called hyperlinks which include directions to the other sections.

Hypertext links or **links**: The words or phrases which can be read by a web browser as directions to other text, images, videos and other elements on the World Wide Web.

Immersive learning environments: Technologically-created 3-D environments that seem to surround the user, used in computer-based games, simulations, virtual reality and data visualization.

Individualized instruction: An instructional method which prescribes the media, content, training materials and pace of learning to be used to accomplished pre-established learning objectives. Self-assessment such as multiple-choice quizzes are often included, to evaluate progress and progress to the next level module.

Industrial model of education: A perspective and practice of education inspired by the industrial assembly line in which students are grouped by age and grade or subject-matter cohorts, and advance as each group concludes the year or semester. Based on testing or other forms of assessment, most will progress while perhaps some will fail and repeat or leave the system. It has been the norm in educational institutes since the start of the 19th century, with the rise of industrialization and the concomitant need for mass literacy and the ability to read and follow instructions.

Instant messaging: Text-based computer messaging that takes place between two people synchronously (i.e., in "real time")—when both participants are online at the same time. The text is transmitted using devices connected to a network such as the Internet.

Internet: A global network of computers which allows users to communicate and share information using technologies such as electronic mail (email), instant messaging, file transfer and file sharing. A section of the Internet is the World Wide Web which includes pages of text, images and other media that include links to other similar elements on the Web. Data on the Internet is transferred using "packet switching" whereby data is broken up into many "packets" for transmission and then reconstituted at the receiving end. The transfer of the packets is completed according to the TCIP/IP set of technical rules and procedures. Physically the Internet consists of millions of public, private, academic, government and business networks which are linked by copper wires, fiber-optic cables, wireless connections and other technologies such as satellites.

Internet-based application: A software tool that is accessed or used via the Internet. Many applications are operated through a web browser. Common web applications include email, online retail sales, banking systems, wikis and computer conference/forums.

Knowledge community: Refers to groups associated with a particular field or discipline. It is the work of the members of a knowledge community to define the state of the art and to advance that state in a particular discipline or field of work.

Learning management system (LMS): See **Content management systems**

Listserv: Launched in 1986 Listserv was the first emailing list software application, a tool for sending emails to many addressees. It was one of the early systems developed for group mailing lists, and was used to create online communities. The list serving computer has an email address to which members of the list send their emails. The server then distributes the emails that it receives to all members in the list. It works somewhat like an Internet forum, but the messages are sent and received as emails. The term listserv is often used to refer to email list applications, but Listserv is a commercial product. Other email list programs exist.

Many-to-many communication: A communication paradigm which describes a process by which many people can use shared technologies to send and receive information to each other via the Internet. The technologies used to put the process into action include file sharing and wikis.

Mixed-mode or **mixed mode learning:** See **Blended learning**

Moderator: A person responsible for initiating, guiding, monitoring and evaluating discussions in computer conferences or forums. In an educational setting the moderator may be the course instructor or a student or group of students. If the course is being conducted according to collaborative learning principles participants are often asked to take on the role of the moderator for sections of the course. Moderating an educational forum involves setting tasks for the group, providing resource materials, creating weaving comments to summarize the discussion and steer it in new directions, ensuring that participants behave according to policies such as mutual respect, helping with technical problems and gauging the amount of conceptual change (learning) which has occurred.

MySpace: A social networking site which allows users to create networks of friends, create personal profiles, operate blogs and communicate in groups plus store photos, music and videos. It is owned by Fox Interactive Media, a unit of News Corporation. A similar service is **Facebook**.

Online: In computer technology online refers to a state in which a system (for example, a personal computer) is connected to a communication network such as the Internet and is operational. The term has been expanded to refer to activities (such as educational computer conferencing/forums) and people—who are described as "being online" when they are communicating via the Web or Internet.

Online collaborative learning (OCL): Learning theory and practice based on collaborative learning and knowledge-building discourse modeled on knowledge communities. The role of the instructor is as representative of the knowledge community, inducting students into the conceptual framework and terms and their applications in solving problems and creating knowledge and innovation, constructing plans or developing explanations for phenomena.

Online courseware (OC): Also known as Online Computer-based Training (OCBT); refers to the use of self-paced and modular courseware (pre-packaged content) prescribed by an instructional designer that can be accessed by the learner online.

Online distance education (ODE): Primarily based on traditional 20th-century distance education delivery models, but replaces postal-mail delivery with the cheaper, faster and more efficient email delivery of course materials and tutor feedback.

Online education: Learning or training conducted via a computer network, such as the Internet and the World Wide Web, a local area network (LAN), or an intranet (a closed private network). Related terms are educational CMC, elearning, online learning. See **Educational CMC/Elearning**.

Online forum: Online discussion site open to all members of the network or made private to a subset. The sites are asynchronous which means that users enter and read messages in the forums at times of their choosing, not at the same time as the other forum members. Facilities are provided for filtering messages according to date, author, subject and other factors. Online forums are used by social networking sites, institutes which provide education that have discussion components (as in online collaborative learning) and technical support services. See **Computer conferencing/forums**.

Online learning: Learning that involves the use of computer networks such as the Internet, World Wide Web or Local Area Networks. It can be synchronous (for example, using videoconferencing) or asynchronous (i.e., using computer conferencing), instructor-facilitated or solely computer-based. Related terms are educational CMC, elearning, online education. See **Educational CMC/Elearning**.

Open-source software: Computer software that is available free of charge and for which the programming source code is available for modification and redistribution in the modified form. It is released under various software licenses, which permit people to use, change and distribute the software in ways that would normally be determined by copyright restrictions. It is often developed by communities of programmers working publicly and collaboratively. Its historical development has resulted in the use of a number of terms. It was first termed "free" software in 1983 in order to emphasize the social and political as well as technological issues related to producing software that could be used, modified and redistributed without charge. The term "open source" was coined in 1998 to de-emphasize the social and political aspects. Both streams are often recognized with the use of the phrase "open source, free, software." Other descriptors are FOSS (free, open source software) or FLOSS (free, libre, open source software).

Packet-switching networks: Communication systems in which messages are divided into packets before they are transmitted. The packets are sent individually and can follow different network paths to their destination. When all the packets which make up a message arrive at their destination, they are reconstituted into the original message. The Internet is based on a packet-switching protocol (a set of technical rules and regulations) called TCP/IP.

Podcasting: Online radio shows or audio broadcasts that can be produced by and downloaded to an iPod, MP3 player or smartphone. Anyone with access to these devices can broadcast their digital audio and video files on the Web. The term comes from a linking of iPod (the MP3 player produced by Apple Inc.) and broadcast. A podcast can refer to a file or related set of files or the content of those files. The person who creates the files is called a podcaster.

Qualitative scientific research: Research which uses inductive methods and observation in the field in order to develop theoretical constructs which can be used to guide further field work and analysis. The data produced are in the form of words, pictures, audio, video or objects. The aim of qualitative research is a more complete and detailed description than might be provided with the use of solely quantitative research.

Quantitative scientific research: Scientists use the deductive method to make predictions and formulate hypotheses which they test by collecting and analyzing numerical data through observation and experimentation. The data gathered during quantitative research is usually presented in the form of numbers and statistics. Quantitative research has been the main approach applied in disciplines such as natural sciences, applied sciences and such social sciences as psychology, sociology and anthropology.

Roleplay: A learning process in which participants act out roles or characters in an educational situation provided by the instructor or devised collaboratively by the students. Also used to refer to adopting a character and playing a role in an online computer game.

Search engine: A computer program that retrieves documents, files or data from a computer network (such as the Internet) or a database. There are two basic kinds of Web-based search engines: *general* (also called generic or horizontal) and *specialized* (also called topical or vertical). General search engines, such as Google, Yahoo! or MSN, are aimed at indexing the whole Web. Specialized engines are focused on a specific number of sites chosen by a person or team working within a particular topic or discipline.

Second Life: A virtual world accessible via the Internet which allows users to interact with one other through the use of avatars (graphic, text, video or icon representations of themselves). Users can explore the virtual world, socialize with other users, create and trade virtual property and services (content which exists solely in the world) and participate in group activities.

Simulation: The technique of representing the real world by a computer program. For example, a flight simulator is a computer program that simulates the conditions of flying an actual airplane.

Skype: A commercial application of a Voice Over Internet Protocol (VoIP) technology that allows users of the service to place audio calls to each other and call telephones not connected to the service. In addition to standard telephone calls, Skype enables file transfers, texting (the sending of short text-based messages), video chat and videoconferencing. The service is available for personal computers and other mobile devices, including cellphones.

Social networking: The process of participating in a social structure consisting of individuals, groups or organizations which are connected by one or more types of interdependencies such as friendship, kinship, sexual relationships, commercial ties or particular ideas, goals, values and visions. Online social networks as a genre began in 2004 with MySpace and the rise of what is known as Web 2.0, although social networking online has been a major use of the Internet since its earliest Arpanet and Bitnet days.

Synchronous communication: Originally a reference to computer operations synchronized by the use of a clock but expanded to refer to communications between people in real time. Telephone calls are examples of synchronous communications. Chatting on computer systems (the sending of short text messages by people on the system at the same time) is also synchronous.

Text-based communication: Online communication which utilizes solely text such as emailing, computer chats and cellphone twitters and texting.

Totally online mode: (Educational) activities conducted completely via a computer network such as the Internet or Local Area Networks (LANs), as contrasted with *blended* which refers to the use of both face-to-face (onsite) interaction and online communications in an educational situation.

User-generated content: Various kinds of media content that are produced by end-users, as opposed to traditional media producers, licensed broadcasters and production companies. The content may be news, gossip, opinions, research or other material presented or contributed by the end-user of a medium or service on that medium. The technologies involved in the generation of end-user content include blogging, digital video, podcasting, photography, wikis, forums and question–answer databases.

Weaving: The summing up of discussion in a computer conference/forum which refers to ideas and information in the contributions made by participants in order to categorize them, point to similarities and highlight agreement or disagreement with a view to moving the discussion in new directions, such as the next section of a course syllabus.

Web 1.0: Refers to the state of the World Wide Web and any website design style and technology used before the advent of the **Web 2.0**.

Web 2.0: Refers to the movement away from static web pages (which simply present information to the reader), to a Web characterized by dynamic information (information which changes), shareable content and social networking.

Web-based forums: See **Computer conferencing/forums**

Web-based technology: Technologies such as browsers, search engines and computer languages that utilize or enhance operations on the World Wide Web. A browser is a web-based technology, which allows the information on web pages to be seen in various ways. A search engine is a technology that can be used for indexing web pages. An example of a Web-based language is XML (Extensible Markup Language) which is a format for creating structured computer documents, primarily on the Web.

Web browsers: A computer program which allows users to view and interact with text, images, videos, music, games and other information typically located on a web page at a website on the World Wide Web or a Local Area Network.

Web-mediated communication: The use of the World Wide Web for communication including web-based email, social networking sites, forums, instant message and other systems for transmitting information.

Website: A collection of computer files on a computer attached to the Internet. The files are formatted with codes defined by the Hypertext Transfer Protocol (HTTP) or extensions of it such as XML (Extensible Markup Language) which provide a set of rules for exchanging files (text, graphic images, sound, video and other multimedia files) on the World Wide Web. Web pages often include hypertext links which are used to provide connections between elements such as text or images on a web page sitting on the serving computer or other computers connected to the Web.

Wikis: A wiki is a collection of web pages designed to enable anyone with access to contribute or modify their content using a simplified markup language that provides formatting commands and codes. They are often used to create collaborative websites such as the collaborative encyclopaedia Wikipedia.

World Wide Web: A collection of Internet sites which use the Hypertext Transfer Protocol (HTTP) to present text, graphics, sound, animation resources and video which can be read by a web browser. Sometimes, incorrectly, used as synonymous with the Internet.

YouTube: A video-sharing website where users can upload, view and share video clips.

Notes

1 Introduction to Learning Theory and Technology

1. *Handbook of Education Psychology*, volume I and II.

2 Historical Overview of Learning and Technology

1. The term incunabula refers to the earliest printed books of a genre, often used exclusively to mean those printed before 1501. It is derived from the Latin word *cunae*, meaning "cradle" (http://north-woodsbookshop.com/bkterm.htm).
2. The prefix "hyper" (from the Greek prefix meaning "over" or "beyond") signifies overcoming the limitations of linear text by a system that creates linkages and enables multiple pathways through text or media. Hypertext is used to cross-reference collections of data in online documents, software applications or books and can develop very complex and dynamic systems of linking and cross-referencing. Many consider the most famous implementation of hypertext to be the World Wide Web.

3 Behaviorist Learning Theory

1. Phlogiston refers to a hypothetical substance once imagined to be the cause of all combustion and the principle of fire. *Vis anima* is related to the divine spark of life, the inner self, the life force.

8 OCL Cases of Institutional Innovation

1. Association of Public Land-grant Universities, formerly known as National Association of State Universities and Land-Grant Colleges (NASULGC).

9 OCL Scenarios: Online Communities of Practice

1. GEN was related to projects studying online education, funded by Canada's TeleLearning Network of Centers of Excellence (Harasim, 2006a).

10 In Retrospect and In Prospect

1. Samuel Morse, 125 years earlier, had sent the first telegraph message: "What hath God wrought?".

References

Allen, B. S. & Otto, R. G. (1996). Media as lived environments: The ecological psychology of educational technology. In David H. Jonassen (Ed.), *Handbook of research for educational communications and technology* (pp. 199–225). New York: Macmillan.

Allen, I. E. & Seaman, J. (2003). *Sizing the opportunity: The quality and extent of online education in the United States, 2002 and 2003.* Needham, MA: The Sloan Consortium. Retrieved November 26, 2009 from: www.sloan-c.org/publications/survey/pdf/sizing_opportunity.pdf.

Allen, I. E. & Seaman, J. (2004). *Entering the mainstream: The quality and extent of online education in the United States, 2003 and 2004.* Needham, MA: The Sloan Consortium. Retrieved November 26, 2009 from: www.sloan-c.org/publications/survey/pdf/entering_mainstream.pdf.

Allen, I. E. & Seaman, J. (2007). *Online nation: Five years of growth in online learning.* Needham, MA: The Sloan Consortium. Retrieved November 26, 2009 from: www.sloan-c.org/publications/survey/pdf/online_nation.pdf.

Allen, I. E. & Seaman, J. (2008). *NASULGC–Sloan national commission on online learning benchmarking study: Preliminary findings.* Needham, MA: The Sloan Consortium. Retrieved November 26, 2009 from: www.sloan-c.org/publications/survey/nasulgc_prelim.

Allen, I. E. & Seaman, J. (2010). *Learning on demand: Online education in the United States, 2009.* Needham, MA: The Sloan Consortium. Retrieved January 18, 2010 from: www.sloanc.org/publications/survey/pdf/learningondemand.pdf.

Allen, I. E., Seaman, J. & Garret, R. (2006). *Blending in: The extent and promise of blended education in the United States.* Needham, MA: The Sloan Consortium. Retrieved November 26, 2009 from: www.sloan-c.org/publications/survey/pdf/Blending_In.pdf.

Andre, T. & Phye, G. D. (1986). Cognition, learning, and education. In G. D. Phye & T. Andre (Eds.), *Cognitive classroom learning.* Orlando: Academic Press.

Ashburn, E. (2006). Online courses fuel growth in colleges' continuing education programs. *Chronicle of Higher Education.*

Bacsich, P. (2005). Lessons to be learned from the failure of the UK e-university. Retrieved November 26, 2009 from: www.odlaa.org/events/2005conf/ref/ODLAA2005bacsich.pdf.

Barab, S., Kling, R. & Gray, J. (Eds.) (2004). *Designing for virtual communities in the service of learning.* Cambridge: Cambridge University Press.

Barab, S., MaKinster, J. & Scheckler, R. (2004). Designing system dualities: Characterizing an online professional development community. In S. Barab, R. Kling & J. Gray (Eds.), *Designing for virtual communities in the service of learning* (pp. 53–90). Cambridge: Cambridge University Press.

Bates, A. W. (2000). *Managing technological change.* San Francisco, CA: Jossey-Bass.

Bates, A. W. & Poole, G. (2003). *Effective teaching with technology in higher education: Foundations for success.* San Francisco, CA: Jossey-Bass.

Bates, A. & Sangra, A. (2010). *The integration of technology within universities and colleges.* San Francisco: Jossey-Bass.

Belanger, M. (2007). *Online collaborative learning and the training of union staff in developing countries.* PhD dissertation. Simon Fraser University, Vancouver, Canada.

Bereiter, C. & Scardamalia, M. (2003). Learning to work creatively with knowledge. In E. De Corte, L. Verschaffel, N. Entwistle & J. van Merriënboer (Eds.), *Unravelling basic components and dimensions of powerful learning environments.* EARLI Advances in Learning and Instruction Series. Retrieved from http://ikit.org/fulltext/inresslearning.pdf.

Bereiter, C., & Scardamalia, M. (2006). Education for the knowledge age: Design-centered models of teaching and instruction. In P. A. Alexander & P. H. Winne (Eds.), *Handbook of educational psychology* (2nd ed., pp. 695–713). Mahwah, NJ: Lawrence Erlbaum Associates.

Berners-Lee, T. (1999). *Weaving the Web: The original design and ultimate destiny of the World Wide Web by its inventor.* New York: Harper Collins.

Bloom, B., Englehart, M. Furst, E., Hill, W. & Krathwohl, D. (1956). *Taxonomy of educational objectives: The classification of educational goals. Handbook I: Cognitive domain.* New York, Toronto: Longmans, Green.

Bodner, G. M. (1986). Constructivism: A theory of knowledge. *Journal of Chemical Education, 63,* 873–878.

Bredo, E. (2006). Conceptual confusion and educational psychology. In P. A. Alexander & P. H. Winne (Eds.), *Handbook of educational psychology* (2nd ed., pp. 29–42). Mahwah, NJ: Lawrence Erlbaum Associates.

Brown, J. S. & Duguid, S. (2000). *The social life of information.* Cambridge, MA: Harvard Business School Press.

Bruffee, K. A. (1999). *Collaborative learning: Higher education, interdependence, and the authority of knowledge,* 2nd ed. Baltimore, MD: Johns Hopkins University Press.

Bruner, J. S. (1962). Introduction. In L. S. Vygotsky, *Thought and language.* Cambridge, MA: MIT Press.

Burton, J. K., Moore, D. M. & Magliaro, S. G. (1996). Behaviorism and instructional technology. In D. H. Jonassen (Ed.), *Handbook of research for educational communications and technology* (pp. 46–73). New York: Simon & Schuster Macmillan.

Bush, V. (1945). As we may think. *Atlantic Monthly, 176*(1), 101–108.

Calfee, R. C. (2006). Educational psychology in the 21st century. In P. A. Alexander & P. H. Winne (Eds.), *Handbook of educational psychology* (2nd ed., pp. 43–57). Mahwah, NJ: Lawrence Erlbaum Associates.

Chomsky, N. (1959). A review of B. F. Skinner's *Verbal Behaviour. Language, 35*(1), 26–58.

Clark, A. (2001). *Mindware: An introduction to the philosophy of cognitive science.* New York: Oxford University Press.

Collison, G., Elbaum, B., Haaving, S. & Tinker, R. (2000). *Facilitating online learning: Effective strategies for moderators.* Madison, WI: Atwood Publishing.

Cross, J. (2007). *Informal learning: Rediscovering the natural pathways that inspire innovation and performance.* San Francisco, CA: Pfeiffer.

Dede, C. (2009). Immersive interfaces for engagement and learning. *Science, 323*(5910), 66–68.

Dewey, J. (1896). The reflex arc concept in psychology. *Psychological Review, 3,* 357–370.

Driscoll, M. P. (2005). *Psychology of learning for instruction,* 3rd ed. Boston, MA: Allyn & Bacon Publishers.

Duffy, T. M. & Cunningham, D. J. (1996). Constructivism: Implications for the design and delivery of instruction. In D. H. Jonassen (Ed.), *Handbook for research for educational communications and technology* (pp. 170–198). New York: Simon & Schuster Macmillan.

Engelbart, D. (1962). *Augmenting human intellect: A conceptual framework.* Summary Report, Stanford Research Institute. Retrieved November 26, 2009 from: www.dougengelbart.org/pubs/augment-3906.html.

Engelbart, D. & Lehtman, H. (1988). Working together. *BYTE, 13*(13), 245–252.

Farrell, M. P. (2001). *Collaborative circles: Friendship dynamics & creative work.* Chicago: University of Chicago Press.

Fletcher, J. D. (2009). Education and training technology in the military. *Science Magazine, 323*(5910), 72–75.

Gagné, R. M. (1985). *The conditions of learning and theory of instruction.* New York: CBS College Publishing.

Gagné, R. M. & Driscoll M. P. (1988). *Essentials of Learning for Instruction,* 2nd ed. Englewood Cliffs, NJ: Prentice-Hall.

Gagné, R. M. & Medsker, K. (1996). *The conditions of learning: Training applications.* New York: Harcourt Brace and Company.

Gardner, H. (2008). Wrestling with Jean Piaget, my paragon. In *What have you changed your mind about?* Edge Foundation, Inc. Retrieved November 26, 2009 from: www.edge.org/q2008/q08_1.html#gardner.

Greenfield, P. M. (1984). A Theory of the teacher in the learning activities of everyday life. In B. Rogoff & J. Lave (Eds.), *Everyday cognition* (pp. 117–138). Cambridge, MA: Harvard University Press.

Greenfield, P. M. (2009). Technology and informal education: What is taught, what is learned. *Science, 323*(5910), 69–71.

Hafner, K. & Lyon, M. (1996). *Where wizards stay up late: The origins of the internet.* New York: Simon & Schuster Macmillan.

Harasim, L. M. (1990a). Online education: An environment for collaboration and intellectual amplification. In L. M. Harasim (Ed.), *Online education: Perspectives on a new environment* (pp. 39–66). New York: Praeger.

Harasim, L. M. (1990b). *Online education: Perspectives on a new environment.* New York: Praeger.

Harasim, L. M. (1993). Collaborating in cyberspace: Using computer conferences as a group learning environment. *Interactive Learning Environments, 3*(2), 119–130.

Harasim, L. M. (1999). A framework for online learning: The Virtual-U. *Computer, 32*(9), 44–49.

Harasim, L. M. (2002). What makes online learning communities successful? The role of collaborative learning in social and intellectual development. In C. Vrasidas & G. V. Glass (Eds.), *Distance education and distributed learning* (pp. 181–200). Charlotte, NC: Information Age Publishers.

Harasim, L. (2004). Collaboration. In A. DeStafano, K. Rudestam & R. Silverman (Eds.), *Encyclopedia of distributed learning* (pp. 65–68). Thousand Oaks, CA: SAGE Publications.

Harasim, L. (2006a). A history of E-learning: Shift happened. In J. Weiss, J. Nolan & P. Trifonas (Eds.), *The international handbook of virtual learning environments* (pp. 59–94). Netherlands: Springer.

Harasim, L. M. (2006b). Assessing online collaborative learning: A Theory, methodology and toolset. In B. Khan (Ed.), *Flexible learning in an information society* (pp. 282–293). Hershey, PA: Idea Group Publishing.

Harasim, L. M., Hiltz, S. R., Teles, L. & Turoff, M. (1995). *Learning networks: A field guide to teaching and learning online.* Cambridge, MA: MIT Press.

Henri, F. & Pudelko, B. (2003). Understanding and analysing activity and learning in virtual communities. *Journal of Computer Assisted Learning, 19,* 474–487.

Hiltz, S. R. (1999). Visions of virtual classrooms. In L. M. Harasim (Ed.), *Wisdom & wizardry: Celebrating the pioneers of online education* (pp. 31–32). Vancouver: TeleLearning Network of Centers of Excellence.

Hiltz, S. R. (1994). *The virtual classroom: Learning without limits via computer networks.* Norwood, NJ: Ablex Publishing.

Hiltz, S. R. & Turoff, M. (1978). *The network nation: Human communication via computer.* Reading, MA: Addison-Wesley Publishing Co.

Hrdy, S. B. (2009). *Mothers and others: The evolutionary origins of mutual understanding.* Cambridge, MA: Harvard University Press.

Interactive Educational Systems Design (IESD). (2009). National online survey of district technology directors exploring district use of Web 2.0 technologies. Retrieved January 31, 2010 from: www.lightspeedsystems.com/researchsurvey.

Jonassen, D. H. (1994). Technology as cognitive tools: Learners as designers. *Instructional Technology Forum, paper #1.* Retrieved November 26, 2009 from: http://it.coe.uga.edu/itforum/paper1/paper1.html.

Jonassen, D. H. (1996). *Computers in the classroom: Mindtools for critical thinking.* Upper Saddle River, NJ: Prentice-Hall.

Jonassen, D. H., Beissner, K. & Yacci, M. (1993). *Structural knowledge: Techniques for representing, conveying, and acquiring structural knowledge.* Hillsdale, NJ: Lawrence Erlbaum Associates.

Keegan, D., Lössenko, J., Mázár, I., Michels, P. F., Paulsen, M. F., Rekkedal, T., et al. (2007). *E-learning initiatives that did not reach targeted goals. Megatrends Project.* Betteskua, Norway: NKI Publishing House. Retrieved November 26, 2009 from: www.nettskolen.com/in_english/megatrends.

Kuhn, T. S. (1970). *The structure of scientific revolutions.* Chicago: University of Chicago Press.

Lave, J. & Wenger, E. (1991). *Situated learning: Legitimate peripheral participation.* Cambridge: Cambridge University Press.

Leahey, T. H. & Harris, R. J. (1997). *Learning and cognition,* 4th ed. Upper Saddle River, NJ: Prentice-Hall.

Licklider, J. C. R. (1960). Man–computer symbiosis. *IRE Transactions on Human Factors in Electronics, HFE-1,* 4–11. Retrieved November 26, 2009 from: http://groups.csail.mit.edu/medg/people/psz/Licklider.html.

Limón, A. A. (2006). Tecnológico de Monterrey in México: Where technology extends the classroom. In C. J. Bonk & C. R. Graham (Eds.), *The handbook of blended learning* (pp. 351–359). San Francisco, CA: Pfeiffer.

Logo Computer Systems Inc. (2002). XXX. Retrieved January 18, 2010 from: www.microworlds.com.

Lohr, S. (2009). Study finds that online education beats the classroom. *New York Times.* Retrieved November 26, 2009 from: http://bits.blogs.nytimes.com/2009/08/19/study-finds-that-online-education-beats-the-classroom.

MacLeod, D. (2004). NHS University axed. *Guardian.* Retrieved November 26, 2009 from: www.guardian.co.uk/education/2004/nov/30/highereducation.uk3.

Martin, H.-J. (1994). *The history and power of writing* (L. G. Cochrane, Trans.). Chicago: University of Chicago Press.

Mason, R. (1989). An evaluation of CoSy on an open university course. In R. Mason & A. Kaye (Eds.), *Mindweave: Communication, computers, and distance education* (pp. 115–145). Oxford: Pergamon Press.

Mason, R. & Kaye, A. (1989). *Mindweave: Communication, computers and distance education.* Oxford: Pergamon Press.

Mayo, M. J. (2009). Video games: A route to large-scale STEM education? *Science, 323*(5910), 79–82.

Mazur, E. (2009). Education: Farewell, lecture? *Science, 323*(5910), 50–51.

McGinley, W. & Tierney, R. J. (1989). Traversing the topical landscape: Reading and writing as ways of knowing. *Written Communication, 6,* 243–269.

Means, B., Toyama, Y., Murphy, R., Bakia, M. & Jones, K. (2009). *Evaluation of evidence-based practices in online learning: A meta-analysis and review of online learning studies.* US Department of Education. Retrieved November 26, 2009 from: www.ed.gov/rschstat/eval/tech/evidence-based-practices/finalreport.pdf.

Muirhead, B. & Betz, M. (2002). Faculty training at an online university. *USDLA Journal, 16*(1). Retrieved November 26, 2009 from: www.usdla.org/html/journal/JAN02_Issue/article04.html.

Munari, A. (1994). Jean Piaget (1896–1980). *Prospects: The quarterly review of comparative education, XXIV*(1/2), 311–327. Retrieved November 26, 2009 from www.ibe.unesco.org/fileadmin/user_upload/archive/publications/ThinkersPdf/piagete.PDF.

Nelson, T. H. (1974). *Dream machines.* South Bend, IN: The Distributors.

Nelson, T. H. (1987). *Literary machines.* South Bend, IN: The Distributors.

Oakeshott, M. (1962). The voice of poetry in the conversation of mankind. In *Rationalizism in politics.* New York: Basic Books.

Palloff, R. & Pratt, K. (1999). *Building effective learning environments in cyberspace: Effective strategies for the online classroom.* San Francisco: Jossey-Bass.

Palloff, R. M. & Pratt, K. (2001). *Lessons from the cyberspace classroom.* San Francisco: Jossey-Bass.

Palloff, R. M. & Pratt, K. (2003). *The virtual student. A profile and guide to working with online learners.* San Francisco: Jossey Bass.

Palloff, R. M. & Pratt, K. (2005). *Collaborating online: Learning together in community.* San Francisco: Jossey-Bass.

Palloff, R. M. & Pratt, K. (2007). *Building online learning communities: Effective strategies for the virtual classroom.* San Francisco: Jossey-Bass.

Papert, S. (1999). What is Logo? Who needs it? *Logo philosophy and implementation.* Logo Computer Systems Inc. Retrieved January 31, 2010 from: www.microworlds.com/support/logo-philosophy-papert.html.

Piaget, J. (1969). *Science of education and the psychology of the child.* New York: Viking.

Picciano, A. & Seaman, J. (2009). *K-12 online learning: A 2008 follow-up of the survey of U.S. school district administrators.* Needham, MA: The Sloan Consortium. Retrieved November 26, 2009 from: www.sloanconsortium.org/publications/survey/pdf/k-12_online_learning_2008.pdf.

Pickett, A. M. (2007). *5 key elements for success: Best practices from online faculty development.* Retrieved November 26, 2009 from: www.slideshare.net/alexandrapickett/aln2007-workshop?src=related_normal&rel=590101.

Pressey, S. L. (1926). A simple apparatus which gives tests and scores—and teaches. *School and Society, 23*(586), 373–376.

Riel, M. (1993). Global education through Learning Circles. In L. Harasim (Ed.), *Global networks: Computer and international communication* (pp. 221–236). Cambridge: MIT.

Riel, M. & Polin, L. (2004). Online learning communities: Common ground and critical differences in designing technical support. In S. A. Barab, R. Kling & J. Gray (Eds.), *Designing for virtual communities in the service of learning* (pp. 16–50). Cambridge, MA: Cambridge University Press.

Romiszowski, A. J. & Ravitz, J. (1997). Computer-mediated communication. In C. R. Dills & A. J. Romiszowski (Eds.), *Instructional development paradigms* (pp. 438–456). Englewood Cliffs, NJ: Educational Technology Publications.

Roschelle, J. (1992). Learning by collaborating: Convergent conceptual change. *Journal of the Learning Sciences, 2*(3), 235–276.

Sack, W., Soloway, E. & Weingrad, P. (1994). Re-writing Cartesian student models. In J. E. Greer & G. I. McCalla (Eds.), *Student modelling: The key to individualized knowledge-based instruction* (NATO ASI Series ed., vol. 125, pp. 355–376). Berlin: Springer-Verlag.

Salmon, G. (2000). *E-moderating: The key to teaching and learning online.* London: Taylor & Francis.

Salmon, G. & Lawless, N. (2006). Management education for the twenty-first century. In C. J. Bonk & C. R. Graham (Eds.), *The handbook of blended learning* (pp. 387–399). San Francisco, CA: Pfeiffer.

Santrock, J. W. (2008). *A Topical Approach to Life Span Development.* New York: McGraw-Hill.

Scardamalia, M. (2003). Knowledge building environments: Extending the limits of the possible in education and knowledge work. In A. DeStefano, K. E. Rudestam & R. Silverman (Eds.), *Encyclopedia of distributed learning* (pp. 269–272). Thousand Oaks, CA: SAGE Publications.

Scardamalia, M. (2004). Instruction, learning, and knowledge building: Harnessing theory, design, and innovation dynamics. *Educational Technology, 44*(3), 30–33.

Scardamalia, M. & Bereiter, C. (1993). Technologies for knowledge-building discourse. *Communications of the ACM, 36*(5), 37–41.

Scardamalia, M. & Bereiter, C. (2003). Knowledge building. In *Encyclopedia of education* (2nd ed., pp. 1370–1373). New York: Macmillan Reference.

Scardamalia, M. & Bereiter, C. (2006). Knowledge building: Theory, pedagogy, and technology. In K. Sawyer (Ed.), *Cambridge handbook of the learning sciences* (pp. 97–118). New York: Cambridge University Press.

Scardamalia, M., Bereiter, C., McLean, R. S., Swallow, J. & Woodruff, E. (1989). Computer supported intentional learning environments. *Journal of Educational Computing Research, 5*, 51–68.

Schwartz, D. (1999). *Ghost in the machine: Seymour Papert on how computers fundamentally change the way kids learn.* Retrieved January 31, 2010 from: www.papert.org/articles/GhostInTheMachine.html.

Seaman, J. (2009). *Online learning as a strategic asset, volume II: The paradox of faculty voices—Views and experiences with online learning.* Washington, DC: Association of Public and Land-grant Universities. Retrieved November 26, 2009 from: www.sloan-c.org/news/APLU_online_strategic_asset_vol. 2.pdf.

Seymour, E. & Hewitt, N. M. (1997). *Talking about leaving: Why undergraduates leave the sciences.* Oxford: Westview Press.

Shute, V. J. & Psotka, J. (1996). Intelligent tutoring systems: Past, present and future. In D. H. Jonassen (Ed.), *Handbook of research for educational communications and technology* (pp. 570–600). New York: Simon & Schuster Macmillan.

Skinner, B. F. (1948). *Walden two.* Indianapolis: Hackett Publishing Company.

Skinner, B. F. (1953). *Science and human behavior.* New York: Macmillan.

Skinner, B. F. (1964). New methods and new aims in teaching. *New Scientist, 122.*

Standridge, M. (2002). Behaviorism. In M. Orey (Ed.), *Emerging perspectives on learning, teaching, and technology.* Retrieved November 26, 2009 from: http://projects.coe.uga.edu/epltt/.

Tapscott, D. & Williams, A. D. (2006). *Wikinomics: How mass collaboration changes everything.* New York: Portfolio.

Tomasello, M., Carpenter, M., Call, J., Behne, T. & Moll, H. (2005). Understanding and sharing intentions: The origins of cultural cognition. *Behavioral and Brain Sciences, 28*, 675–691.

Turing, A. (1950). Computing machinery and intelligence. *Mind, LIX*(236), 433–460. Retrieved November, 26 from: http://loebner.net/Prizef/TuringArticle.html.

Turkle, S. (1995). *Life on the screen: Identity in the age of the Internet.* New York: Simon & Schuster.

University of Phoenix. (2009). Campus and online learning formats. Retrieved January 31, 2010 from: www.phoenix.edu/students/how-it-works/learning_formats.

von Glasersfeld, E. (1982). An interpretation of Piaget's constructivism. *Revue Internationale de Philosophie, 36*(4), 612–635.

Vygotsky, L. S. (1962). *Thought and language* (E. Hanfmann and G. Vakar, Ed. and Trans.). Cambridge, MA: MIT Press.

Wasley, P. (2008). U. of Phoenix lets students find answers virtually. *Chronicle of Higher Education, 54*(48), A1.

Watson, J. B. (1913). Psychology as the behaviorist views it. *Psychological Review, 20*, 158–177.

Wenger, E. (1998). *Communities of practice: Learning, meaning and identity.* Cambridge, MA. Cambridge University Press, 2008.

Wenger, E., McDermott, R. & Snyder, W. M. (2002). *Cultivating communities of practice.* Boston, MA. Harvard Business School Press.

Wilson, B. G. (1997a). Thoughts on theory in educational technology. *Educational Technology, 37*(1), 22–27.

Wilson, B. G. (1997b). Reflections on constructivism and instructional design. In C. R. Dills & A. J. Romiszowski (Eds.), *Instructional development paradigms* (pp. 63–80). Englewood Cliffs, NJ: Educational Technology Publications.

Winn, W. & Snyder, D. (1996). Cognitive perspectives in psychology. In D. H. Jonassen (Ed.), *Handbook for research for educational communications and technology* (pp. 112–142). New York: Macmillan.

Index